FRANZL II

From 4 years on the Russian Front, 1941-45, to standing on the Olympic podium in 1948

AN AUTOBIOGRAPHY by FRANZ X. GABL

To; The good people of the office of Dr. Tetrich,

Franzl II

Andrianne's Restaurant

The Ultra-Modern Restaurant in Canada's Premier National Park ☆ Banff, Canada

FRANZ GABL-1957, Mt.NORQUAY,
BANFF,CANADA. (PHOTO Bruno Engler)

FRANZL II

FROM 4 YEARS ON THE RUSSIAN FRONT, 1941-45, TO STANDING ON THE OLYMPIC PODIUM IN 1948

AN AUTOBIOGRAPHY BY FRANZ X. GABL

Franz Gabl and friend Rudi Alber
St. Anton, Austria, January 1943

PICTORIAL HISTORIES PUBLISHING COMPANY, INC.

L.C. CONTROL NUMBER 00 132196

ISBN 1-57510-073-8

First Printing: April 2000

Printed in Canada

Cover Graphics: Egeler Design
Typography by Jan Taylor
Missoula, Montana

Edelweiss - a perennial plant (genus Leontopdium) *of the composite*
family, found at high altitudes in the mountains of Europe, Asia
and South America. It has woolly-white floral leaves and
small yellow disk flowers surrounded by silvery bracts.
It is esteemed in Europe as a symbol of purity.
ELECTRIC LIBRARY @ ENCLYCLOPEDIA.COM

PICTORIAL HISTORIES PUBLISHING COMPANY, INC.
713 South Third West, Missoula, Montana 59801
Phone (406) 549-8488 FAX (406) 728-9280
phpc@montana.com

Preface

This book tells the story of my life from my birth in 1921 to the year 2000.

It tells of the immense joys of my early years skiing in my hometown of St. Anton in the Austrian Tyrol, my early racing with the very primitive equipment, climbing mountains and haying in the fields, berry-picking in the fall and playing soccer.

But in 1938 a cloud appeared on the Austrian horizon. Hitler's *soldiers* marched into Austria and annexed it amid jubilation into the Third *Reich*.

In 1941 a dark cloud appeared in my life. I was sent to the Russian Front as "cannon fodder" for Hitler's madness—Hitler who wanted more *Lebensraum* for the German people.

One cannot adequately describe the hardships the German *Landser* (G.I.) endured, especially the infantry man. It was inhuman, to say the least.

With immense luck I was able to see my home again. It was as if a higher power had a hand in it.

Two and a half years after coming home from a Russian P.O.W. camp, I won the first Olympic medal in skiing for Austria.

Bellingham, Washington, 2000

The story of Franzl *is dedicated to my comrades on the Russian Front in World War II who didn't have a chance and were bedded in Russian soil.*

Franz Xaver Gabl

Introduction

FRANZL is the story of Franz X. Gabl, a Tyrolean mountain boy. Franzl has survived equally well the twin experiences of his youth as the first Austrian winner of an Olympic
medal (a silver in the downhill at St. Moritz in 1948) and a
survivor as a machine gunner for the German *Wehrmacht* on
the Russian front for four years. Few skiers match the skill
and daring of Franz Gabl. Of his youth in St. Anton, Franz
writes, "We were seven children with one pair of skis. But I
had a one-track mind, and that was to become one day a great
ski champion." He succeeded as an aggressive no-holds-barred
skier on the world stage of the 1930s 1940s.

His World War II years on the three-thousand-kilometer-
long Russian front were as important to Franz's development
as his years on skis.

In March of 1938, Hitler's army marched into Austria and
annexed it. In 1940, Franz was drafted into the
Reichsarbeitsdienst, a pre-military organization, and sent to
France to build an airport. In May of 1941, he was drafted
into the *Wehrmacht*, joining the *Gebirgsjaeger* battalion near
Innsbruck. At the end of September 1941, his battalion was
sent to Russia as "cannon fodder." In his diary he wrote on
the date October 4, 1941, "crossed the border" 75 kilometers
west of Kiev, "a sad sight."

Daily marches of from fifteen to forty kilometers with sev-
enty-pound rucksacks steeled the already-toughened
Gebirgsjaeger even more. Within weeks, the dusty roads became quagmires. Forward progress was sometimes only two
or three kilometers a day. At the end of October, the cold
Siberian winds brought the coldest Russian winter in a hundred years. On Christmas Eve, 1941, Franz went into battle
for the first time. Within a month, not a man of his battalion
was left fighting. All were either dead, wounded, sick, or had
frostbite, including Franz. There was no winter clothing.
Franz was sent to a hospital in Kursk. In July 1943, he was
wounded seriously for the first time. Before the war's end,
his body was pierced five more times, besides having con-
tracted malaria, yellow jaundice, and strep throat. His last

wound came on March 17, 1945, outside Danzig (now Gdansk). On May 2, 1945, he was captured by the British army in a hospital in Luebeck. On July 1st, all in the hospital were turned over to the Russians. The Russians left them alone until July 17th, when they were marched to a regular P.O.W. camp. Franz and Willy, his friend since May 2nd, escaped and were recaptured. The same day they escaped again at midnight. They made their way east to Berlin and then down south to Dresden-Chemnitz-Plauen. Willy and Franz said good-bye and wished each other luck.

On August 2 he crossed the border into the American zone in Bavaria. On August 7, 1945, in the evening, he arrived home. As he stood on the kitchen threshold, his sister asked, "Who are you?" She didn't recognize her bald-headed and tattered brother, who weighed hardly one hundred pounds. He still has his diaries, the fifteen letters home that his mother kept all those years and many certificates of battle given to soldiers for valor.

Franz was declared a war invalid and received a pension of 25.50 Austrian *Schillings*, approximately $1.05 US a month.

He then resumed his work with his father's painting business and the family farm. Strength regained, Franz gained serious notoriety by winning the 1947 annual Austrian Grossglockner Glacier race. Racers hiked the day before the race to an overnight hut on the highest mountain in Austria. It required a three- or four-hour uphill trek with skis on their shoulders.

Franz took the race with an 11.8-second margin over second place. He was on his way to the 1948 Olympics in St. Moritz, the 5th Winter Olympic Games. The downhill course at St. Moritz was designed for risk takers. Several artificial ridges dotted the course. "In training, I used to jump from one ridge over the next one, landing on the fall-away side as a cushion," says Franz. When he earned his silver, the racers' strategy was to take a few steps and then crouch.

"Very seldom did we have to stand up and worry about the turns," he writes today. There was only one control gate, at the start. The finish line was down below, and the fastest time down was the winner. In the three *Steilhangs*, one could take chances and many racers did. And many didn't finish either. There was 4.1 seconds between first and second place, twenty seconds between first and thirtieth. Today places are separated by hundredths of a second.

In 1950 Franz went with the Austrian team to Aspen, Colorado, for the alpine world championships. He then went to Banff, Canada, to take over the ski school there and in the summer drove limousines for the Brewster Gray Line Sight Seeing Company. A picture of Franz scaling a mountain face graces a 1950s menu for an upscale Banff restaurant. Banff was one of the favorite places in his life, but the winters were just too cold. In the 1960s, by then married, Franz moved to Washington state's Mt. Baker to open a summer racing camp and have the concession for the ski shop, rentals, and the ski school. Today he is retired in Bellingham, Washington, and can be seen skiing at Mt. Baker or Steven's Pass or the long runs at Whistler, B.C. In the summer he plays golf and goes on trips, visiting his daughter Rosemary's family in Alberta and Sarah's in British Columbia and sight-seeing around the Pacific Northwest.

The writing of this autobiography traces its inception to 1958. Franz was working with Lowell Thomas on a movie in Alaska, and the two became good friends. Thomas said at the time, "Franz, you must write a book about your life."

The idea churned in his mind for 20 years. He began writing in 1979, and voila , sixteen years later in 1995 his proud book was ready . And now *FRANZL II*, including the sequel, 1948 to 2000, is here.

Why did it take so long?

For one thing, he did most of the writing on a typewriter, before the computer years. For another, he wrote it several times. He'd finish a manuscript and seek advice. "Not enough skiing," he was told one time. "Not enough on the war years," said another advisor. Franz followed others people's advice so many times that it was no longer his own book. A close friend and editor gave him the best advice. "Franz, you must be you. Tell your own story."

Here it is.

Steve Giordano
Bellingham, Washington
February 2000

Contents

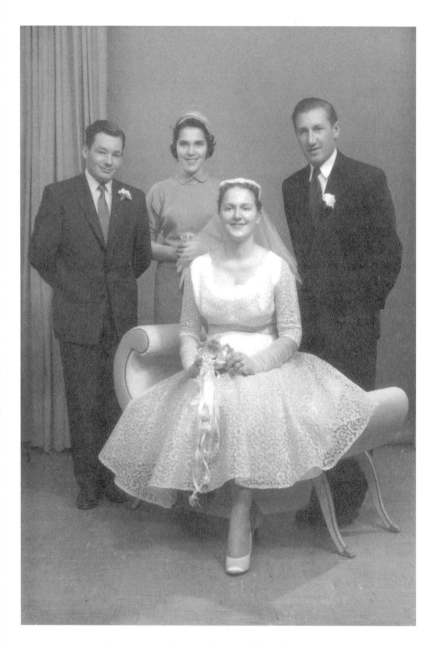

Erich Sailer and Joan Smith with bride and groom
Franz and Audrey Moorman Gabl on their wedding day in Vacouver,
British Columbia, 1956.

My Early Years

It was on a Sunday morning, in February 1929, when I was standing at the starting gate of my first ski race. My heart was pounding with excitement like I had never felt before. It was a first taste of competition—a sensation I would experience many times in the next years, culminating on a mountain above St. Moritz, Switzerland, nineteen years later. But now I had just turned seven, and the junior downhill race of the annual Ski Club Arlberg Championships in St. Anton am Arlberg was the only thing in the world that mattered. This was the big event, the one day of the year when the best skiers of the most famous ski region in the world would be crowned. There were about fifteen of us boys, all between ages six and nine, lined up on that starting line. We looked down the slope, about 400 feet to the finish line. The adults were standing at the bottom, enjoying the spectacle of these young skiers dressed in their best clothes, no doubt laughing at our seriousness as we pictured ourselves as the champion racers of the day. Our parents watched as we trudged up the side of the hill—there were no lifts in those days. We carried our skis over our shoulders, just like the adults, and when we got to the starting line, we strapped on our skis with their primitive bindings. My skis were old wooden hand-me-downs, surplus from World War I. The one pair in our family, shared by all seven children, they featured metal and leather bindings that barely held our hiking boots to the skis. They had no metal edges because those were about to be invented later on in the year, two hundred miles away in Salzburg by a certain Dr. Lettner. There was a big chunk of wood broken out of the tail section on one of them, but they were skis, and I was determined they would take me down the slope faster than anyone.

I had practiced ski races with some of the neighbor boys because we loved to make our own downhill and slalom courses. For slalom flags we gathered twigs and stuck them into the snow. For a timer I snitched my father's large pocket watch, and for prizes—there had to be prizes for the winners— we pooled treasures from our homes: erasers, pencils, souvenirs, even a flashlight once. The winners would ceremoniously receive their prizes, usually in my bedroom. Of course, for the next race we would have to pool the same prizes again. But this time, on this particular Sunday, it was no make believe race; this was the real thing.

Hermann Tschol Jr., the official starter, was trying to get all the young skiers organized into an imaginary starting line. Someone would fall over, someone else move too far forward. Then he began to count, *"Achtung, Fertig,"* but before he could get to *"Los!"* our signal to start, several got an early jump, and he had to get everyone back into line. Again, *"Achtung, Fertig,"* and again someone would jump. Finally he said, *"Achtung, fertig, los!"* as fast as he could, and we were off.

The race was a straight line downhill, and there was a heavy layer of new snow. Few of the young skiers could go straight. There were collisions, yelps, skis flying off, poles scattering, faces plowing into the fresh powder, tears and cries of "Mama" and "Papa!" It was chaos, but I dug my poles hard into the snow and kept my eyes on the finish line. There were three or four of us near the front now; I bent lower trying to pick up speed. I could see I was pulling ahead and dipped lower, letting my knees come up to absorb the bumps. Now the finish was just a few yards ahead. Disaster! The leather strap came loose off my bindings, and my ski went off in a different direction. Ludwig Dellasega, a schoolmate, sailed past me as I sat in the snow. Desperately, I reached for the lost ski and grabbed it, half skiing and half running I crossed the finish line to the laughter and cheers of the parents, older skiers and my ski heroes. I came in third. My first official ski race, and it taught me a lesson: take good care of the equipment. I was disappointed, but the ski jumping contest was still to come in the afternoon.

By the time of the 1929 Ski Club Championships, skiing had already gripped my life like nothing before or since. Our family was one of the first in the neighborhood to get skis, one pair among seven children. I was the second youngest and the smallest of the brood, so I had to fight for my share of time on the skis. Fortunately for me, girls in those days did not do much skiing. There were no ski pants, and girls found it immodest, let alone uncomfortable, to ski in skirts. Besides, the view then was that girls should be home helping mother with the housework. That left Karl, Pepi and me to fight over the skis. Karl was seven years older, Pepi just a year older than me. Because of his age and corresponding size, when Karl wanted to ski there was little we could do except continually yell after him, "My turn, Karl, my turn!" But Karl didn't have the same passion for skiing that Pepi and I had, so we usually argued it out between the two of us. Karl was a gentle brother, he never let on to be bossy.

Because of the sharing, I was pretty protective of my skis when I had them. I was skiing with some friends one day when Franz Schutz, an older boy from the neighborhood, asked if he could use them for a run. I reluctantly agreed to one run. But he didn't just take one run, he took many. No matter how I yelled at him, he wouldn't give them back. I was furious, but he just laughed. After all, he was much older and I was short, even for my age. In a fury I went home and got one of my father's souvenir bayonets from the first world war. I climbed back up the hill, determined at least to scare him into giving me my skis back. Neighbors watched this furious little boy with his jaw stuck out and called to me saying the police were on the way to arrest me. That was too much. I ran home and hid behind our *Kachel-Ofen* or closed-in fireplace. I begged my older brother Karl and my sisters to protect me from the police, and to bribe them into protecting me, I even offered to eat the tail of the pig we had slaughtered the day before. For many years afterwards, I would have to listen to this story laughingly retold by my sisters.

Whenever we would change skis, the bindings would have to be adjusted. Uncle Albert, my mother's brother who lived with us, would help me tie the leather thongs, then I'd push open the front door of our house with the ski pole, jump over the threshold down the few steps onto the snow, and sail downhill toward the railroad embankment just a hundred feet away. Across from our house the railroad had an elevated dam about forty feet high and quite steep. Perfect for practice. To shuss straight down in unpacked powder was a challenge and a thrill to a six or seven year old skier. Toward the west end of the dam, it got higher and steeper, and I gradually moved farther and farther over until I was near the tunnel. I kept pushing myself to get that thrill of adrenaline rushing through me. I loved challenging my buddies to steeper and steeper runs, and discovered that I loved taking chances and seeing if I had greater courage than anyone else.

Jumping was best of all. To me it was the spice of life, the most exhilarating thing the world could offer. There were a great many hills on the mountain sides surrounding our village of St. Anton, almost all of them perfect for building ski jumps. My favorite was less then 200 hundred yards from my home, the one we called *Gonda*. The inrun was not too steep, and in the middle was a hump where we built our jump. The landing could have been steeper and there was lots of room for the outrun. When my friends and I jumped, our young imaginations flew with us.

"Look!" I'd yell at the top of the jump. "I'm Birger Ruud!" Birger was the king of ski jumping, the Muhammed Ali, Michael Jordan, and Joe Montana of our day, all rolled into one. Skiing, after all, to Austrians was bigger than any other sport by far, and Birger Ruud was the greatest name in ski jumping having won the Olympic gold in 1932 and 1936. We'd all claim the names of our heroes: the Norwegians Reidar Andersen, Radmond Sorenson, Sigmund Ruud (Birger's brother), Recknagel and Glass of Germany.

Birger's fame was such that we loved hearing the story about how he came to Innsbruck to jump in a contest on the big Berg Isel hill. The first place trophy was placed in a sports store window in town days before the event with this inscription: 'Birger Ruud, first." He won. It was like Babe Ruth pointing out his next home run before hitting it.

Those early days I jumped hundreds of times in my mind, each time flying flawlessly through the air, landing far down the flat, perfectly on both skis with my arms held gracefully high and still. Years later, in adulthood, sleeping on the frozen Russian steppe and at home in the Pacific Northwest of the United States, I would still dream the same dream. The push off into heavy air, the long endless flight, a sweet dream interrupted by fear about the landing. To jump is to take a risk. I loved the challenge, but I was never fearless.

I certainly wasn't without fear as I faced my first real ski jump in competition on that crisp day in February of 1929. I had my Sunday best on—without today's high fashion ski clothes, competitors wore their best church clothes to competitive events. I had just turned seven, my birthday being

December 29, 1921. The young skiers from St. Anton and neighboring St. Jakob had gathered, and now we were going to see who was the best ski jumper between the ages of six and nine. With my disappointing loss in the morning downhill run still very much in mind, I must have been a very determined boy as I stood on top of *Schweinbuehel* (pig hill), the site for the afternoon jumping event. I knew that I could win because no one could match me in daring. I pushed hard, jumped with just a fleeting thought of worry for the landing, and sailed far past where any of the other kids had landed.

"*Tatti!*" I said to my father when I got home, "I won the jumping." He clapped me on the back and laughed with his jolly, good natured laugh. After politics, sport was the next important thing in my dad's life, and he would be perhaps my greatest supporter.

That afternoon was the *Preisverteilung* (awards ceremony). It was held at the *Bahnhof* Restaurant in St. Anton. Each winner would get a trophy and some merchandise that had been collected from the merchants in our town. The restaurant was packed to the rafters with the townspeople, young and old alike, and all us children ogled the glittering prizes lined up on the restaurant tables. They also had been displayed all week in the window of Hannes Schneider's Sport Shop. Now we waited for the arrival of Hannes Schneider, the king of Austrian skiing, already one of the most famous ski legends throughout the world. Finally, Hannes marched in, the crowd quieted, and everyone looked at him with awe. He opened the ceremony with a brief speech. Hannes was born in a neighboring village a few miles away. For all his fame he was not a boastful man and gave a short speech. It was fine with me. I was eager for my prize.

After the speech by Hannes, the winners were called, one by one, to the head table. I heard my name called, a little applause from the crowd, and in a daze and blushing I went forward. I had won. It was just the most junior of the divisions, but I had won and now Hannes Schneider himself was handing me my prize. It was a small silver ski pin with the engraving "*Jgd. Sprg. 1929, I,*" but it was the most beautiful thing I had ever seen and I treasure it to this day. Nothing I ever experienced in life, not even climbing the Olympic award platform, could match the exhilaration I felt on that day.

In 1921 when I was born, St. Anton, pronounced: "Sankt-ann-ton" was a typical Tyrolean farming village even though it was now becoming famous as a ski resort. The reason was one man: Hannes Schneider and the great skiing terrain of the Arlberg region of Tyrol and Vorarlberg, the two most western provinces of Austria. St. Anton, about halfway between Innsbruck, the capital of Tyrol, and Zurich in Switzerland, has an elevation of 4,200 feet, the surrounding mountains reaching heights of over 10,000 feet. The village is nestled in a narrow valley between the jagged peaks and wide open, treeless, alpine meadows which would become a paradise for alpine skiers because they are one of the snowiest in all the Alps. This had been a common travel route between Paris and Vienna for many centuries. The high Alps provided a huge barrier to travel, and the 6,000-foot Arlberg Pass was the shortest route. St. Anton, just four miles east of the pass, was strategically located, and at no time was this more important than in winter when many a hapless traveler trying to make it through the heavy snow carrying burdens on their back, fell into the cold snow only to be found in springtime.

There is a small rise, a few hundred yards from where I was born, known as *Schlosskopf,* or castle hill. In the 1300s, an impressive castle stood here, *Schloss Arlen*, the home of the *Schlossherr* (count). The story is told that one day a newborn baby was found on the castle steps, a foundling. It was not uncommon for babies born out of wedlock to find themselves thus deposited. Young mothers, desperate in their plight and desperate with hope for their child, would place them on the doorsteps of nobles hoping they would find a better life than the mother could offer. This baby was fortunate. The *Schlossherr* took him in and treated him kindly, calling him *Heinrich Findelkind,* Henry, the found child.

Young Heinrich tended the *Schlossherr's* pigs when he was a teenager, but his character was noble if his genealogy was not. He was troubled by the fact that in many winters when the snows got very deep on the Arlberg Pass, many travelers would find themselves stranded and succumb to the deep snow and exhaustion. So he got up the courage to ask his foster father to help him build a shelter for winter travelers at St. Christoph, just a quarter mile away on the border between Tyrol and Vorarlberg, the westernmost Austrian province.

His foster father agreed and not only helped him build the shelter, but provided him with giant, gentle St. Bernard dogs that would help find stranded travelers and tend to them until the human rescuers could reach them. These dogs became world famous, although it is a little doubtful they carried whiskey bottles around their necks at that time.

A few hundred yards from where the Arlen Castle stood in the 1300s, you can find house #14 in St. Anton. In these Austrian villages houses are numbered not by where they are located on the street, but by when they were built. Each new house built in St. Anton to this day will get the next higher number from the previous one built. Our house was built early in the 1700s and was the fourteenth built in St. Anton. It was in the middle between houses #13 and #15; in fact since these houses were built together, they were in effect one building. The barns which sheltered the animals were built onto the backs of the houses, so you could go down a hallway directly from the house into the barn. The houses were wood with stone basement walls almost three feet thick. The living quarters had double windows and shutters and the roof was covered with shingles that were not nailed but held down with logs placed at three feet intervals and heavy stones to keep the logs from moving.

When one thinks of a picturesque, mountain village it is easy to imagine a peaceful, flat meadow with little houses huddled in the middle and surrounded by rolling hills that rise higher and higher to the guarding mountains. But that is not St. Anton. The valley where St. Anton is located is more like a ravine. There are few gentle meadows, and the valley floor is too narrow for the cozy cluster of homes. Instead they are strung along the hillsides, paralleling the railroad and the highway. The railroad passes right through the middle of town, and along side of it, the main street. The railroad was completed in 1884 when the seven-mile-long Arlberg Tunnel was dug, making the passage through the Arlberg mountains as easy as a walk across the street. In the very bottom of the valley flowed the Rosanna, a small river that could become treacherous when swollen with snow melt when the temperature rose too quickly or after heavy rain. When that happened in the springtime, it was usually accompanied by heavy rains, and the creek that flowed down the *Zwoelferkopf* would become the route that avalanches preferred. We'd hear the distinctive low rumble that quickly turned to a roar, and all inhabitants would rush to the windows, watching the mass of snow quickly gather speed on the treeless, upper part of the mountain, disappear into a gully, then fill it up and drop with the sound of thunder over a high waterfall, finally slowing and dying as the gully flattened out coming into the Rosanna river.

In the Winter of 1921, on December 29th, just a few hundred yards from where *Schloss Arlen* once stood, my mother went into labor yet again. Kreszenz Weissenbach-Gabl, my mother, was a gentle and strong woman who understood only one thing in her entire life: work. She was also born and raised in house #14, in St. Anton. Her father came to St. Anton from the town of Warth, two miles from Lech, and mother could trace her ancestors to that town since 1676. Warth was just twelve miles northwest of St. Anton, on the other side of the Arlberg pass. My father, Joseph Gabl, was from the town of Kauns near Landeck, about twenty miles east of St. Anton. His family came to the area in 1737, so you could say that my roots run very deep into the Arlberg mountains. Father was born in 1881, and he and mother married in 1908.

On my father's side, trades were strong in his family background, and he had a strong artistic streak and decided that he wished to paint, preferably frescoes for churches, houses and inn's. In about 1899 he went to study art in Munich. He went with three others from Kauns, who also wanted to be artists; they were called the "cloverleaf boys of Kauns." They were characters as history books revealed, we assumed. When he finished school he then did some painting in churches for several years but soon gave that up and went to St. Anton to become a house painter. Ironically, it was a few years later that another Austrian, this one from the northeast, also an aspiring artist went to Vienna in hopes of launching an art career. This young man, who blamed Jewish control of the art market for his failure to make it as an artist, would have a profound effect on not only my life, but the entire world. His name: Adolf Hitler.

My father was wiser. After moving to St. Anton he realized that a struggling artist would have great difficulty in supporting a large family, so he applied to the town authorities in 1906 to have the right to be a commercial painter. A couple of years after being granted this license, he married my mother and started his family. The family business is still operating in St. Anton, owned now by my niece's husband. The ads in the local paper proudly say, "Since 1906."

In Austria at that time, and still to a certain extent today, enterprise is not as free as in North America. The town authorities determined who received a permit to practice a trade, and the right to that business was passed on to succeeding generations. If someone new applied and the town fathers determined that it would harm the livelihood of a townsman who already owned a permit, especially if he had a large family, the applicant would be denied the right to practice that particular trade.

The security meant that my father could spend a good part of his time in *Weinstuben* (the local pups) talking politics, the weather, trying to solve problems of the day and drinking wine or beer with other license holders of other trades. They also didn't have to worry about competition. It also meant that my future was quite sealed: I would apprentice with my father and become a painter in the family business. Being a commercial painter meant that one did interior and exterior house and building painting, decorating, wall papering, signs and in the fall gold plating family iron crosses in the cemetery. He also sold paint by the quart or gallon, all hand mixed at our home because there was no store in town to sell paint.

Father never discouraged my skiing and would watch Pepi and me through the window as we skied down the railroad embankment. He was also the one to settle the disputes: "*Tatti*, Pepi (or Franz) is already over an hour on the skis. It is my turn now." Later, when Pepi and I both became known for our skiing success, my father was proud and happy. I will never forget him wishing me luck at the train station as our train pulled out for St. Moritz in 1948.

Mother was the strength of the family. Slim and wiry, she knew just one thing in her life from the day she could help care for her family to the day she died when she was 92 years old, and that thing was work. Unlike my father, she had little time or patience for jokes or fooling around. But with seven children and two men—her brother Albert lived with us—she had plenty to keep her busy. Household chores had a different meaning then than they do now, and life in a mountain village, especially during the long winter months, was hardly easy. We also raised a few cows, some pigs, chickens, sheep and goats. Uncle Albert, when he wasn't on a binge, shared the responsibility for the animals with my mother and with some help from us children. Every morning and evening, for example, the cows would have to be taken to the neighborhood communal drinking trough to be watered, then milked, fed and cared for.

Uncle Albert lived with our family his entire adult life. He was a kind and good man who never had a family of his own because, being left without land or livelihood, he could not afford to raise his own family. So we were his family. He would be of great help to the widows in town who had lost husbands in the first world war to help with haying, bringing in the harvest, cutting wood and other chores. They would pay him sometimes with *Schnapps*, a reward he did seldom refused. While I remember him helping me lace up my leather binding thongs to hold those wooden skis to my hiking boots, I also remember that once he started into the *Schnapps* he would be on a binge for as much as two weeks. When it was over he would get the shakes and return again to being one of the nicest men in town, until next time, perhaps three or four months later. I thought of him as just a simple farmer and an essential member of our household.

Then, when I was already out of school I found out that he had been a skier. In fact, he won the Ski Club Arlberg Championship in 1903, two years after the club was formed and the first time the ski club held an official race. True, it was more like Nordic or cross country skiing, and even involved what is now known as orienteering, but still, he was a ski champion. I never thought of him in quite the same way again, though I never saw him, my father or my mother on skis.

Perhaps the reason I never saw him ski was the first world war. Uncle Albert served in that conflict on the Italian front where he was wounded in battle three times, one time severely. Fortunately, his wounds were not crippling. Our father, who served on the same front as an artillery observer, didn't talk much about the war either. Once I remembered when I was a little boy, I asked him questions how it felt being under fire, he couldn't give me a satisfactory answer, and later on in life when I am asked this same question I have a hard time of what I should say.

Father liked best of all to talk about politics and sports, especially skiing. He would just come alive talking about sports, and to me that was just fine. I would much rather hear the latest about the skiing heroes of that era rather than about some war heroes from an old, forgotten war.

Karl was the first, born seven years before me in 1914. Then there was Maria, Hedwig, Kathi, Pepi (Joseph), me and finally, Hilda. Karl was a true big brother—serious, hard working—but hardly a playmate, more like a half-parent. He began his apprenticeship with my father early on. Fortunately for me, that meant he didn't compete often for the one pair of skis we had to share.

My sisters were also busy helping around the house and on the farm. Since girls didn't ski much in those days, they also offered little competition for the skis. I do remember my sister Kathi entering the ski club competition for girls one year and winning it. The next year she entered again and came in dead last. She never raced again. She had to bear

Josef Gabl, his wife Kreszenz Weissenbach-Gabl, and their seven children. Franz sits at his father's, in front of his sister Hilda.

the teasing of all her brothers and sisters for years about this. We loved to remind her that she came in fourth in a field of three. Maria and Hedwig didn't care for skiing. Thinking back on it now, if we had all loved skiing like Pepi and I did, I don't think I would have had the chance to develop the skills needed to compete.

I have many pleasant memories of growing up in St. Anton with my family. Certainly there was work and plenty of it. There was always much wood to cut because everything was done with wood—heating, cooking, building and repairing the roof of the house and the hay barns in our meadows outside of town. Our house had electricity since 1912 when the town built a dam to harness it for a power station which was a boon to the towns folk.

The work in summer revolved around cutting wood. We had in one of our meadows a sizeable forest, and haying in the summer and fall. We needed to put away as much hay for the animals, so we could tide them over during the snowy months which would last from November to late May or even later. Of course there were no machines. The only tools we had were a scythe with a big sharp, curved blade and our strong, young arms. Hour after hour, working in a row with other men and boys, we would swing the heavy scythe back and forth through the mountain grass and wildflowers. And, you must remember, these are not all flat farmer's fields we are talking about. Some are high, alpine meadows where you don't stand level and where walking is more often vertical than horizontal. But the hard work was compensated in part by the incredibly beautiful flowers that bloomed from early spring through the haying season. Forget-me-nots, dandelions, *alpen rosen*, and, of course, edelweiss. My heart would fill to overflowing with the sights and smells in these meadows, but still I preferred them to be covered over with snow so I could ski. And I remember very well when I looked at the green hills and mountains during the summer months, thinking, "If I only could hibernate like bears during the summer and wake up when the first snows covered the grassy hills.

In late summer we would make our annual trek to cut hay in the high, alpine meadows. My father leased some of these, and there were shelters like a hay barn to store the hay until the first snows arrived. Other *Schober* (shelters) consisted of four poles and a roof that was raised to accommodate the ever-rising pile of loose hay we would store underneath with no walls. Since getting to these meadows involved a hike of one to two hours, we stayed up there from Monday through Saturday afternoon. We always returned on Saturday so we could go to church on Sunday. When we hiked up we usually carried heavy packs on our back with food and tools, often carrying lumber to repair or build more hay shelters. And we took our goats with us up the mountain. After all, without them we wouldn't have fresh milk for our coffee. Black coffee was unthinkable; one would have to be very desperate to drink it, or so we thought. Then all week long, for three weeks, it was swing the scythe back and forth and pack the hay on our backs up or down the steep hills to a shelter. In some areas the hill sides were so steep we had to wear crampons, and more than once these saved us from deadly falls. We slept in the hay in the shelter at night, and sometimes neighbors would come over to our barn. There were some good storytellers, but we had a hard time swallowing their BS. The cooking was done in an area where the roof of the shelter extended or under a rock outcropping. It was hard, hard work, but it made us tough and gave us physical and mental endurance.

A few years later, laying on my back in a Russian hospital and wondering why I was surviving when so many of my comrades were not, I credited some of my ability to survive to the toughness I had developed and learned on those beautiful mountain meadows high above my little town of St. Anton.

You might wonder, why keep the hay in shelters on the mountain? For the simple reason that it was easier to take the hay down after the snows had come because some of these mountain meadows were three or more miles from our home. Then we would ski the hay down. It may sound like fun, but it could be very dangerous. When the first snows fell we would get the neighbors together, walk up to the stored hay barn on the mountain, make square bundles weighing 200 kilos, tie them securely with lots of rope, then ski them down on a contraption called a *Ferla*. These were like two-by-sixes, bent up in front like skis and connected in front with a strong cross bar. Coming down from some of the mountains it was so steep, at times 60 degrees, that it was not unusual for a bundle to get out of control and go careening down. More than one farmer got killed in this process, so it was common practice for the farmer and his helpers to bow down in prayer around a bundle of hay before beginning the quick trip down the mountain.

It wasn't all work, though. Late summer was also the time when the edelweiss were in full bloom. Many people know this from the famous song in the movie *The Sound of Music.* We knew it as a beautiful, delicate, white starlike flower that grew in isolated patches high up between walls of rocks. We knew that to get at the edelweiss you might have to risk your life on these treacherous mountainsides. We also knew that if you delivered a precious bunch to a special young lady in town, you could be quite assured of some return affection. Finally, in the late 1930s it was against the law to pluck edelweiss.

A favorite family activity in the fall was hiking up the mountains in search of berries. My mother loved this as much as I loved skiing. It was a real family treat to pack a picnic lunch, which usually consisted of a loaf of bread, sausage, cheese and *Speck* (smoked bacon). Then we would top it off high above the town with the sweet taste of the mountain berries—*Preiselbeeren*, blueberries and raspberries.

A highlight of the summer was *Sonnwendfeier* (which means, the sun turned south again). It was the longest day of the year, and it was celebrated with the young people going high up on the mountains to gather as much wood as possible for a bonfire. Some would pile the wood onto one big pile; others would make patterns of hearts or crosses. Then, after dark, the wood piles would be lit, and the villagers would come out and look at the spectacle of the fires on the side of the mountains. Of course, we had to have contests to see which group had made the biggest or most spectacular fire. This fun custom took on an uncomfortably political nature in the mid 1930s that forever removed its childlike innocence. You now could see *Hackenkreuze* (swastikas), burning on the mountain sides.

Alber Rudi was one of my best friends, although a little younger than me. He lived in a house just below the *Schlosskopf,* and often we would play together, including chasing the sheep and the goats, playing cop and robber, things which young boys indulge in. I don't remember that too well, but I do remember one incident painfully well. We were playing in our woodshed ,and one of us had found a small piece of bread. Bread, like all food, was very precious in those days. It had almost a holy quality to it. For certain it was not to be eaten except at meal times, and every crumb was to be treated with the kind of respect given to those things on which life itself depended. But now we had a small piece of bread, the end of the loaf. It was small and it was very hard; try as we might the two of us could not divide it. We pulled at it, tried to break it and did everything we could to try and divide it. It wouldn't give. "Here," Rudi said. "Try the axe." The axe was heavy and sharp, and I knew better as a five year old to play with it. But the bread was solemnly placed on the chopping block, and Rudi looked while I hefted the axe as high as I could. At the last moment Rudi's conscience must have got the best of him about how we were about to treat the bread, and he tried to grab the bread back. But the axe was coming down, and my young arms were not strong enough to stop it. Three of Rudi's fingers were dangling, held onto his gushing hand by just strings of flesh and muscle. Rudi screamed and ran out of the woodshed up to the street yelling at the top of his lungs, "Franz cut off my fingers! Franz cut off my fingers!"

It was the end of the world as far as I could see. "My God, what have I done?" I did the only sensible thing I could think of and ran, ran far and fast into the forest with Rudi's screams being left farther and farther behind. Here I would stay and would live out what was left of my pitiful life. Hiding in that dark forest I wished that the trees or the whole world would just fall in on me. I could only imagine what trouble lay in store for me if I ever were to return home.

Late that night fear of the dark and hunger overcame my fear of home, so quietly I stole into the house. The whole family was waiting for me. Mother grabbed my arm with a vicious squeeze and took my pants down in front of the mirror in the living room. Then she picked up the *Pragger*, a large, flat bamboo tool used to beat the dust out of carpets. Now situated so that I could inspect the damage being done to my bum, my mother spanked, and I saw red almost as bright as Rudi's blood every time the Pragger came down. It was the only spanking I ever remember getting from my mother, and after she heard the whole story and not just Rudi's abbreviated version of it, she felt awful. All through her life that good woman insisted the worst thing she ever did in her life was to spank me after I almost cut off Rudi's fingers.

As for Rudi, he was taken quickly to the village doctor who prepared to finish the job by cutting through the muscle and skin that still held the little fingers to his four year old hand. Rudi's mother would have none of it. She was quite certain that Rudi would have need of his fingers later in life and took him home. There she carefully made splints of wood and bandaged the fingers tightly. She applied stone oil into the bandages, a home medicine that was used frequently to treat a variety of injuries. It must have some miraculous qualities because Rudi's fingers were saved. Although he never had full movement of them, he became the finest accordion player in St. Anton. And Rudi remained my best friend in my childhood and a lifetime friend.

School and Skiing

After winning the ski jumping event in the 1929 Ski Club Arlberg Championships on Sunday, I got to wear my winning silver ski pin to school the next Monday. I couldn't have been prouder. My only regret was that the etiquette of the times allowed me only one day of glory when I could proudly show off the ski-shaped, silver pin fastened to the lapel of my school jacket. Wearing it any more than that would be a sign of a prideful braggart. I had just started school that fall and was not happy about it. I would have much preferred my simple life of chasing goats and sheep through the meadows, hunting moles, picking berries with my family and playing with Rudi and friends, all in anticipation of the coming glorious winter when I could once again strap on the old skis with part of the tail end missing, build jumps and set slalom courses with twigs. I said to my father, "*Tatti*, you know ski champions really don't need to bother with school?" With twinkling eyes he answered me, "Franz, a smart man knows he has a lot to learn. When you are older you will, I am sure, agree with me. When times are tough, you will be glad you learned a trade." There was no arguing with him; I knew he would be proven right, and he was.

The worldwide depression was still years away, and I often thought of my father's wisdom and foresight. School was a ten-minute walk from my home, unfortunately, there was no need to ski to school when the snows came in November or December. The routine was monotonous: at 6:30 mother would wake us, wash our faces and hands, comb our hair and then feed us a breakfast of fried potatoes, bread and jam and white coffee and send us off to church for the 7:30 mass. I remember we had two Jewish boys, the sons of the Gomperz family, Rudi and Hansi, who didn't have to go to church because of their religion. At 8:00 we would be sitting at our desks, facing *Fraeulein* Seirer in the little school room. At 11:00 a.m. we were free to walk home for a lunch of soup, bread, meat and vegetables. Then we'd slowly wander back to school in time for the afternoon session from 1:00 to 3:00.

For each pair of pupils, there was a bench with a table in front which had a little ink bottle and under the top room for books etc. It was like a prison to me; having roamed the meadows, the nearby forests and the small creeks, was freedom which I would never experience the same way.

In school it was expected that we would stay firmly planted on our seats. If one needed to go to the bathroom, one held the right hand high with the forefinger straight out. If the teacher was in a bad mood, you just waited a bit longer.

In winter it was difficult to keep the mind on the subjects we were learning. More than once I would be called back to the real world of high German when my mind had drifted off into the crisp, dry powder snow. We studied reading, math, history, geography, all the normal things a child is supposed to learn. In spite of my reluctance and lackadaisical attitude toward school, I did remarkably well. Learning came easily to me, as it did to most in my family. My report cards in my first two years there were only "1s" in all the subjects. It didn't mean that much to me. Geography I enjoyed more then any other subject. I learned the names of all the provinces of Austria, rivers, high mountains and most capitals of the European countries. My interest started to fade east of Poland and Hungary; it seemed the land just stretched endlessly with little meaning or purpose in the vastness that would swallow up any humanity. If I had only known the desperate years I had to endure in that vastness of the Russian steppe, I would have found the study of the Bug, Dniepr, Donez, Don and Volga most fascinating.

Fraeulein Seirer was my teacher the first two years of my school life. She was an elderly spinster, heavy set and very tolerant. In those days every schoolboy and girl was expected to show only the greatest of respect for their teacher, even those who were hopelessly naive. Teachers were always greeted formally on the street, and this applied to adults as well as children. Men and boys lifted their narrow brim hats off their heads when passing a teacher, and God help the young boy who might forget.

"*Aber Franzl*," the teacher would ask with a stern frown. "Do you have sparrows under your hat?" The offender would quickly pull off his hat and stammer an apology while shamefacedly backing his way down the street.

I have a warm spot in my heart for *Fraeulein* Seirer, partly because I think back now with some sadness on the abuse she received from some of the rowdy and nasty boys in school, and partly because of the fervent prayers she led daily on my behalf when I had a severe accident in my first year of school. It may be, too, because I was one of her favorites. I always did well in school and learned quickly, only running into serious trouble with her once.

It had been a beautiful mid-winter afternoon, and I succumbed to the temptation of the fluffy powder. But I had a stack of homework to do and figured it out there was only one way to get my homework done and get some skiing in at the same time. "Anderl," I said and approached one of my father's employees. I sought him out because I knew him to be a bright fellows. "It is a beaufiful afternoon for skiing, don't you think. Maybe you could help?" Anderl agreed with a laugh—my love for skiing was already well known in my home—and off I went to the slopes with just a little worry spoiling an otherwise perfect afternoon. The next day, no doubt looking guilty, I handed in the homework assignment.

"*Aber Franzl,*" *Fraeulein* Seier said with a stern voice in front of the entire class. "This is not your handwriting, is it?" My embarrassment would have been punishment enough. Unfortunately, it wasn't, and I never, ever cheated again.

"Bubi" was one of the boys who was born with a streak of trouble and a brain which was underdeveloped. He had a terrible time with numbers and assignments. In fact, he couldn't even read numbers on a clock translated into the time of day. Added to his lack of scholastic ability, he also had a streak of trouble in him. Frequently *Fraeulein* Seirer found it necessary to apply her favorite punishment to "Bubi." This punishment consisted of having the offender kneel in front of the blackboard with arms extended out wide. Then the *Frauelein* would place a heavy round stone in each hand, and he was expected to hold the stones for a certain length of time until she felt he had been punished enough. On occasions Bubi would drop one arm, letting the stone fall down with a crash, while she shoveled to the other side to put a stone on the other hand. This game could go on for sometime until the good teacher either felt he had been punished enough or was just outsmarting her. At any rate, after the little game was

over, Bubi got his revenge by dipping his ink pen in the inkwell
and spattering ink on her rather generous bottom as she
walked by him down the aisle.

The ink spatter was just one of the common tricks played
on this well meaning teacher. Even more cruel were the times
when a swift leg appeared out of nowhere in the narrow aisles
between benches, and the heavy woman would come down
with a horrendous crash. Some of these kids were real
Spitzbuben (bad boys). Nonetheless, anyone graduating from
her class could be assured quality education.

Three o'clock in the afternoon was freedom. It was a beautiful day in June 1929. I was seven, a first grader, and summer was almost here. Soon we would be out of school, and we
could look forward to *Sonnwendfeier*, to hiking with family
and friends, chase goats and sheep, haying in our own meadows, all the delights of summer. School was out at 3:00, and
most kids walked across the street to the front lawn of the
Habicher house, like hundreds of times before. In front of
that house grazed daily a big brown horse with a black spot
on its side. He was called Max. Auto traffic at that time was
in its embryonic state, in St. Anton. There was only one private car, owned by the Schuler family of the Hotel Post and
one by Probst Taxi. Max was neither fenced in nor tied up.
Just then a gravel truck came up the street, its engine roaring, its chain drive rattling and its airless rubber tires clat-
tering on the gravel. Max somehow panicked, and kicked at
the thundering racket. Unfortunately, at that instant I found
myself directly between Max and the swiftly moving truck.
There were at least another two dozen kids in front of that
house. In an instant Max kicked me with his hoof into the
wheels of that gravel truck. Of course I can't remember anything about that, only after I was at Dr. Santeler's office did I
wake up with tremendous pain, which I remember very well.
Dr. Santeler looked at my leg and hip and said I needed to go
to the hospital in Zams, 20 miles away, at once. Walter
Schuler's was the only car then in St. Anton, and he obliged
at once to have me driven to Zams.

My mother had taken the train to visit her sister Maria in
Bludenz that morning, also twenty miles away in the opposite direction. About six in the evening she arrived back at
the railroad station in St. Anton. The accident had taken

place after 3:00 p.m., right after school. As soon as she stepped off the train, a well meaning villager stopped her and said, "*Oh Frau Gabl, Franz hat beide Fuesse ab!*" Now here is a little problem with our Tyrolean dialect. Literally translated that means, "Mrs. Gabl, your son Franz has both his feet (or legs) off." But it could just as well mean, "Franz has broken both legs." This was the first serious accident my mother experienced in our family of seven children and uncle Albert, her brother. But my poor mother, who was known to think the worst from time to time, was certain that her youngest son was now legless. In her frantic state of mind she rushed to the hospital in Zams to see me and cried piteous tears, in fear and relief, when she saw that I still had my legs, however damaged they might be.

My fear, of course, was: will I ever ski again? I must have pestered everyone constantly with the question, but who could answer it? My mother visited just as often as she could, and she would remind me that *Frauelein* Seirer was having the whole class pray for me daily as I lay in the hospital bed for over three months. It was a real trial for her because after every visit when she left, I would cry for a long time, begging her to come back quickly. I was such a mama's boy.

I watched the lazy summer pass by me from my bed in the hospital at Zams. It was no place for a lively seven-year old, not when his friends were roaming the meadows and woods or going on hikes. On the other hand I didn't have to worry about chores or school work.

Finally I returned home at the end of summer, but my worst fears were realized. My knee, it seemed, had suffered permanent damage. I felt constant pain, but nothing could keep me from the snow once it covered the mountains and meadows in town. I still pictured myself as ski champion of sorts and would build jumps and set slalom courses with my friends again and hand out prizes to each other. In spite of the damage to my knee, I would take home downhill and jumping silver ski pins to wear them to school for one day. When local people inquired about the accident and asked my father if he was going to try and have the Habicher family made responsible for this accident, my father just answered: in a small town like this I don't want to make enemies or something to that effect. I never received one *Schilling*.

By springtime, my knee was not getting better. I was limping and so was glad that my parents decided I should go to Innsbruck during summer school break and get treatment at the University Hospital. The next two summers I spent in Innsbruck. Living so far from my family—sixty miles—could have been a hardship, but I lived with my uncle and aunt Johann and Theresa Weissenbach and their two children Franzl and Lisl. Life was quite exciting. After I walked to the hospital every day to get treatment for the knee, I was free to spend my time as I liked. My cousin Franzl was only a few years younger, and together we would explore Innsbruck with all its shops and sights.

Innsbruck was a very big city for a young country boy. It was filled with endless delights, and I liked nothing better than walking the streets and avenues enjoying the trinkets and merchandise in the store windows. Here I discovered that I had an endless fascination for tools. Hardware stores mesmerize me to this day. I like nothing better than to tinker with all kinds of tools in my workshop. To have a motorbike was my greatest wish, and I knew it would be many years off. When my father told me, that after my school years I would have to have a trade, I told him, "*Tatti*, if I have to have a trade, I want to be a mechanic." He kind of smiled; he knew that I would be a painter in his business.

By Christmas 1931, I had received quite a few Ski Club Arlberg silver ski trophies. My father must have decided that his youngest son had some talent for skiing because before Christmas that year when he tinkered in his shop he looked at me and with a twinkle in his eyes asked, " So, Franz, what would you like *Christkindl* to bring you this year?" "Hickory skis," I said without a moment's hesitation. "Well, I don't know if it still has any left," father said, with a smirk on his face. I had a feeling that maybe I might get hickory skis. The old hand-me-downs with part of the tail end missing that were used by everyone in my family had carried me to as much glory as my young mind could imagine.

Christmas in St. Anton was a magical time, as it is for most children throughout the western world. We did not get many toys or things during the year; after all there were seven children. But at Christmas our parents were very generous. We not only received toys beyond our modest dreams, but sweaters, socks, hats, all hand knitted by mother or sisters. These were exciting times because in St. Anton the snow season had just began and our winter clothes were needed to keep us warm and made us look sharp as we stood at the start line of our yearly ski club championships in February.

Christmas eve 1931 I was nine; children eleven and under waited in the barn with the animals while the older members of the family prepared the traditional Christmas tree in the house. Presents were all hidden, but once in a while somehow we would catch the older ones while trying to hide them, then, with a frown we would be told, "Get going, don't snoop around." The whole process took two to three hours, and it was a long, long wait, filled with excitement. Finally we would hear the tinkle of a little bell that was the signal that the angels had finished their work in our house and were on their way to another house to bring glorious presents. For us it meant a fast dash up from the barn, through the hallway, and then bursting into the living room to see what wonderful gifts were ours this year. As soon as I entered the room my eyes fell on a brand new pair of hickory skis standing in the corner behind the tree. They were finished in a green stain, and one could easy distinguish the hickory wood. There were thin lines carved in lengthwise. For me it was one of the most unforgettable moments in my young life. Hickory skis at the age of nine were unheard of. The only other boy in town who could have gotten hickory skis was Herbert Schneider, the son of Hannes, who was a year older than me.

My father then said; "Franz, these skis might be a bit long for you now, but they should last you for a few years and some ski club championships. One doesn't get hickory skis every year. Tomorrow you take them to Hannes' ski shop and tell them to mount a binding for you.

Bindings in these primitive early days of skiing consisted of metal toe irons. A hole would be drilled through the middle of the ski from one side to the other, then a flat piece of metal the size of three and a half inches by six inches long and one sixthth inch thick inserted. After it was inserted, on each side the metal would be bent up 90 degrees, but at the front it would be narrower so that the boot then would get stuck in it. Near the top of the toe iron was a slit for the strap to keep the boot from pulling up and out of it. About six inches back a

small hole would be drilled through the ski through which to
insert a leather strap which would be wound around the boot
to keep it on the ski, called long thongs. It also wouldn't release in case of a fall. Ski accidents were common, but the
thrills one could experience on skis were worth the risks.

Christmas 1931 was unforgettable. Unfortunately, so was
new years day 1932. I was now a ten-year-old, my birthday
being December 29th. My new skis had not yet had the pleasure to experience a downhill run when after lunch friends
and I climbed up a moderate hill in herringbone fashion. As
we stood there, another group with girls just started the climb
up. I turned my new skis for their first run downhill—probably a bit show-offish—and tried to make a parallel christy
and come to a stop. The snow was a bit crusty, and one ski
got caught on the icy crust while the other flew on. I heard a
sickening crack as my left leg snapped. Pain seized my body
as I lay there in the snow and screamed in agony and, no
doubt frustration. The screams echoed against the mountain
walls. My friends rushed up to me trying to help, but were
not sure how to. Some of the boys went to my home to get a
toboggan and to tell my family that I got hurt. The girls stayed
trying to comfort me. It was an hour before they returned
with the toboggan and then loaded me gingerly—there was
no splint or painkiller—onto the toboggan and tried hard to
prevent unnecessary bumps. Still the broken bones, tibia and
fibula, did rub against each other, and I just had to endure
the agony. Finally I was pulled toward house Nr. 14. In the
meantime neighbors were alerted and the local doctor was
called.

January 1st is a big holiday in Austria, and the custom is
that neighbors visit each other after morning mass and wish
each other *Gutes Neues Jahr* (Have a good new year). Also,
each neighbor had to serve *Schnapps* to each well wisher, if
its a man. Not accepting the offer would be considered being
a sissy or conceited. When the doctor arrived, he was already
in good spirits, having visited patients of his and accepted
toasts of Schnapps. *"Ja, ja Franzl*, we will fix your leg, no
problem," he said in his hoarse and raspy voice. Before long
neighbors from house Nr. 15, Adolf and Richard Habicher,
arrived and Albert Strolz from house Nr. 13 and from house
Nr. 16 arrived Alfred Koehle. These four men were the ones

who now had the job of "pulling my leg!" As I lay in my
parents bed, next to the *Stube* (living room), two men held me
by the shoulder while the other two were pulling on my foot
and the doctor with his hands aligned the broken bones. It
sent me into a high orbit of pain which I would only once
more experience in my life as you will read later on in this
book, and that would last less than a minute. My mother and
sisters ran out of the house, crying. For them it must have
been hell listening to my lamentation and misery. Immediately a plaster cast was wrapped firmly around my broken
leg, and that's when my prolonged agony began. The doctor
made the cast tight without allowing for swelling, and very
soon my leg began to swell. One cannot describe the pain.
Day and night I cried, and my brother Pepi who lay in a bed
in the same room called me a sissy and threw once in a while
a pillow at me. He, of course could not have known that the
swelling of the leg and the hard cast caused all this pain, and
I forgive him. My father even went to Innsbruck to buy me a
hand-held jig saw, tool set and wood with monograms, chocolate and lots of sweets, all trying to divert my mind from the
pain.

It was weeks before the swelling started to subside and
my life became bearable. The old cast then was removed and
a new one put on and the pain was all but gone. After four
months finally the last cast was removed, but it was weeks
before I could walk normal again. The painful accident left
me one permanent reminder: my left leg is still over half an
inch longer than my right leg.

In the fall I was back in dreary school and thinking eagerly about the coming winter and skiing and finally giving
my hickory's a good workout. It may seem strange now, but I
never, ever again thought about the broken leg or let the fear
of it daunt my daring on the slopes.

It was likely that during the next ski season, when I was
skiing with friends near the *Schlosskopf* (castle hill) that an
event happened which gave me a tremendous boost of confidence, convincing me that maybe I had the makings of a champion in me. We were a group of dare devil youngsters and
liked nothing better than challenge each other for daring es-
capades. Pepi Jenewein was the unquestioned leader of our
group. He was short like me but absolutely fearless. Pepi

would rather die than have anyone beat him in our game of daredevilry. He was over two years older than I and had great style. His father Joseph Jenewein had been a ski champion and knew how to select and prepare skis for his son. He knew all about waxes and in his ski repair shop mounted steel edges which only a few years earlier were invented by Dr. Lettner of Salzburg. Pepi's father's advice and taking care of his equipment was well rewarded when Pepi became world champion in the alpine combined in 1939 in Zakopane, Poland. Pepi proved to have more talents than just skiing as we will find out later, on the Russian front in World War II.

One day we were skiing on the *Schlosskopf* where *Schloss Arlen* stood before it turned into a ruin, where Heinrich Findelkind was deposited on the steps by a unmarried mother in the 1300s. Just below the *Schlosskopf* was the home of my friend Rudi Alber, who had by this time pretty much forgiven me for almost cutting three fingers off a few years earlier. The *Schlosskopf* was chosen for our exploits because it was close and very steep. We were all skiing and having a great time when somebody suggested , "Hey, let's see who can shuss down from the highest point of the hill?" For non skiers, shussing of course meant going straight down the steep part of the hill without turning from side to side to slow your speed. To shuss *Schlosskopf*—that would be a true test of daring.

We started from the bottom of the hill and marched up together part of the way. The brave young skiers looked over their shoulders as the valley floor dropped farther and farther below. One by one they turned and with a sigh pointed their tips straight down and shussed. To decide to turn and go was an admission of defeat. Higher and higher we went. And the higher we went, the fewer of us there were. The ones at the bottom were looking up, shaking their head, pointing and laughing. Still higher we trudged. Then suddenly, it was just Pepi Jenewein and I. I looked at Pepi, he looked at me, and we took a few more steps. Finally, Pepi turned his skis and shussed straight down, building tremendous speed. I don't know what craziness came over me, but I wanted to go higher and looked up the steep slope to where a fence marked the end of the meadow and the ruins of *Schloss Arlen* were still visible. In the distance far below I could hear my friends yelling. Then quickly I pointed the skis straight down with a little worry. It was sheer exhilaration and a personal triumph. Pepi was the best, the bravest of us young Arlbergers; he set the standard, but little Franz Gabl had out skied him that day. It gave me confidence. I would never forget it, and at moments when I would doubt myself, my ability or my guts, I would remember the sight of Pepi Jenewein turning and shussing in front of me.

Until 1934, the only races I ran were the Ski Club Arlberg championships held every year in February. After having won more than my share of the silver ski pins, by 1934 I was through with my injuries and ready for more challenges.

"Du, Gabaly!" Hannes Schneider called to me as I walked past his ski shop. "Gabaly" is what I was most frequently called in St. Anton, but it always had a special meaning coming from my hero, the great ski pioneer Hannes Schneider. "Do you want to go to Kitzbühel for the Austrian Youth Championships?" Hannes asked. I couldn't believe my ears. "*Ja! Ja!* of course, Hannes," I said, still not believing what I was hearing. "Then go home and tell your parents you will take the Arlberg Express train on Thursday to Kitzbühel. You, Pepi Jenewein, Albert and Karl Pfeifer, Rudi Moser and Herman Ladner are going to represent our Ski Club at the Austrian Youth Championships this weekend. Make sure your equipment is in good order and take some Sohm and Bilgeri ski wax with you. Herman Schuler will go with you as manager and don't forget to wear your gray club pullover with the red and white stripes on the sleeves." I almost ran home and said to my father, *"Tatti,* Hannes told me that I could go with our team to Kitzbühel for the youth races." I thought I saw a smirk come over his face.

I didn't need a second invitation. Kitzbuehel! The Austrian National Youth Championships in 1934! I was just twelve and now going to the national championships! Not only that, but Kitzbühel had already a cable car to the top of the Streifalpe, so we wouldn't have to hike up. A cable car came to the Galzig three years later, in 1937. Kitzbühel was already famous as a ski destination, although from a ski terrain standpoint it was minor league compared to the wide open spaces and endless runs in our Arlberg region.

That Thursday, the "hotshots" Pepi Jenewein, Karl and Albert Pfeifer, Rudi Moser, Herman Ladner and myself were gathered at the train station with all our skis, equipment and luggage. Herman Schuler was running around like a hen trying to keep his brood close by and organized. A sizable crowd of locals had gathered at the train station to send the local boys off to the national championships. My father came to join with the send-off, and we could hear the chorus of *Hals und Beinbruch! Hals und Beinbruch.* Literally translated that means: break your neck, break your leg, which sounds more like a curse than well-wishing, especially considering the frequency with which skiers broke their legs and sometimes their necks in those days. But it was and still is in Austria the common way to say "Good luck!" Just as in the theater, it is only common courtesy to say to an actor before the play begins, "Break a leg!"

We arrived in Kitzbühel later that evening and got settled into our rooms. It doesn't take much to imagine the excitement of still school boys getting ready for the biggest adventure of their young lives, trying to play cool and professional on one hand, and on the other hand acting just like little kids let loose in a video arcade. The next morning we walked from our hotel to the cable car. On the way we walked past a little airfield near town that had been made into a primitive airport, and that's where I saw my first airplane close up. You must understand that to a young boy in love with tools and everything mechanical, and whose high aspiration in life— other than becoming a champion skier—was to own a motorcycle, seeing a real life airplane close up was a never-forgotten thrill. To this day ask me about Kitzbühel in 1934 and I'll tell you quick as a wink, "That's where I saw my first airplane."

It was another thrill to ride the cable car to the top of the *Hahnenkamm* (rooster comb). From here we needed to locate the downhill start. The downhill went down to Kirchberg another town on the bottom of the *Hahnenkamm* mountain through some clear alpine meadows, then dropped into the forest with some clearings. These were farmer's meadows and were marked with fences which had openings. Most were closed off with cross beams, and when we started to remove them the farmer would come out and yell at us, do not trespass on my field. We then had to ski around it, and on some fences we just removed the cross beams so we could get through it. The local boys knew all the shortcuts; they had a easy time and of course did well in the race. As for me, it was an experience I shall never forget, though the results I rather would.

The next day in the morning was the slalom, and after only a few gates a ski came off and I disqualified. In the afternoon was the jumping competition, and that's where my heart really was. The Innsbrucker Franz Mair came in 1st with Hans Bucher 2nd and me 3rd. In 1941, seven years later, I would meet up with Hans again, and we would march together into Russia to serve as cannon fodder for Hitler's madness.

We were not particularly pleased with ourselves as we returned to St. Anton on Sunday night. There was no hero's welcome awaiting us. Instead, we had to put up with a fair amount of teasing. Even Hannes Schneider joined in the fun. *"Du, Gabaly!"* he called to me from his house the next day as I walked past his. "I think I shall have to send you all to Paznaun." It was an old joke and painful now. To threaten a Arlberger ski racer with exile to the Paznaun was a true insult. Paznaun was another mountain valley nearby; however, it was not blessed with anywhere near the same caliber of skiing terrain as we had on the Arlberg. Every time when Hannes told us we should pack our skis and move to the Paznaun was like telling a major league hitter that he should go back to the lowest level in the minors. Ooh, it hurt! Of course, it was all meant to be a joke. But, thank God, it wasn't our last chance to bring glory to St. Anton. The next year in 1935, I was sent by the ski club to represent the club at the All-Tyrolean Youth Championships held in Wattens, near Innsbruck. Now thirteen years old, I was entered into the twelve to fifteen year old group. I won in my age group in the downhill race, and in the jumping I not only beat my age group, but also the next higher one as well, including Pepi Jenewein.

Perhaps my most memorable ski race in those early days of my career was in Innsbruck in 1936. It was not a national championship exactly, it was more like an All-Austria Youth Ski Festival. Over 700 young skiers from every region of Austria gathered on the famous Patscherkofel for the alpine events and for the jumping on the *Berg Isel* of "Napoleonic" fame, where Norwegian Birger Ruud had more than once soared to

international fame. Racers were divided into two age catego-
ries, twelve to fifteen and fifteen to eighteen. I was fourteen
now, so I still raced in the younger category. On this trip I
was lucky to have with me my good friend, Herman Ladner.
Herman was known as the skiing farm boy. He came from
our sister town St. Jakob, adjacent to St. Anton. Herman
was a few month older than me, but he literally towered over
most in our age group. He had a constant grin on his face as
if life was just a picnic. He was one of the most optimistic,
jovial, person I've ever known. His good humor buoyed me,
not only on this weekend but on much more difficult days
much farther east five and half years later. Herman and I
were from the Ski Club Arlberg and proudly wore our grey
pullovers with the red and white stripes on the upper arms,
the Tyrolean colors. The racers from the Arlberg had a great
reputation, with the likes of Pfeifer, Harrer, Werle, Matt, Willy
Walch and others bringing home championships from all over
Europe. Hannes Schneider of course started this tradition
before World War I. We were so proud to represent the
Tyrolean colors against the other eight provinces in Austria.

We arrived in Innsbruck on Friday, accompanied by
Hannes's right hand man Herman Schuler. Herman was our
manager and was to take care of the logistics. He was not a
coach in a sense we understand it today. His job was to get
each age group to the right place at the right time, hopefully
with all our equipment intact and in good shape. Races simply weren't well organized. Saturday was the downhill. We
hadn't seen the course, never having been on that mountain.

We awoke Saturday at 6:00 a.m. and hurried out without
breakfast. A bad mistake. Herman Ladner, Rudi Moser and
I walked for half an hour from our hotel on the *Maria Theresien
Strasse* to Igls where the cable car would take us up to the
Patscherkofel. What we found there was sheer madness.
Many hundreds of skiers with all their equipment, plus all
the tourists and well wishers, and all were waiting in line for
the cable car to take them up the steep mountain. There was
pushing and shoving and swearing. Thinking about it later,
we realized we would have been much better off climbing to
the starting point, but we didn't know at that time that we
would have to wait for several hours to get on the cable car.
About noon, when we finally arrived at the top, we were abso-

lutely famished and rushed to the hotel for a quick bite of
Heisse Wuerstl (wieners). Then we had to find our starting
point for the downhill. It was windy and snowy and cold at
the top. At a table we got some bibs, and they told us to go
downhill to the left a few hundred yards; that's where the
start was supposed to be. Finally we arrived and we waited
and waited. Name after name was called for their time to
start, but frequently no one came forward. Their trip up, combined with the cold and snow, had turned many competitors
into frozen stiffs, and they had left. But Herman, Rudi and I
had no quit in us. We had spent too many summers on those
mountain meadows with heavy scythes in our hands, not caring about weather. But as they say, the spirit was more than
willing; the flesh, unfortunately had become quite weakened
by the ordeal of the morning and the lack of hearty food.

I felt quite queasy as I got to the starting line after 2:30
p.m. From here we could see some distance down, above timberline. After the broad open expanse the course disappeared
into the woods, following a logging road with many
switchbacks back and forth down the mountain. It was on
the same ski run as the Olympic course in 1976, 40 years
later, when another Franz, this one was Franz Klammer, became world famous. Of course the run was totally different.
Big swathes of trees were removed, the run widened and
smoothed out like a golf course. Five-four-three-two-one, and
off I went with a hard push on my ski poles. It was a good
start, but my legs were shaky ,and my stomach was turning
like a boulder. I made it in good time down the open area and
hit the woods in high speed. On the second switchback my
stomach had had enough, and I was leaning into the uphill
side of the road and vomited. A moment later the skier who
started behind me raced past. I was sicker than I could remember and had every reason to give up, go back to the hotel
in Innsbruck and climb into a soft, warm bed. Then another
racer passed me. Suddenly I got angry, very angry. These
were competitors passing me while I vomited onto the side of
the road. I didn't come to Innsbruck for this. I tore after the
one who had just passed with everything I had. I saw that I
had gained some distance, but knew there was no way I could
make up the time difference to the finish line.

In those days, downhill courses were somewhat loosely

defined. There were no gates or boundaries to follow. There
was the top of the mountain and way down the bottom, and
the winner's medal would go to the skier who got from the top
to the bottom in the shortest amount of time. If there were
three feet of new snow overnight, you raced in three feet of
powder. Packing a downhill course at that time was unheard
of. You need to understand that what I did next may have
been foolish, it may have been creative, but it was not cheat-
ing. I was about to give up in despair when I noticed a log
shoot to my left. This is a path straight down the mountain
that is carved through the trees by logs crashing down from
above where they had been felled and is only useful for this
purpose, and another use for a desperate ski racer to make
up time. As I eyed the chute, I couldn't help to get the itch
and try to slide on my skis down, sitting on my bottom and
with hands held out sideways to try to slow down. There
were no logs in the chute and by letting myself falling sideways a few times, I cut many switchbacks, and as I cut across
the road almost wiped out one of the two guys who passed me
when I vomited high up. I can only imagine the thoughts in
his head as he saw out of the corner of his eyes this fool coming straight down the mountain like a log. As I neared the
bottom of the hill I saw an opportunity to get back on the
logging road, and a hundred yards later I crossed the finish
line in a deep Hannes Schneider crouch. I was ever glad this
ordeal was over. My heroics, or foolishness, managed to win
me third place in my age group, a position that brought bright
smiles of joy to my father's face but still left me disappointed.

The *Preisverteilung* (awards ceremony) was unbelievable.
I had never, ever seen such riches in all my life nor would I
ever see it again. It was held in the largest auditorium in
Innsbruck, and that Sunday night it was filled to the rafters
with racers, skiers, parents, officials and Innsbruckers. The
tables on the stage and the walls were filled with hundreds of
trophies and merchandise.

Is it then any wonder when every youngster in Austria,
who was a ski racer, wanted to be a champion? For trophies
there were four Leica cameras—the finest camera in the world
then, and truly a prize to break one's neck for—plus bicycles,
skis, boots, poles, bindings, pack sacks, pullovers, hats and
waxes. And all these prizes for boys from twelve to eighteen

years of age. There were no girls competing then. I received a small camera for my efforts, but the reputation I earned as a do-or-die competitor was more valuable to me. I had gotten to the point where I wanted to be a champion. It is out of such hunger that champions are born, I believe. Where I got this desire, I couldn't say, but am sure this experience instilled in me then, that I wanted to be a ski champion.

After the races in Innsbruck, I had to think of my future. In April, my school principal *Herr Oberlehrer* Hofer called me to his office and said, "Franz, your father wants you to begin as an apprentice in his business as a painter. You are one of my best pupils, and I will let you out of school April 15th instead of June 30th, so you can join your father." I was not too happy and did not like the painting business at all, but father convinced me if I didn't join his business and wanted to be a mechanic, I could not be an apprentice instructor for Hannes Schneider. I than said, "Yes, *Tatti*, I will join you as an apprentice," and I became his helper.

Hannes Schneider & St. Anton Become World Famous

In the mid 1930s, St. Anton was a world-renowned ski resort. The rich and famous would invade our town, crowding the few hotels and spilling over into the spare rooms of nearly all the business and some farmer's houses in the village. To accommodate all these tourists, nearly every extra bed had been turned into a guest room, and still there was often not enough room. Royalty mixed with movie stars and wealthy business tycoons. Other than the excellent skiing terrain and snow conditions, there was really only one reason for St. Anton's fame in the growing ski world—Hannes Schneider.

If you are a skier, you probably already know of Johann "Hannes" Schneider, one of the greatest names in the history of skiing. He was born in 1890 and grew up in the town of Stuben in Vorarlberg, the western-most province of Austria and adjacent to the Swiss border. Stuben is only about eight miles west from St. Anton, and it shares much of the same great ski terrain. Hannes became famous for his skiing talents early, even though the sport was in its infancy at the turn of the century. He had as his teachers the likes of Victor Sohm, also from Vorarlberg, and Wilhelm Paulke from Germany. Sohm and Paulke spent several weeks of every winter in the mountains at Stuben or at St. Christoph on the Arlberg Pass. Hannes, as a boy, would watch these two skiers any time he had a chance and ogle their skis when they had them stuck in the snow next to the entrance of the Fritz Family Inn in Stuben. Before long these two gentlemen invited young Hannes and taught him the basic rudiments in their new found sport. It didn't take Hannes long to master this sport, and before long he would leave Sohm and Paulke in the "dust."π

From these teachers he learned the standard skiing techniques of the day. Turns on skis were accomplished mainly by the Starsky method. With this technique the skier would remain upright and steer through the turn using only one ski pole which was passed from one hand to the other as needed.

It was hardly elegant or effective and the high center of gravity resulted in a great many spills at reasonably high speed. From the Telemark Valley in Norway came another popular method of turning. The Telemark turn consisted of bending both knees with one knee in front of the other. The heel of the front ski was pushed out, thus initiating a turn. This forced the trailing ski to turn in the direction of the front ski at an angle. With practice it could be quite effective and elegant. Schneider mastered these techniques and turned his skills into championships throughout Austria, Germany and Switzerland. But he was an innovator and soon tried using two ski poles for balance instead of one and found that by crouching down and lowering his center of gravity he could achieve much higher speeds, especially through turns. Neither with the Telemark nor Starsky method could he achieve high speeds. At that time ski boots were the usual hiking boots, without nails at the edges. The lateral ankle support was nil, but there was no packed snow then, and hard or icy snow would be avoided like the plague.

If an artist were to paint a portrait of the ideal ski hero of the time, that picture would be Hannes—tall and lanky, his dark, curly hair provided a veritable crown to his high forehead. He had a strong, Romanish nose, and his skin was always a deep bronze from the days spent on the sunny ski slopes in winter, hiking and mountain climbing in summer and during the fall hunting chamois, deer, elk or marmots. The last mentioned were hunted not so much for meat but for their fat which was a home remedy for some ailments.

In later years Hannes' face took on a deeply weathered, leathery look like a well worn saddle. He had a quick smile with a dashing and daring that appealed to the adventurous tourists who were taking up skiing as a sport.

Karl Schuler owned the *Hotel Post* in St. Anton in 1907. By this time Schneider's reputation was spreading throughout the European skiing world and operators from Switzerland were appealing to him to come to one of their areas and open a ski school. Schuler went to visit Hannes and his parents in the nearby village of Stuben where Hannes lived and asked him to come to start a ski school in St. Anton. Hannes was just seventeen, but his parents realized that if they didn't say yes to St. Anton, it would only be a matter of time before

Hannes would leave to some more distant area, most probably Switzerland where some ski resorts offered him a position as a ski instructor. Pay at that time would have been room and board and a few Swiss *Fraenkly*. So they agreed, and Hannes left home for St. Anton. Our little village would never be the same.

Hannes applied in 1907 for operating a ski school in St. Anton, and the city council gave their approval. The first few years, as expected, there weren't line ups for lessons. Business was slow, and Hannes could devote a lot of his time to improve his own skiing and his teaching technique. He even had to do chores for the Hotel Post, like helping with luggage to be carried from the *Bahnhof* to the Hotel 30 yards away.

He was naturally gifted for skiing, and that's when he developed his style—low crouch, two poles and high speed skiing. He also was an innovator in ski teaching. When there were enough students, he would hire extra teachers—they were the best skiers from St. Anton—and divide them into classes. The first grade "beginners" would start with straight running and snow plow on a very flat hill. Then in the next higher class he started the pupils with a snowplow turn. Gradually he made them do stem turns and then stem *christianias*. Within a few years Hannes perfected his own, high speed parallel turns. These turns made the Starsky method and the Telemark turns superfluous. This method then became the Arlberg Technique which for more then a half century was taught world wide. In some regions of Austria there were a few jealous men who tried other methods of teaching, but these never amounted to much.

As Hannes reputation grew, so did St. Anton's. Both reputations were given a tremendous boost in the 1920s and early 1930s when Dr. Arnold Fanck of Germany made some of the world's earliest ski movies. He was a sort of pioneering Warren Miller. Naturally, many of the films starred the dashing Hannes Schneider of St. Anton where many of these movies were made. They featured fast-moving footage and fantasy-style photography to create a romantic view of winter in the mountains and of skiers of heroic proportions. The films were a roaring success and were seen by millions in Europe and all around the world. As a result, the rich and famous crowded into our sleepy little village when the snows hit and didn't leave until spring when the brown patches of bare grass showed. It was wonderful to see the new pupils arrive at Hannes Schneider's Ski School meeting place. They had traveled from far away places, sometimes thousands of miles away. They even came from America and Japan. After getting settled in, they would gather with their fellow students at the ski school meeting place every morning at ten o'clock, and you could feel the anticipation and excitement in the air. While they talked excitedly together, a tall imposing man would enter with some ceremony. Slowly the students would realize that the man they had come so far to see was right in front of them. You could see by the look of awe in their eyes and by the hush that spread that they could hardly believe they were in the presence of the man they had admired on the big movie screen.

Hannes' fame reached new world wide heights when he traveled to Japan. The visit in 1930 was a result of Hannes' fame in the movies made by Dr. Arnold Fanck and Hannes' friendship with world-famous German stunt pilot Ernst Udet. During the second world war, Udet became a general for Hitler's *Luftwaffe*, and when Hitler's fortunes went awry he committed suicide.

On his way to Japan, Hannes travelled through Siberia on the Russian railroad. Eventually he was imprisoned by the Russians on the border of China. Only by the intervention of the Japanese Foreign Ministry was he freed. During this visit, Hannes met with many high ranking government officials and taught ski lessons to the Japanese, where on one occasion 500 pupils lined up for his lessons on Mt. Fuji. There are many photos of him from this time demonstrating his now famous Arlberg Technique. The newspapers of Austria and Germany followed the progress of Schneider and the overwhelming response of the Japanese people to this engaging hero and ski pioneer. Today there is a handsome bronze monument of a well dressed Hannes Schneider on skis in Japan—a monument of a grateful people to a ski pioneer who taught the Japanese how to ski.

When he returned home to St. Anton following a round the world tour, Hannes was treated with a degree of awe reserved for world leaders. This was our own Hannes Schneider, whom the world idolized. This is the man who brought the beauty and skills of our beloved skiing to a world hungry for the thrills,spills and excitement of this growing sport on skis.

Hannes' ski shop in the village center, near the Hotel Post, could rightly be called St. Anton's spiritual center, at least as far as us hot shot young skiers were concerned. Here the latest in ash and hickory skis were displayed and sold along with the newest in ski fashions—there were no stretch pants then. It was here that my father went on Christmas 1931 to pick out a brand new pair of hickory skis as a Christmas present for me, and some day I hoped to become one of those lucky young skiers who might be working for Hannes.

A happy tradition began in the mid-thirties when a rich Hollander Mr. Oskar Janssen from Amsterdam, one of Hannes' early pupils, decided to leave a portion of his will to the young skiers of St. Anton whose parents could hardly afford new skis for them in the deep depression. The future champions from St. Anton were already practicing on world–class ski runs, and now they would have the equipment to bring more glory to the Arlberg. The generous bequest would provide the funds to buy promising young skiers top notch equipment, and Hannes Schneider was the executor. Every year or two he would offer brand new pairs of skis, ski poles and bindings to a small group of lucky youngsters who showed promise to be future champions. I was one of them.

It wasn't too many years after winning my first Ski Club Championships in 1929 that Hannes called to me as I walked by his shop. *"Du, Gabaly,"* he said brusquely but with a twinkle in his eye. "Come and get your new skis." And every year or two after that it was the same. "Gabaly, get your skis!" It was no surprise then that my fondest dream at this time of my life was to become one of Hannes' ski instructors. A ski instructor had everything a fifteen-year-old boy could possibly want: virtually unlimited time on the slopes, all kinds of practice time, working with godlike Hannes Schneider, and last but certainly not least, being able to teach the ski bunnies how to ski. These were the many cute, young girls who flocked to the slopes and idolized the ski instructors. Who could want anything more, or so I thought as a happy young Austrian teenager.

When the first snows of winter came in late 1936, I decided it was time I should try to become an apprentice ski instructor for Hannes. To become an instructor, one had to apprentice for two years, assisting with the classes and thoroughly learning the now famous Arlberg Technique. My brother Pepi had become an apprentice the previous year, and I was dying with jealousy. I had won more than my share of races; I knew I could ski, but would Hannes accept me? I was shy and afraid to ask him. I had no idea how to go about this.

"Just go to his house in the evening when he is home and ask him," my father advised simply. So with fresh snow on the ground I nervously walked the few blocks from our house to the Schneider house located in the middle of the village. I could see the light was on in the house as I approached, but instead of walking straight up to it, I kept on walking past. Finally, I said to myself, Franz, don't be a fool, just go and ask. I marched up to the door and knocked. It was if he had been waiting at the door because in an instant the door was open and there stood the now middle-aged ski pioneer. "Hannes," I said nervously, "Can I be an *Hilfsschilehrer* (an apprentice) for you, Hannes?" All the townspeople would address Hannes Schneider as "Hannes" where as any outsider would address him as "Mr. Schneider."

"*Selbstverstaendlich!* Of course," he said with a warm smile. "Be there tomorrow at 9:30 sharp at the ski school meeting place, and I will send you with one of my regulars." I was to be a ski instructor for Hannes Schneider! All my dreams were coming true. It was December 22, 1936, and I remember it like it happened last week.

While becoming a ski instructor apprentice was very exciting, I soon found that it was not all fun and games. We gathered every morning on the slopes on the north side of the Hotel Post, across the railroad tracks, where the ski school meeting place was centered. The students would be assigned their instructors, and the apprentices were there to assist the instructors. My friends Herman Ladner and Rudi Moser along with myself were the newest apprentices that year. Since we were new, we were assigned to assist the instructor with the beginning students on the gentle slopes just across from the *Bahnhof* (railroad station).

We were ski racers, so we had our eyes on the Galzig, the mountain northeast of our village with a challenging three-mile-long downhill run and the site of many famous races including the Arlberg Kandahar. But instructing on the Galzig was reserved for the more experienced instructors, so we were left to help the beginners at the base of the hills. Of course, there were no chair lifts or rope tows in St. Anton in 1936. Beginning skiers had to learn to climb the slopes using herringbone or sidestepping techniques. Students who were able to climb the higher peaks used seal skins on their skis to keep from sliding backwards after each step. The instructor carried first aid equipment, just in case—at that time on all the mountain ski runs there was only one ski patrol man Alois Petter to take care of injured skiers. For beginners whose time on skis was limited to a few hours, those treks up even the smallest hills were a challenge. The instructor flitted about his class of about anywhere from 15 to 20 pupils, sometimes over 30 beginners, shouting instructions and encouragement.

As apprentices, it was our job to pick up those who had fallen, try to help them gain their feet and in one way or another get them to the top of the hill. Some of the women just waited for their apprentice to help them up; we felt some of them did it on purpose. When the rookie skiers had finally made it to the top of the slope, they received their instructions on the basics of the Arlberg Technique—how to keep your center of gravity down low, how to turn keeping your weight firmly above the downhill ski and push the heel out, press the inside edge of the ski hard, how to use your poles for balance and control; then we would watch them tumble down. We skied after them, picked them up, tried to force out words of encouragement and finally got them to the bottom of the hill. Then it was time to turn around and do it all over again.

However frustrating it seemed for us at times, we reminded ourselves that at least it was better than apprenticing in a dirty machine shop or dusty cabinet maker's shop. We were on skis, and some of the students were pretty young girls who admired our skills on skis. Many were eager for romance, and in the evenings instructors had a hard time to decide which blonde to accompany to the five o'clock tea and dance in one of the many hotel bars.

In the mid-thirties was also the time when ski equipment started to change. Up to then, skis were made of ash wood, and few had steel edges; they were just invented in 1929 by a certain Dr. Lettner of Salzburg, and the metal edges were mounted in local ski shops after their purchase. Years later, almost all skis were sold with steel edges already mounted in the factory. On the tip, plastic edges were mounted. At that time skis were very thin at the "shovel,"so as not to "dig" into the deep snow, there was hardly any "hard piste," and the plastic edges did not scrape at the tips like metal edges would have done and wear them out. Skis then broke frequently at the tips and Jenewein's and Pangratz's ski repair shops in St. Anton did all the repair of broken ski tips. A new invention came on the market, too—metal skis. They were immune to breaking and warping, but once they were bent out of shape, they were ready to be discarded. From Norway came then the Marius Eriksen skis. They were laminated and made of hickory and were almost immune to warping which happened frequently to skis not laminated. They were the Cadillac of skis then.

At that time the rule to select the length of skis was very simple: with an arm extended, one reached to the tip of the ski; the hollow of the hand was supposed to touch the tip. If you were tall, you were told to get long skis; it was generally 210 or 215 cm. If a person was shorter, the skis were shorter also; there was not much allowance made for ability. The reason then was: if you were tall, your weight would have had to be considered; the greater running surface kept the heavier skier higher on the unpacked snow. Many years later when every ski area used packing machines, the weight ratio was no more a problem, and male skiers would get started with six and a half-foot-long skis, women about three to six inches shorter ones. These days it would be unthinkable to learn to ski on 210 cm skis, even 205 cm. Naturally with short skis one could learn skiing much faster, especially on groomed slopes.

After the second world war plastic skis were introduced, and also one of the greatest invention was the slippery, soft plastic base on skis. The first one was called Kofix (Kofler-fix) and was patented by a certain Dr. Kofler of Innsbruck, Austria. These bases didn't need to be waxed and were much faster then the previous hard plastic or wood bases, even if they had been waxed.

Bindings in the late twenties and early thirties were the Huitfeld—a hole was drilled through the ski just behind the toe irons, then a leather strap inserted and a buckle attached on the outside which was to tighten the binding and push the boot forward into the toe iron. On the outer side, the strap could be adjusted for length. (The toe irons are described in Chapter 2.)

By the mid-thirties a new invention took over. Mr. Bildstein, a ski jumper from the province of Vorarlberg, invented the *Bildsteinstrammer.* This binding was replacing the Huitfeld binding. Onto each end of the leather strap a spring the shape of a "U" with a tightening buckle was attached.

By the mid 1930s yet a newer kind came on the market. It was called Kanadahar binding. This had a spring, the same shape as the *Bildstein Strammer* in the rear but no buckle and was connected to a cable which ran along the sides of the skis which had cable guides and in front of the toe irons was an adjustable tightening buckle. These bindings then were used by the very majority of skiers until after the war when manufacturers experimented with release bindings. Ski poles were made out of bamboo or plain wood, and on the bottom end a two-inch-long iron tip was screwed in. Through a hole on top of the handle a thin, leather strap was attached. The baskets, made of a bamboo ring and crosswise a leather strap, were attached about four inches from the bottom up. In the early thirties steel poles took over—we called them *Schwedenstahl*(Swedensteel). After World War II, steel poles were adjustable, and grips and baskets were made out of rubber or plastic. Eventually plastic poles became the fashion.

As we apprentice instructors gained more experience, we were often called to assist the advanced classes. This involved a bus ride to St. Christoph, then a half hour hike up to the Maiensee and then down the *Waldschneise,* a three-mile run back to St. Anton. The snow was often deep powder or a breakable crust, so the trip down was usually chaotic for these more advanced students. The ski instructor would lead the class of students down the slope and the apprentices were left behind to help the stragglers. We were called *Knochensammler* (bone collectors). The name was appropriate. We would dig students out of deep snow, try to find out if there were any injuries, help them to their feet and try to get them back down the hill in the right direction.

On one of these trips, one of the *Knochensammlers* was a young apprentice with a fairly short fuse. P.A. was stuck with a middle-aged French woman who probably had no business on even this moderately difficult slope. She was continually falling, and he, of course, was left to dig her out and get her going again. After picking her up for the umpteenth time, his temper got the better of him, and he swore at her using four letter words in German. What he didn't realize was that she was well versed in fluent German, even gutter German. The woman went to Hannes, and the apprentice was immediately dismissed, no questions asked. Hannes knew that the student was the customer, and the customer was always right. And we knew that Hannes would not tolerate discourtesy to his students.

Life in St. Anton during the winter season of 1936–1937 was hard to beat. I was fifteen. Hannes Schneider was my boss. I spent my days on the slopes, working in as much hard skiing practice as I could between the lessons and discovering on a daily basis that after Hannes created such a glamorous image of Arlberg ski instructors, that many of the young ladies came not so much for the thrills on skis as for the romance of the ski instructors and romance in general. This was a lesson my friend Herman Ladner seemed to learn a little quicker than me.

Still, a dark cloud was brewing. Although St. Anton was a bustling little community in Winter, thanks to its world reputation as a ski center, the rest of Austria was suffering unbearably. It started in 1934 when Adolf Hitler, the new German *Reichskanzler* imposed a *Tausend Mark Sperre* (1000-Mark tax) on any German tourists traveling to Austria. The 1,000 *Reichsmark* tax was imposed ostensibly as punishment for the outlawing of the Nazi party in Austria after their members had assassinated the Austrian Chancellor Dr. Engelbert Dollfuss, in Vienna. In reality, the tax was intended to put extreme pressure on the Schuschnigg regime, which came to power after Dollfuss was murdered.

After World War I, the Austrian Republic was born, but we Austrians had little experience in democratic government. After all, Austria had been the proud seat of the Habsburg empire for seven hundred years before it crumbled finally into the abyss of the first world war. As a result the Austrian chancellors held tremendous powers and were in effect also quasi dictators. This needs to be understood if one is to understand the willingness of many Austrians to accept the dictatorship of Hitler. Schuschnigg was hardly popular although many in the *Weinstuben* (taverns) of St. Anton and other towns and villages of Austria defended him for resisting the increasing pressure to legalize the National Socialist German Workers Party and allow them to become part of his government. Without the German tourists Austria could hardly exist; a great percentage of Tourists coming to Austria were Germans.

The German tax wreaked havoc on the Austrian economy. It was said that beggars crowded the streets of Vienna and other cities and that people were dying of hunger and cold. We in St. Anton were not immune to the suffering. Beggars were constantly going from house to house. Years later we found out that beggars seldom missed our house. They had a secret code. With chalk they would mark a spot which indicated that in this house they would almost certainly get something to eat. It was thanks to our mother, this good woman had a heart of gold; she would rather not eat then turn away a beggar. Business was slow, as most owners of houses couldn't afford painting, even though my father then employed already from six to eight journeymen during the summer.

The owner of a trade seemed to have lots of time, and many of these men would spend a lot of time during the day in the *Weinstuben* to discuss politics or what was happening in general. My father was one of them, and I began to hear stories of him defending Hitler and talking about how the Nazis might bring stability and prosperity to Austria.

There was talk of *Anschluss* (annexation). Non-Germans tend to think the word means something like a forcible takeover, something akin to rape. In reality, *Anschluss* means merger, so the discussion was whether Austria should remain totally independent, or whether it should become part of a now resurgent and greater German Third *Reich*. Good men and thoughtful men stood on both sides of this increasingly hot issue. For my part, I paid little attention to all this, my interest being absorbed by the summer activities of painting, haying, hiking, berry picking and, most of all, skiing when the blessed snow finally came. I remember still when at times

I wished I could hibernate during the summer month and only wake up when the blessed snow covered the hills.

In the summer of 1937, a great structure began to take shape on the flower covered steep meadows just above St. Anton to the northwest. It was the steel towers and wheels, cables and motors of the *Galzigbahn*, the great cable car that would carry skiers from around the world from the ski school meeting place in St. Anton to the top of the mighty Galzig, a mountain that towered almost 3,000 feet above the village and more than 7,000 feet above sea level. The Galzig came to the attention of the skiing world in 1928 when it became the location for the world's first international alpine combined ski race a downhill, slalom and a combined. Trophies were handed out for each event, but the winners trophy was for the alpine combined. It was sponsored by the well known, British ski pioneer Sir Arnold Lunn. Lunn was an early promoter of ski racing and invented the slalom race in 1922 in Switzerland when I was just one year old, and it remains essentially the same today. The race was named by Lunn after a city in India, Kandahar. To this day the Kandahar remains one of the great names in alpine ski racing, its name ringing with the poetry of great tradition and glory like Wimbledon in tennis or the Holmenkollen Ski Jump in Oslo, Norway.

The *Galzigbahn* would prove to be a godsend to me and the other aspiring racers from the Arlberg. It meant, instead of having one run a day, now, maybe half a dozen or more. Before this, skiing the Galzig meant a bus ride to St. Christoph and a hike of one hour on seal skins. Without the opportunity to ride the cable car, I have no doubt that we would not have developed the skills necessary to compete against the class of the world. Our duties as instructors kept us very busy in our second season as apprentices, but at every possible opportunity we would rush over to the *Galzigbahn* to get to the top. It cost money to ride the cable car when not in ski school, but we were given a special rate as *Einsheimische* (locals). But even this would have made it difficult to ride as much as we wanted if it were not for the fact that many of the operators were good fella's from St. Anton whom, I suppose, decided they were investing in the future glory of their home town ski heroes and frequently looked the other way as we walked past the gate, and the likes of Flunger, Alber, Schutz and others looked the other way. I am still grateful to them for their support of us young, eager skiers.

It was December 17, 1937, when the giant cable car system was completed, just in time for the new ski season. My first ride, unfortunately, was all too memorable for it got Rudi Moser and me into hot water with our idol and boss Hannes. We had decided that we would make a run on the Galzig before classes began in the morning. So we entered the big glass-enclosed cable car and swung dizzily up the mountain. What a thrill to dangle and sway hundreds of feet above the snow, rocks and cliffs instead of riding the busses, which had tracks in the rear instead of wheels, to St. Christoph and climb for an hour with seal skins on skis to the Galzig. We got to the top and found it foggy. We had climbed and skied this mountain many times before, but the station at the top was in fog, and we got lost. We knew we had to hurry to make it to class at 10:00 a.m., so we headed blindly down hoping we would find landmarks on the way. We finally found familiar territory. Down we schussed as fast as we could, wondering of the reaction of Hannes for being late. When we got to the top of Pig Hill above the ski school area, only one figure stood at the bottom looking our way. All the classes had left ,and the tall stern figure could only be one man: Hannes. He watched us schuss pig hill and motioned us toward him. "Come over here you two *Spitzbuben*," he said.

"You, Franz, go to the *Galzigbahn* and join Franz Schranz's class, and you, Rudi, you are to be *Knochensammler* for Edmund Schutz's class. Now go!"

The thought of Hannes dismissing the apprentice the year before for cursing at a student was fresh in my mind. We were still employed, and I knew I would do just about anything to keep from getting into trouble with Hannes again.

Anschluss to the Third Reich

The winter of 1937–38 passed as idyllic times. It was the second year for me as an apprentice for Hannes. Now the instructor in charge of the class would let us apprentices take over for several runs, and we would demonstrate and correct the pupils. In turn the instructor would criticize us. It was a great way to learn to be a teacher. Hannes would often sit high up on a hill and watch classes with binoculars, or he would show up and watch his instructor while giving lessons. There were no meetings after ski school. Knowing Hannes' watchful eyes were on us was enough not get too playful with the students. What we young apprentices liked best was, when Hannes said, "*Buaba* (boys) this afternoon you can go and train, you can ride the cable car once free, then you can train slalom on the slalom hill." He was very supportive that we would some day become champion racers and bring glory to the Ski Club Arlberg.

By mid-March 1938 the snow in the streets was already melting, but we still could ski from the Galzig all the way down to the village. It was now March 12th, 1938—a fateful day for Austria. As I walked toward the village center in the morning, carrying my skis on the shoulder, I noticed some red banners hanging from balconies and windows. Each had in the middle a white circle with a black *Hackenkreuz* (Swastika). It was quite unexpected, even though rumors had been circulating for weeks that Austria might become part of Germany. As I walked past Hannes Schneider's house, I saw a black spot on the side of his house. It looked like a glass of ink was thrown onto it. A small group of locals were standing there, talking, I assumed it was about the ink spot. When I arrived at the ski school meeting place at 9:30, my friends Herman Ladner and Rudi Moser were there already. They at once came over to me and said, "They have taken Hannes to a jail in Landeck," the county seat. I didn't understand what was going on. "Why would they take Hannes to jail?" I asked. Herman then said, "He might have been a friend of Schuschnigg," the Austrian Chanceller. Hannes was taken then from the jail in Landeck to Garmisch-Partenkirchen in Germany, about 15 miles from the Austrian border and was forbidden to come back to St. Anton. An old friend of Hannes who had the guts took Hannes in as a guest in Germany! That same morning we also learned that Karl Moser, who was dismissed by Hannes a few years earlier because of his then-illegal Nazi activities, came back from his German exile and was now installed as the Mayor of St. Anton. He and the other local Nazi leaders were afraid that many locals would still show loyalty to Hannes and it might cause embarrassment to them. Eventually Hannes was allowed to emigrate to the USA in 1939 with his family, wife Ludmilla, son Herbert and daughter Herta, through the efforts of a Mr. Gibson who had an interest in a ski resort in North Conway, New Hampshire. Mr. Gibson was a banker and had something to do with the U.S. government to reduce reparation payments which Germany owed to the Allies after World War I. I felt my plans, my future might take a completely different course and wondered if we still had a ski school, especially when I heard that many tourists were gathering in hotel lobbys with suitcases packed ready to leave, maybe forever. The instructors were sober, some even a bit fearful. No one knew "what now?" St. Anton was one of the few towns in Austria which had not felt the depression and hardships many of the cities and villages had gone through. Mainly responsible for this was one man—Hannes Schneider. Because of him, St. Anton was the Mecca of skiing.

In the evening of March 12th, as we all sat down for our family dinner, our father explained that it was a mistake to take Hannes away, because he was the one who attracted skiers from all over the world. But things will now get a lot better in all of Austria. "You will see some big changes now, and I will bet the beggars in all of Austria will disappear, maybe not overnight but pretty soon. We will have two or three tourists from Germany coming for every one leaving now. And you Pepi and you Franz can flirt with the *Fraeuleins* who will flood Austria, to your hearts content." Father laughed and his belly jiggled. Next day, on March 13th, a meeting of all instructors was called by two new men we didn't know, one from Innsbruck, by the name of Hubert Salcher, the other from Salzburg with the name of Hans Aichinger. They were now co-directors, and the name of "Hannes Schneider Ski School" was changed to "St. Anton Ski School."

Human emotions fired by anger fade when they are not fanned, even the strongest ones, and life resumed a semblance of normality. Partially this was due to our new co-directors of the ski school; though strong Nazis, we assumed, they seemed two decent fellows, and at no time were we coerced to join any of the Nazi Party organizations. It seemed they didn't want to ruffle feathers so quickly after taking over Hannes job. A few times, though, Mr. Ernst von Tilzer, the local party big wig, asked me to join the S.A.; it was only to race for them in the regional championships to bring glory to St. Anton and his local S. A. Party organization. Each time somehow, I managed to have an excuse.

One has to understand that "Nazi" is the abbreviated version of

NATIONAL SOZIALISTISCHE DEUTSCHE ARBEITER PARTEI
(National Socialist German Workers Party).

We would also learn soon of a change in policy. Hannes had made it a rule that instructors had to get permission from him to go to bars or for dinner with their ski school pupils. I don't remember if Hannes ever disallowed an instructor to dine or go with pupils in the bar. The new ski school directors told us that we were on our own as long as we maintained order in the classes and kept our mind on instructing during lessons.

Immediately after the *Anschluss* (annexation) German tourists flooded Austria, especially ski resorts. The mood of the population turned increasingly more euphoric. Now swastikas were displayed almost on every house in every town. The name *Oesterreich* was changed to *Ostmark*, to erase any feelings for the past 700 hundred years of Austria's existence under the banner of the Habsburg Empire. Some of the older folks were very disappointed, though there was nothing they could do. I was busy helping my father painting on huge white sheets of cloth *Führer befiel, wir folgen dir* (Leader order us, we will follow you). These were displayed on balconys, on buildings and even on the side of bridges. But the greatest disruption in Austrian life involved the traditional greeting between men on the street: a doff of the hat and a pleasant *Gruess Gott, Guten Morgen, Guten Tag, or Guten Abend* (good morning, good day or good evening). The new greeting called for an outstretched right arm and a barked, *"Heil Hitler."* It was real comical. Every time you passed a man on the street, and that could be twenty times during one walk through town, a good Nazi would throw his right arm straight up and bark a fairly loud, *"Heil Hitler."* The lesser the Nazi, then the right arm would be angled somewhat sloppily at 90 degrees from the elbow up and a *"Heil Hitler"* you could hardly hear. Women were not required to use the Nazi *Salut*, though there were a few fanatics who did as the men did. There were a few citizens who didn't bother with right arm or *Heil Hitler.* They were the strong Catholics or very old people. It became so bad that many men, even Nazis, would use a meadow path to walk to the center of town to avoid using the Hitler *Salut* with outstretched right arm. It seemed that overnight the male population was in one uniform or another. The *Gauleiters* (governors) of each province wore uniforms; some of these men looked like big fat slobs, like Goering, and paraded around like peacocks.

Sturm Abteilung (S.A.) were the brown-shirts, the original Nazi party members. The civilian *Schutz Staffel* (S.S.) in black uniforms, *Hitler Jugend* (Hitler Youth) where I belonged, wore brown shirts and an armband with the swastika flag and shorts. *Bund Deutscher Maedel* (B. D. M.), girls from 14 to 18 years of age, wore white blouses and dark skirts. These organizations marched two to three times each week through town to playing fields, marching and singing. There were very few 14-to 18-year-olds who didn't join the Hitler Youth or B.D.M.

Before long even our father got a bit tired of *"Heil, Heil."* He even told a story he had heard; an old woman complained that there was no more butter in the stores. A Nazi official heard this woman complaining and told her to repeat ten times, *"Heil Hitler*, we have enough butter." After a few repeats she said *"Heil* butter, we have enough Hitler." It was true, when Germany *anschluss*-ed Austria, the Germans came from the *Altreich* (original Germany) with hundreds of trucks to buy Austrian foodstuffs. Another story was told that when an old farm woman came to the voting place, she complained about that the new order did not respect the church, the attendant told her, "Just cross out "*Ja.*" Of course that meant yes.

Their factories were humming to capacity, not to produce foodstuff in abundance, but for armaments. Austria had foodstuff in abundance, but little money to buy it. For most Austrians these were exciting times. The economic doldrums were replaced with a bustling enthusiasm, almost as if a pall had been lifted. The family breadwinners with several children who had little or no work for many years now had all they could handle and plenty of food on the table. An Austrian family man of German stock doesn't want to live on the dole. It really was no wonder that the enthusiasm for the new regime was at an all time high.

Tourists from Germany now invaded our Austria and with their ready cash gobbled up the merchandise in short supply in Germany. Our village would never be the same. This influx of money rippled through the business community, and my father could hardly fill all the painting contracts on order.

Right after the German's marched into Austria, Hitler called for a plebiscite for April 10th with one question: "Do you agree with the *Anschluss* of Austria into the German Reich?— Yes or No." I remember it very well. I was not yet 18 and couldn't vote. I went with my Hitler Youth group by train to Innsbruck. Bernhard Wasle was our leader. His family had long been Nazi-oriented. We knew Hitler was coming on April 10th and would drive through the main streets of Innsbruck in an open car. It was about noon, and a few of us were standing on the steps of the *Proxauf Loden* store in the *Museum Strasse*. There were masses of people as if the population of all Innsbruck and the Tyrol were gathering to see this man. Finally, Hitler rode in an open Mercedes through the *Museum Strasse* toward the *Maria Theresien Strasse*. Every few seconds he lifted his right arm, angled at 90 degrees, up. There was pandemonium. *Heil– Heil–Heil* echoed back from the Patscherkofel and Seegrube. I don't think God could have had a more enthusiastic reception then Hitler did. I thought to myself then, why does this man get a reception of such proportions; he didn't do much so far for Austria?

One of the reasons that I was not too happy, was I wanted so badly to buy a bicycle in Germany where they were much less expensive then in Austria. But we Austrians had to pay duty until October when buying things in Germany. The border was still controlled; it was very unfair. The Germans could buy now all they wanted in Austria without paying duty and take it back. I realized later, Hitler brought work and bread on the tables to the hundreds of thousands of near destitute Austrian families. When the votes were counted, Austria voted overwhelmingly for *Anschluss*—if I remember right, it was 97%. In St. Anton, surprisingly the vote was similar. I also remember that many villages and towns voted 100% for *Anschluss*. They were mentioned in headlines of the daily news papers. Sure, there was some swindle, because the voting booth had an observer near the half-open curtain and could easily see the way the person voted. But despite that, when one heard and saw the enthusiasm of the population, it didn't surprise anyone. Of course after the war, when Nazism was finished, you could hear, "Well, I really never was a Nazi." To be honest, there were very few Austrians who didn't mind having Hitler *anschluss* Austria into the Third Reich. Had all those people known then that Hitler was committed to war, the enthusiasm wouldn't have been as it was. In his speeches, he always mentioned, "We do not want war;" he was fooling the population. Hitler with his Nazi party came to power in Germany on January 30, 1933. His party had only 44% of the votes, but it was the largest party. Hitler at once used all kinds of intrigue, had all communists and some social democrats jailed to prevent them from being able to vote in the *Reichstag* (congress).

Less then two month later, on March 23, 1933, Hitler was given dictatorial power through the Enabling Act. He was now a dictator. From now on until the end of the war Hitler's word was the law. The corporal of the first world war would now make all decisions not only for the German armed forces, he would now also direct the economic program for Germany, even though he never commanded a squad of men before.

Hitler was a dispatch runner in the first world war in the German army on the Western front and won the iron cross first class, at that time a very high decoration for a corporal. Hitler was not a coward.

In a speech to the *Reichstag* he said, *"Gebt mir zehn Jahre Zeit und Ihr werdet Deutschland nicht wieder erkennen!* (Give me ten years time and you shall not recognize Germany again!)" He kept his word.

After that, the *Reichstag* never met again. His minister of propaganda and enlightenment, the clubfooted Joseph Goebels, used every trick to make Hitler look like one of the greatest man in German history, greater then Frederick the Great, founder of the First *Reich*, or Bismarck of Second *Reich* fame.

Not long after Hitler's legions entered Austria on March 12, 1938, many Germans moved to Austria to buy homes, have homes built for them or bought businesses or invested in one or another venture.

The local population had now a bit of a problem with the newcomers, and that was language. In Austria each region has their own dialect. Sometimes the dialect changed from one town to the other, even if it is was only a few miles apart. In one instance, St. Anton is only three miles west of the town of Pettneu. In St. Anton when you say *elfi* it means *elf* (eleven.) In Pettneu, *elfi* is pronounced *alfi,* and God help you if you don't use the dialect of your own home town. You would almost be considered conceited or an outsider.

The influx of German capital into Austria was a boon to the economy, and my father had so many new contracts to fill, that he needed journeymen from Germany. He told us that he was going to hire some from the *Altreich,* the Germany before the *Anschluss.* It was difficult hiring Austrian employees because of shortage. Before long some of them would arrive; there were two from the Rhineland, one from Zell am Ellis, in Thuringia, and one from East Prussia whose name was George. These German painters were way ahead of us when it came to painting in methods and in cleanliness, leaving the work place less messy. Pepi and I were still apprentices, and I preferred to paint with the German journeymen; we learned a great deal from them. In many trades, an apprentice was treated like a criminal. My father wouldn't stand for mistreatment. Until that time it was the custom that a father who wanted his son to learn a trade had to pay the master money, so he could learn. Only after the second year of apprenticeship would the boy earn money, and that was more like a tip. The apprentice also worked many more hours. He had to be on the job before the journeymen and in the evening would have to wash tools, store them etc. At that time there was a sixty-hour work week. From Monday through Saturday, 7–12 and 1–6 p.m.

It was also about this time when Herman Goering, the big, fat, dope-eating *Reichmarshall* mentioned in a speech, "The Austrian *Gemuetlichkeit* borders on laziness." To many Germans, Austrians were not like the hard-working German people. They seemed to enjoy life more. I am sure that there might be some truth to it. He is also the one who said after war broke out on September 1, 1939: if ever an enemy plane trespasses over Germany, my name shall be "Maier" not Goering. He would have to eat these words thousands of time in the next six years of war.

THE NUREMBERG RALLIES

When Hitler came to power in Germany on January 30, 1933, every year after that, party rallies were held on a wide, open field in Nuremberg, Bavaria. It could accommodate 100,000 people. These party rallies lasted for a week, and every day the party organizations from all the *Gaue* (states) in Germany, marched and held sports festivities. The army displayed the newest in weaponry, all this in front of the *Führer*. Now the *Ostmark* also participated with each *Gau* (state) represented. My father, who attended these rallies in September 1938, came home and was very enthusiastic and told us of the weapons on display, the tanks, the artillery, especially the 88-mm antiaircraft guns and of the precision with which the men handled them. No enemy would dare attack Germany now, was his thought. After World War II had ended, adversaries would speak of the "88" as one of the most devastating weapon in the German *Wehrmacht*.

Dr. Joseph Goebbels didn't spare anything to make it a Nazi show case. He would exhort the German youth, "You must be fast like Greyhounds, hard as the steel of Krupp and tough as leather, yes, so must be the German youth of today."

On the last day of these rallies, on Sunday, Hitler gave his final speech, and all of Germany were waiting to hear him on radios. As he mounted the speakers platform, 100,000 in unison gave him an ovation without equal. When the crowd quieted down, he started in a very low voice, slowly first, "*Volksgenossen und Volksgenossinen* (Fellow German men and fellow German women)." Then after a while his voice would rise and he would speak faster. He would rehash all what his Nazi party accomplished since 1933—from 6 million unemployed down now to less then one million. Each time he would get a tremendous ovation. There were very few people in Germany who didn't listen on the radio when Hitler spoke.

It is true of that what he did for Germany in the five years from 1933 to 1938 bordered on a miracle, but there was another side to this miracle. He was thinking of war. By then the armed forces had millions of soldiers conscripted, and the weapons production was going full tilt; it was the main reason for almost full employment of the working force.

After these rallies were over, I waited impatiently for the first snowflakes to whiten the mountain tops, then the meadows, especially the Galzig. For me it was time to get ready for the ski season 1938–39.

Hannes was gone, that was true; but now I would be a full fledged ski instructor without the limitations of an apprentice in the coming ski season. With the return of the German tourists, we figured there would be a very good group of young students, especially the dimpled blond girls. My high expectations were realized and beyond. Hannes had been strict with his instructors. He knew his instructors were mountain boys, relatively simple and unsophisticated. But most of the students were from the city and more worldly wise. He thought it best if the fraternization were kept to a minimum. The new co-directors of the ski school had no such worries. They knew the new students would be almost exclusively German or Austrian and maybe a few Italians. Certainly, they expected proper deportment on the slopes, but what an instructor did on his own time was his own business.

The winter season 1938–39 was to be the busiest ever in the newly named Ski School St. Anton. German tourists flocked not only to our ski resort but to all resorts in Austria. It was like an avalanche. There were so many women—and many were eager for romance—it was a man's paradise, and the moral standard, you might say, was considerably lowered. The churches were still attended to, but less then before.

Hitler needed soldiers, and that meant Germany needed children. He was thinking of the 1000 year *Reich*. I remember well when in the newsreels he was shown giving mothers who had born more then 15 children a decoration called the *Mutterkreuz* (mother cross). The cross was hung around their neck like the Knights Cross for soldiers.

One day, two young students apparently decided that I was to be their instructor. They kept asking for demonstrations that required me to put my arms around them or grab them by the arms to help them up. They asked for private lessons after regular ski school and then asked if I'd join them for dancing later in the evening. With apprehension I agreed and met them later that evening for dancing in the bar of the Hotel Arlberg. They said they'd like to show me some pictures of their hometown in Germany if Id come to their room.

"Oh, please do," said one of the sweet things. Before I could answer they took me by the arms and were ushering me up the stairs. As we got to the door of their room, my courage left me, and I went down the stairs, calling up to them, "I am supposed to help at home tonight." The owner of the Hotel Arlberg Otto Ennemoser knew me, and gave me a wink. After the war, Otto and I would laugh over this incident. As for the sweet young students, they soon latched onto another instructor who seemed more amenable to teaching them the particular moves they were interested in.

WORLD WAR II

It was after midnight of September 1, 1939, when I heard a pounding on the door downstairs. It wakened both Pepi and me, and we ran downstairs. There, in the hallway stood my father and one of his employees George, the East Prussian, in his night clothes. They were talking to Rudi Schmid, the son of St. Anton's baker and an enthusiastic Hitler Youth. "But why come in the middle of the night?" my father asked, clearly irritated that the sleep of the household had been disturbed.

"The situation is urgent," answered Rudi Schmid officiously. "These are your orders," he said to George who was standing there silent. "Be at the railway station before noon. *Heil Hitler!*" he said as he turned on his heels and left the house quickly. "What's this about, father?" I asked, not daring to think. "For some reason George has been called into the Army. They are acting as if it is some big hurry. I tell you, I sometimes don't understand how these Nazis operate, that's for sure."

We went back to bed, awakening in the morning to the news that Germany was at war with Poland. Two days later, France and England in turn declared war on Germany. The news was electrifying. The talk on the street was that Polish troops had attacked a radio station on the German-Polish border city of Gleiwitz and killed the men guarding it. The German *Blitzkrieg* (lightning attack) was in retaliation for the brutal Polish provocation. In reality, German *Gestapo— Geheime Staats Polizei*—under the leadership of a certain sergeant Alfred Herman Naujoks had a few of their own criminals outfitted in Polish uniforms and killed in that radio station in Gleiwitz, this side of the German border. Now they put the blame on the Poles to have an excuse for a declaration of war. "What are we supposed to do? Let the Poles or anybody just run over us?" was the question of many.

But my father seemed troubled by it. Rudi Schmid had made a comment to father about the Poles forcing Germany into war. But how could he know about this before it happened? It seemed too much of a coincidence. Regardless, George was gone. Leaving our house the same day to an uncertain future and leaving my father with one less journeyman. A few weeks later, my oldest brother Karl entered the regular German army. As for George, he was killed on September 13th, less than two weeks after he stood in our hallway in his nightclothes, and just a few days into the fighting in Poland, his family from East Prussia wrote us. One of the first, but not the last, of the sons of St. Anton sacrificed to satisfy our *Führer's* appetite for war.

As usual, I busied myself with working for my father. From that fateful September until the snows came in early December, it was just thinking about skiing. After December, it was ski, ski, ski. As long as I was skiing, life was fine.

About Christmas time, *Bürgermeister* (mayor) Moser approached me at the ski school "I want to talk to you Franz?" "To me, *Herr Bürgermeister*?" I asked in confusion. "Yes, you. I want to ask if you would like to be in a movie? A movie director from Innsbruck called me, and he is looking for good skiers because there is to be lots of skiing in it. Are you interested?"

"*Ja natürlich, Herr Buergermeister*" I answered. After finding out it was to be a promotional movie for the Hitler Youth, I was thrilled to the idea of skiing in a real movie—just like Hannes Schneider in the movies many years ago, the *Sun over the Arlberg* and the *White Intoxication.* "Will they film it here, and how long will it take? I need to get permission from the ski school and my father," I said. "I've already talked to your father and the ski school. You'll be gone for about two months, in Ladis." Ladis was a village about 20 miles east from St. Anton. The main feature there was an old castle, a ruin called *Schloss Laudegg.* It was perched high above a vertical wall on a hill top, and this was to be the site for the movie. Two weeks later I was in Ladis and finding out all about the glamour of movie making. Besides Franz Fahrner, Ludwig Moser and myself from St. Anton, came Otto Felbermeier from Landeck. There were twenty other young skiers from near Innsbruck and some from the *Altreich,* the Germany before the *Anschluss,* participating in this movie.

Dr. Franz Wieser from Innsbruck was the producer and director. Franz Fahrner was to be the hero in the movie who was not yet 14 years of age and wanted badly to join the Hitler Youth. The purpose of the film was to glorify the Hitler Youth, to make young people yearn to join this organization. To get this message across, the plot involved two small Pricipalities at war with each other.

Young Franz Gabl as a movie stunt skier in a 1939 Franz Wieser film promoting the Hitler Youth.

One Principality, the *Frundsbergers* (that was our castle *Laudegg* of Ladis) was besieged. The *Geyersbergers* were the besiegers. Unless someone could escape and get help from another, friendly castle, the *Frundsbergers* were doomed. So a commando team inside the castle planned a daring escape which involved a brave young boy, who wouldn't be eligible yet for joining the Hitler Youth, because of age. The underage boy volunteers by jumping over the castle's high wall and skiing through the *Geyersbergers* territory and get help. He wore all white bed sheets covering him for camouflage. The hero of the story Franz Fahrner succeeds, and the *Frundsbergers* of castle *Laudegg* are saved, and as a grand reward, the hero is honored with entry into the Hitler Youth despite his age. I had two roles, one to be the leader of the commando who planned the escape, and one as a stunt double for the hero, which meant I was the one who had to perform the dangerous jump from the castle wall.

The jump itself was not much more challenging than many I had conquered in the mountains above my home and in the ski contests where I had competed. But, the landing was very tight. There was very little room on the steep hill, in between the trees, and I was concerned about how to come to a stop. The day came for filming the jump, the cameras were set up and rolling. I jumped, but my thought was on the landing and it was not a great jump. Dr. Wieser called me aside. "Franz," he said with his arm over my shoulder, "You are jumping like you are afraid. You're not letting yourself go. You must forget about the landing and think only about the flight."

"Don't give the landing a thought. The real landing will be filmed on the Patscherkofel in Innsbruck later on when we finish the scenes here. We just want to film the takeoff and flight here. It doesn't matter how you land. Let yourself go!"

With those instructions I returned to the castle wall determined to focus only on the takeoff and flight. As I approached the take off I felt myself go free and sailed through the air. When I hit the ground I tried hard to brake to avoid hitting the trees, but I totally lost control and plowed heavily into the snow. "Perfect! cried Dr. Wieser. Let's do it again."

If it was so perfect, I thought to myself as I was dusting off the heavy snow, why do I have to do it again? But I remembered the director's instructions: let yourself go, and again I flew through the air freely and with abandon, and crashed again with a thud between the trees. But I learned something important. My best performance was based on a total abandonment to my instincts and skills that had been practiced and perfected during the countless hours on the slopes. The skills were there. Now I had to conquer my own mind and the limitations it created.

The filming was over within two months, and Fahrner, Moser, Felbermeier and the other boys from Tyrol and Germany and I returned to our homes for more skiing. But not for long because the spring ski racing season was now here.

International ski racing had all but disappeared since the outbreak of war in 1939. But our Ski Club Arlberg ski team was invited to race against the best German and Italian skiers on the Feldberg, in the Black Forest in Germany. These were some of the best skiers in the world, and it was my first opportunity to compete against elite skiers. It was also my first time out of my homeland of Austria, now called *Ostmark*. My excitement was great and my confidence was at an all-time high. Our team of Pepi Jenewein, my brother Pepi, Robert Falch, Rudi Moser, Herman Ladner, Rudi Alber (Fingers), and I went by train to Freiburg and then by bus to a hotel on top of the Feldberg, the highest hill in the Black Forest.

All that changed when we reached the downhill course. It was like no downhill run I had ever seen before. It was a suicide run. I had never before feared a mountain, but these very steep drops were like cliffs and then turned into steep logging road. After a half mile you had to jump to the left into a cut forest where the stumps were still two to three feet high and not completely covered. Here you had to wangle your way through it, thanks that the snow was deep and one didn't get too much speed. Finally there was another short steep run to the finish line and no place to slow down; you had to fall to come to stop. Have I lost my courage? I thought. Maybe it's just me. But one glance at world champion Pepi Jenewein, my teammate standing next to me, and I knew that I had every right to be afraid. This mountain was a killer.

The mountains of the Black Forest were very different from our craggy Alps. The Feldberg, where we were to race, was simply the tallest of these big hills. The hotel was located at the top of the mountain and to get to the downhill start area, instead of walking uphill like we were used to, here we had to ski downhill. This was the most ridiculous downhill run of my life. We were allowed just one training run. Then of course we had to walk up to the start. There were no lifts on this mountain. Now, anyone designing such a foolishly dangerous course would be committed to a mental hospital or worse. But these were the early days of ski racing, and the thinking must have been, if you are foolish enough to participate in this sport, the world probably doesn't need you anyway.

Skiing has always been a dangerous sport. But in these days of high-tech equipment, safety-minded course planning, and emergency evacuation and treatment, it may not be understood what ski racing in those days was like. For a typical Kandahar race, the annual race held on the Galzig above St. Anton, there might be 120 men starting in the downhill, and by the time it was over only 40 of those had finished, many ended up at a doctor's office or in a hospital, broke a ski, or lost one, or just plainly gave up. Even the ones who finished were often injured in one way or another, blood streaming down their faces.

The women raced a much shorter downhill course, and the injuries were less then the men's. Ski injuries, in those times were simply to be expected. But no one in their right mind asked for them, and this course in the Black Forest was invitation to disaster.

When I found myself at the gate to start the downhill, the fear was with me. It was genuine fear. Down I went, but timidly, cautiously and was not proud of myself when my time was announced. Hannes was gone now, but I could hear him in my mind saying, "Gabaly, move *ins Paznaun*. There was still the slalom the next day, Sunday. I knew I was racing against some of the world's best, but when I got to the bottom on my second run I found that only two of them had been able to get down the course faster than this 110-pound painter's son from St. Anton.

Suddenly I found a crowd of people around me, holding a piece of paper and pencil in front of me, calling my name. I was a surprise to the crowd and the experts. For the first time in my young life I was asked for autographs and found what it felt like to be a hero, to be famous. I must admit, it did nothing to take away my desire to be a true ski champion.

As I was winning some measure of glory for St. Anton in the Black Forest, Germany was also winning. It rolled over Poland in a matter of weeks, in the process introducing to the world new words that would take on frightening meanings in the months and years ahead: *Blitzkrieg, Panzer, Gestapo, Stuka, U-boots, Einkesselung, Holocaust, Konzentrations Lager,* and more. After the victory in Poland the spoils of war were divided between Hitler and Stalin—there is no honor among thieves.

In St. Anton the talk was of peace. "It's all over," my father announced with perhaps more hope than certainty. "Germany has no interest in war with England or France. Surely the French and English understand that. They will just accept things as they are now. They will have to." "That's not what the *Bürgermeister* told me," I answered my father. I had spoken with Karl Moser after I returned from making the film, and he said next year I'd be making a movie in France. Germany would attack France once the thaw was over, he predicted. "No," my father said quite emphatically. "Germany doesn't fight wars just to fight." I noticed my uncle Albert was very quiet in this discussion. The thaw came, and Hitler proved Karl Moser right. In April 1940, Hitler overwhelmed the neutrals Norway and Denmark. Then, in May with the lightning offense that proved so effective in Poland, the *Luftwaffe* and armored *Panzer* columns quickly overran the brave but brief defense of the neutral Dutch, the Belgians and Luxemburg. Now they stood face to face against the French and the British who hid, somewhat securely they thought, behind the fortifications of the Maginot Line. But this great bulwark was built for another war in a previous time. Instead of taking the expected route to the west, right through the well publicized fortified Maginot Line, the German army hid in the Ardennes forest, breaking out upon the unguarded north flank of the Allied Forces through Belgium, Luxemburg and Holland. The French lines were broken, and within weeks the bulk of the French and English armies had been surrounded. Yet the victory was incomplete. The miracle of Dunkirk enabled the British to prevent the annihilation of their army, if not their fighting equipment. Three hundred, thirty-eight thousand British and French soldiers were ferried across the channel and were ready to give the *Wehrmacht* battle again. St. Anton lost one son, Rudolf Koessler, killed in the battles in France in 1940. By the end of the war, 55 more would be buried in foreign soil and 22 are missing to this day.

Of my age group of 11 boys, born in the year 1921 who went to take the physical exam for army life and who went to war, only six would return and one would succumb within months to injuries suffered in the war.

The German victories were spectacular, but there was an uneasiness in St. Anton about how this war had taken on such giant proportions. But because of the victories, it was also viewed that the war would soon come to an end. Some of the young men were worrying not to have a chance to earn the Iron Cross before it was all over. Most were just young and eager to participate in the great events of the times in our lifetime. After all, we were young, and the young never die, or so some seemed to think. That is how I understood the decisions that were made then. My brother Pepi, and his friend Pepi Jenewein, Albert Pfeifer and Othmar Schuler volunteered for the *Luftwaffe* with all the excitement of going out on an extended mountain hike. Only my brother would return and ski the *Galzig* again. The other three gave their life for *Führer* and *Vaterland.* The thought of flying those sleek fighters was enough to make me join them, too. In the *Luftwaffe* they took only volunteers. But I didn't volunteer. I can't say why exactly, although I never had the enthusiasm for the Nazi future that my brothers did. Especially after what they did to Hannes. Within me there was always a question. I can't describe what it was. It may have been an incident which happened in Innsbruck in November 1938 when the Nazis destroyed many Jewish synagoges and stores. I was walking on a minor street, paralleling the *Maria Theresien Strasse*, when I saw on a Jewish store all windows broken, lots of merchandise laying on the street outside and on the walls written, *"Kauft nicht bei Juden ein* (Don't buy from Jews)." It was called *Kristall Nacht* (crystal night). It was November 9, 1938, where in Germany and in the *Ostmark* all the Jewish stores were to be destroyed or damaged on orders of the higher Nazi hierarchy. It just didn't make sense, and honestly I felt very sorry for whoever owned that store.

It wasn't fear, that I didn't join as a volunteer, though, and I knew that, it was most likely only a matter of time before I would be called, and I really looked forward to it.

Perhaps it was that summer of 1940. The sky was bluer, the grass greener, the smell of the hay sweeter than I ever remembered it. I didn't know what the future held if I didn't volunteer, but I knew if I went in, my skiing days would be over for awhile.

In the fall of 1940, on October 2nd, it was my turn. The papers came directing me to Salzburg. I wasn't to join the army though, but the *Reichsarbeitsdienst* (national service). This was a duty required of every young German man and involved four months of training and work meant to provide needed service to the country and prepare us for the army if we should be called. Little did I know when I got my papers what they meant by preparing us for the army.

When I got my papers, the thought went through my head, why are they calling more men when the war is over? But the next day, as I packed my clothes for the trip to Salzburg, I heard on the radio that London and the city of Coventry had sustained a massive bombing, the worst a city had ever received. It hit mostly the workers settlements of London, and civilian population of Coventry which were supposed to stifle the will to resist Germany's war ambitions. In reality, it had the opposite effect. So, there was to be war with England. I packed with a heavy heart.

I soon found out that my good friend Herman Ladner had been called at the same time. There were others from St. Anton—Rudi Moser and Franz Gamper. This made it easier to say good-bye to my family and board the train for Salzburg and an unknown future. We arrived at our assigned barracks in late afternoon and found out that we had been split into two camps. Rudi and Herman headed for Bergheim camp, on the eastern outskirts of Salzburg; Franz Gamper and I headed for Max Glan camp on the western outskirts of the city.

The very first evening we found out what military life was all about. "Get those suitcases out of here! Put your clothes away! Hurry up about it! Don't just stand there and look, get going! Hurry up! What are you waiting for?" In this way our sergeant, called *Unterführer* in the *Reichsarbeitsdienst*, introduced himself to us, but it was just the beginning. I tried to look around to check out my new home and quickly un-packed my suitcase. It wasn't encouraging. There were six double-decker bunks, each with a small locker to store our few personal items, and God help anyone who forgot to lock it. The *Unterführer* would dip the locker forward and then spill belongings onto the floor and kick them with his feet under beds. At one end stood a desk and a few chairs, and here was the sergeant now sitting. He caught me looking in his direction. Big mistake.

"Did I tell you to look around?" He stomped over to me. "What's your name?" "Franz Gabl," I answered. "Franz Gabl what?" "*Arbeitsmann Gabl*," I said, trying to meet his eyes. Other recruits were busily emptying their suitcases. After me the *Unterführer* had his face in a frightened recruit's, and I heard him yelling, "Sir! Sir! Do you understand that?" "*Jawohl Herr Unterfuehrer*," he answered. But the worst part was staying in line to receive the uniforms. The *Unterführer* was a real Prussian; you could almost feel his voice cutting the air like a knife. He threw the clothing into our faces. The issued clothing seldom fit properly, either to big or to small. Most just took it, saying "no way will I go back and exchange it." The next morning we went back. Low and behold this Prussian was like a lamb. I knew then that this was all part of the routine, done to impress the others as much as the poor sucker he was yelling at. It still did little to give me warm feelings about my new life.

We were issued two uniforms, a regular uniform, brown in color and a white work uniform made of jeans–type mate-rial. Our knee-high boots we got to know very well. We were issued two pairs, and they were expected to be spit-shined all the time. It seemed we were shining our boots whenever we had a spare moment from our other work.

After awhile our days took on a certain routine. Up early for calisthenics, then washing with cold water, then break-fast, after that to work building more of the prefabricated barracks like the one we were living in. At the end of the day we had marching practice using flat bladed spades for prac-tice like with rifles. At night we cleaned the barracks, every rafter, every corner, every locker had to be scrubbed. Every bunk was stretched drum-tight and every pair of boots shined like a mirror. Then came the inspection. The *Unterführers* were quite adept at discovering the locker that had clothes out of place or was unlocked. The boots with a speck of mud meant big trouble for all of us. "Everybody! Outside in your work uniform! Now!" We'd form up in a line outside the barracks, he would walk past us all with a cold eye then yell, "Into your dress uniforms, on the double!" We'd run back into the barracks, change our uniforms, and line up outside. "Into your pajamas, now!' Back we'd go to change again. This was called the Masquerade ball, and sometimes this German fashion show would go on for an hour or two. You can believe we'd give the poor sap who had screwed up and caused us all this trouble a piece of our mind after this little game had finally ended. We also realized that these leaders of ours were plain actors. In the military you had to act and be able to yell loud or your promotion would have to wait years. Brains were not important. After a few weeks of this, our *Unterführer* would come with us recruits on Sundays to have a beer in one of the wine cellars of Salzburg.

Two months into our four months of *Reichsarbeitsdienst* we were told we were leaving for France. Now this was a change that was welcomed! Ah, France. O–La–La, Gay Pahree. Wine, women and song. Now life would get better, we thought.

What a disgusting disappointment. The wine was undrinkable, the women were invisible, and Pontoise, northwest of Paris, the city where we were stationed, was as drab and uninteresting as the inside of our barracks. We soon longed for the days of building our prefab barracks back in Salzburg, because in Pontoise we had the job of building an airfield some twelve miles from our cold, unheated three–story high brick buildings. Every morning we marched two miles to the train station. We left at 5:00 in the morning, marching through the city, singing our patriotic marching songs. *"Auf der Heide blueht ein kleines—Blue—melein— und das heisst—'Eee-rika.'"* I often thought why our leaders would wake the local population this early in the morning. I am certain it was to annoy them or to show pride. We rode the train for eight miles, then marched another two miles to get to the airfield to build a runway for airplanes. By now it was early winter 1940, and it was cold. There was no winter clothing. Had we known that within one year we would experience 20 to 40 below zero in our summer uniforms and the Siberian wind howling at 20–30 miles an hour, we wouldn't have complained.

Many times, after a hard day of labor, we would have to march the entire twelve miles back to our barracks. There, we would find cold slop for food and rancid wine that was kept in canisters in the hallway. At the time I thought, how could things get worse.

Still, there were a few highlights. We did get to see Paris almost every Sunday, and as much as I enjoyed window shopping in Innsbruck as a boy, the shops of Paris mesmerized me. This was an occupied country, but the stores were full of merchandise and shoppers. Our highlights in Paris were the shows at the Moulin Rouge and the other Casino de Paris, Sacre Coer, hiking up the Eiffel Tower, visiting famous buildings like Notre Dame, Dom de Invalides. But one of the most memorable moments was visiting the Arc D'Triumph, the great monument of Napoleon that houses the tomb of the unknown soldier. While at the monument we were told it was a soldier's duty to salute. God help the poor sap who happened to forget.

Then, the four months of *Reichsarbeitsdienst* was over. It was January 30, 1941. But we knew the army was most likely ahead for us. Some were inducted in directly after their service was finished. Rudi Moser and Herman Ladner from the Bergheim camp and Franz Gamper and I from the Max Glan camp had been discharged, and we happily headed home. The ski season was still going on, and I returned to the slopes and the ski school with greater appreciation than I ever had before. It felt so good to be home. The mountains surrounding our little village seemed like giant protectors, I felt so comfortable. And the skiing, ah, the skiing. How often I had thought about the joy of gliding down the Galzig, over the deep powder during all those unbearable marches and endless days of work.

Then the ski season was over and soon after that, on May 2nd, 1941 the papers came to join the *Wehrmacht.*

Joining the *Wehrmacht*

Franz Gabl, report to Volders for duty in the German *Wehrmacht*, May 2nd, 1941" said my orders.

But fortunately, again I had friends to go with. Herman Ladner and Franz Klimmer had received the same orders, and we would travel together. Herman was my fellow ski school instructor. He was big, gentle and took a very optimistic view of just about any situation. His broad smile and hearty laugh were a welcome antidote to the drudgery and misery of the days ahead. While Herman was optimistic, Franz was cautious. Also from St. Jakob, we saw Franz frequently because he had to go often to his uncle's hotel Arlberg Hoehe in St. Christoph on the Arlberg Pass, and so he had to walk through St. Anton on his way. At that time there was no bus service, and one had to walk from one end of town to the other.

Franz was about my height with a shock of light brown hair and deep penetrating eyes. Franz thought about things;

Three friends, Herman Ladner, Franz Klimmer and Franz Gabl at Innsbruck in 1941. Klimmer died in Russia in April of 1942. Ladner died there in June.

he pondered the future and the meaning of things. We dreaded the indoctrination into the army. We thought if the *Reichsarbeitsdienst* (worker service to the nation) was as rough as it was, just think what the army must be. But we were wrong. There was no humiliation or masquerades, no long marches. It seemed it was a picnic compared to the *Reichsarbeitsdienst*. Instead, there was a seriousness about our training that communicated to us that this was not a game we were in. There were classes that dealt with subjects like how prisoners should be treated under the Geneva convention, and what to do if we were captured by the enemy—only to divulge name, rank, serial number, under no circumstances the name of division, army and site of headquarters.

Herman, Franz and I shared a room at Volders, a small town east of Innsbruck. Herman and I knew what this training was all about, and we used our experience to help Franz make the adjustments he had to in his new life. Instead of standard army barracks, the training camp at Volders was a converted monastery. The minimum had been done to prepare it for service and glory of a greater Germany, but the religious atmosphere had not all been removed; there were even religious artifacts such as small statues and pictures around. The heavy brick walls made our rooms cool but also somewhat comforting. The long hallways rang, not with choirs or bells, but with harsh calls from our beloved sergeants getting us up, calling us to meals or upbraiding us in one way or another.

We were blessed to have in our group a gangly young soldier by the name of "Hammel." He was tall and awkward with a bony face that would turn bright red whenever embarrassed, which was frequent. Hammel was from a remote valley village area and considered a real hick. The old joke was that he had to walk for two hours downhill just to pick edelweiss. This joke was told not just on Hammel but later on all of us from the mountain areas after we joined a purely German Division. Hammel's naivete was fortunate for us, because he drew the ire of our superiors by his bumbling mistakes and by the bigger mistake of thinking he had the smarts to outwit those with higher ranks.

"Right face!" the drill sergeant would yell. Hammel would click his heels smartly, stick out his chest, drop his chin to his chest and swivel jerkily left. There he would find himself face to face with the soldier who had correctly followed the order, and he would invariably scowl at him, thinking, you fool, can't you follow a simple order. The man he faced would often laugh out loud, also knowing he could be reprimanded. Once he reported himself sick. He was sent to the infirmary and was tested for temperature, it was very high indeed. They then inserted once more the thermometer under the armpits and it showed normal. What he did was rub the thermometer until it was so high that it showed he was near death. In the following weeks Hammel walked more on elbows through the mud then on his feet.

We spent only a week and a half at Volders before being transferred to Rum, a small town outside of Innsbruck, above the city of Hall. Hall was also the place where the insane or other severely handicapped people were sent from around Tyrol. The joke to this day is still when one makes a bumbling mistake, "You ought to be sent to Hall."

This camp in Rum was a normal army camp, and now we found ourselves sharing our barracks with new recruits from around Tyrol, from Vorarlberg and Salzburg. The routine was pretty simple: in the morning it was running a few miles, washing, dressing, then breakfast; after that riding our bicycles, as we were a bicycle battalion, and in the afternoon rifle and machine gun practice.

Several classes were devoted to gas masks. *Feldwebel* Karg, our sarge, would have us marching along and all of a sudden he would yell, "Gas!" Then we would dismount and quickly scramble to put on our gas masks and run 100 feet or more to get away from the gas. By the time we got a safe distance away, we were winded and gasping for air. The intake in our gas masks was limited so when they were on and operating properly we couldn't draw enough air in to run very far or fast. We solved the problem at times, we just opened a valve which would let air in, though, sparingly, we knew if caught, all hell broke loose, and we would walk with shoe tips and elbows.

Sergeant Karg did his best to get us to take seriously the threats of gas warfare. We were told there are three kinds of gas: yellow cross, white cross and blue cross. Yellow was supposed to be the worst; it could eat through the soles of our

leather boots. To walk safely on ground that had been contaminated, we had to put tarps on the ground to create safe
areas to walk on. We felt like we were spreading cloths for a
picnic, and that's about as seriously as most of us took it at
that time. But who could blame us, really. It was early summer of 1941, the threat of war with England was dying down,
the sky was brilliant blue, and we had weekend leaves where
we could go back to St. Anton. All in all, we found army life to
be for the most part acceptable.

The training seemed to get ever more serious and realistic. Ours was a bicycle battalion, so we spent many hours a
day riding our bicycles. Why we drilled for a war to be fought
on bicycles, we didn't know. It was not unusual to ride 65 or
more miles in a day. Still, we didn't complain. Riding bikes
was fun, and it certainly looked better than the mountain
troops. We watched them head for the mountains carrying
huge packs on their backs. We practiced throwing hand grenades and spent many hours at the rifle range with our rifles
and machine guns. I felt comfortable on the range because
we always had rifles at home, and I had spent many hours
shooting as a young boy and had won many medals in competitions. Consequently, I found I was one of the best marks-
men in our group. I especially enjoyed the machine gun. There
was a certain sense of invincibility as you sprayed a barrage
of lead in the sand and dirt ahead of you. No one can get
through that, I thought. Of course, there were the artillery
shells and mortars, and the fact that in the heat of battle men
could be shooting at you from all sides at once. None of that
disrupted my confidence as I clattered away at still imaginary targets. Had I known how many bullets I would shoot
on the Russian front, I would have taken this training more
seriously.

We seldom talked of war but listened intently for any news
about what was happening with the air war against England
or what the latest rumors of invasion might be. Those who
did talk, talked with bravado and expressed fears that their
opportunities for medals and honor might have passed them
by. That was not my thought. I thought of skiing, of the
summer I was missing in the mountains above my village, of
girls and the future and of plucking edelweiss from steep
mountain sides above timberline in the late summer.

JUNE 22, 1941—WAR WITH RUSSIA

One morning I took the street car from Rum to Innsbruck to the train station to head home for a weekend leave. There were about five or six people in the car. A few were quietly talking among themselves when one lady, addressing no one in particular but sounding like a school teacher making an announcement to her class, said, "Did you hear there is war with Russia?" It was June 22, 1941.

It was unbelievable. Russia and Germany had been allies, they had treaties, they both seemed to get what they wanted when they broke up Poland like a couple of lions tearing apart a gazelle. Now, it seemed it was not enough, and they were to tear each other apart.

Back home in St. Anton that weekend I went to the *Weinstube* (tavern) of the *Gasthof Post* to wait for Herman and Franz for our get together. I still had some measure of confidence that perhaps our army could crush Russia like it had the Poles, the French, Belgians, Holland, Norway, Denmark, Luxemburg and Yugoslavia. Sitting in the *Weinstube* I overheard three men in a corner talk openly about the war with Russia. "That's a country to get lost in," one said, with the others agreeing, shaking their heads. "The land is endless. The army will be stretched out for thousands of kilometers until it's too thin to fight." "That's if the winter doesn't kill them all first. Think, what happened to Napoleon."

It was remarkable in this time that men should speak so openly and brazenly in tones that were clearly critical of Hitler. Things were changing. But worse than that, I knew in my heart these men were right. This was a war that Germany could not win. My confidence in Hitler's invincibility was forever gone. It is one thing to head into war with a sense of purpose and a belief in the outcome. But when you leave home to go to a far distant, empty land for a worthless cause that you believe to be futile, the pain and emptiness are nearly unbearable. I decided then, I would volunteer for nothing; I would be no hero. I would do my duty and perhaps survive, but I would not do one thing to extend myself for any great victory or any imagined honor. A deep dread settled on me, and even Herman's lighthearted optimism could not dull it. Day after day we heard bulletins broadcast. The Russian army was in disarray, thousands of tanks and planes were destroyed, millions were taken prisoners.

"Look at this," Herman said after hearing more news. "The war is almost over; all that will be left for us is some mopping up to do." It did seem to be true. The *Stukas* and *Panzers* had rushed into the Russian heartland, and the defenses seemed to collapse in front of them. Even easier than the rout of France. My doubts wavered a little, but only a little. Well, let us hope it will end soon and the dying will be over before our training is. Not all took such optimistic views, however. The eager-beaver Nazis were grumbling about being stuck way back in the *Ostmark* when the iron crosses were being handed out hundreds of miles to the east.

The training in July and August took on an intensity that we hadn't truly felt before. It wasn't just stuff they made us do because they felt like being mean. Now these were exercises that could save our lives. We pedaled hard and practiced at the range trying to imagine what a Russian soldier looked like as we sighted down the barrels of our rifles and machine guns. It still seemed unreal that someday, perhaps soon, we might be shooting at real people, and being shot at with real bullets. When you are young and close to home, dying doesn't seem a realistic possibility.

In late September we received the dreaded news—we were to be shipped to the Ukraine to join the 1st mountain division, a part of Field Marshall von Reichenau's 6th army in the Army Group South headed by Field Marshall von Rundstedt. This army, led by 600 tanks of General Kleist's *Panzer* Group, had faced 5,000 Russian tanks under the command of the heavily mustached cavalry Marshal Budjenny and had driven them back deep in the heart of the Ukraine. In September, they were driving the Russian forces steadily back toward Kiev and the Dnieper river. We were to join the fight as an *Ersatz* (replacement) battalion. Apparently, the brilliant army planners decided there was little need in the Russian heartland for soldiers trained to fight on bicycles so we were declared fully trained mountain troops and appropriately outfitted. We were sent to Salzburg for final outfitting and assembly before being sent east.

We arrived in Salzburg in high spirits. We had no idea, not the slightest concept of the hardships and horrors that lay in store for us for the next four years hundreds of miles to the east. And we were young, filled with bravado and a sense of our own invincibility. Mostly, though, I think our light hearted joking around was a device to hide our deeper fears; deep down we knew we were headed for something much greater than our own individual lives, something very much out of our control.

In Salzburg we received our new uniforms and mountain troop equipment. During the day we put our equipment together and started to adjust to the large packs. In the evening I went to visit my cousins Franzl and Ria Weissenbach and filled up on sweets as much as I could, or joined the other boys in an antique wine cellar of Salzburg for a last beer or glass of wine. A few of the guys even visited a brothel only a few houses away from Amadeus Mozart's birth place. We drank in more than the beer and the wine. We lived knowing that our lives were soon to change, perhaps permanently. If we had known what a life we were heading for, we would have hung onto those days like an eagle grasping its prey.

Shortly before we were to ship out, I took a trip back to St. Anton one more time. My father who was so enthusiastic with the *Anschluss* to the Third *Reich* was sobered by the events in the east. Unlike the war in the west, this fight with Russia made no sense. There were some new doubts about the wisdom of the *Führer*, and there was the unnerving memory of what happened to Napoleon who had so gloriously conquered Europe only to have his greed for more ground to bitterness in the endless Russian steppe and the vicious Russian winter. George, my father's right hand man, was already molding in Polish dirt, killed within two weeks of leaving our house and shortly after the war started in Poland, September 1939.

I found out that Karl, my oldest brother, serving in a mountain division, was posted to Finland. My other brother Pepi and Pepi Jenewein (now a world ski champion), Albert Pfeifer and Othmar Schuler were all volunteering for the Luftwaffe. The two Pepis and Pfeifer were training to become fighter pilots, Schuler to be a bomber pilot. They were stationed in Schwechat, at an air base near Vienna. Only my brother would ski the Galzig again. It was not easy for my father and mother to say good-bye to another son, the last one, about to disappear into the mouth of Mother Russia.

"Herman, Franz and I will take care of each other," I tried to reassure them, and then I said, "Tell the ski school I'll be coming back in the winter so they should plan on that;" Father said he would. "Tell Karl and Pepi to write to me." Then I turned looked up to the mountains where I had spent my childhood and walked to the train.

The Russian Front

On September 27, 1941, a long train of boxcars pulled into the railroad station at Salzburg, and we climbed aboard. The floor was covered with straw, and we were packed in tightly, but we were young men, and it was an adventure. Some were eager to prove themselves and to bring home medals for valor and stories for their sweethearts and families. The Russian army was routed, and it seemed it was only a matter of weeks before the campaign in the east was over.

The iron cross was the most sought-after medal, and some coveted it so much they would be willing to give their lives for our *Führer and Vaterland.* Some were so caught up in the glory of Germany and the *Führer's* propaganda that they felt they were actually doing something worthwhile. I was with fellow Tyroleans and other Austrians who felt we had been pressed into something unnecessary, puzzling and annoying. We had no choice but to see what the next days would bring.; then we could go back home to our families, mountains and skis. Our leaders, from sergeants to the officers, accompanied our *Ersatz* battalion until we were divided up and joined a German infantry division. They then went home to Innsbruck to instruct newly conscripted men in the art of warfare.

We passed through Prague, Czechoslovakia, and north and east into Poland. The rough boxcar bounced us around, and the endless clacking of tracks made a mournful sound as we moved farther and farther from the people and homeland we loved. Some young officer tried to pick up our morale by pointing out that Austrian and Hungarian troops had fought heroic battles in World War I near there at Przemysl and Lemberg in southeast Poland against the Russians.

We were finally allowed out of the boxcars in Lublin and herded into barracks that a short time before had most likely been used by Polish troops. The thought occurred to me that the bed I had slept in, chances were that he was now bedded somewhere beneath Polish or Russian soil.

Lublin was only about 50 miles southeast of Warsaw and near the Ukrainian frontier. In Lublin our leaders decided we should get into combat condition, so we were led on marches of 15–20 miles per day carrying our full combat packs weighing about 65 pounds. In our optimism, we complained that it seemed all rather pointless since the Russians were in full retreat, and it looked unlikely that we would even get into combat before all the shooting was over.

Food was scarce; the ration for each soldier was one liter stew, one pound bread, a piece of sausage or cheese and some pudding. For liquid each soldier received one liter black coffee; there was no sugar. This was the daily food we received for the next four years, except towards the end of the war when the bread ration was cut again to a little more than half a pound. So we found we could keep ourselves well enough fed by trading with the local population in the evening, after we returned from the marches. Each soldier was entitled to six cigarettes a day. They were in high demand, so we traded them for eggs, bread and other items.

At this time we noticed something that struck us as somewhat strange and made us a little uncomfortable. In Lublin there were many Jews, and they were very obvious because they all wore the star of David sewn onto their clothing. They were being singled out and treated differently than the other Poles, although we had no inkling what this separating out meant. I did recall that the two Jewish families who lived in St. Anton. Herr von Stein's had been taken away by the Nazis right after the *Anschluss*. Miraculously von Stein's family returned after the war.

Rudolf Gomperz's family was still allowed to stay in St. Anton, and Mr. Gomperz was allowed to report the weather. The non-Jewish Mrs. Gomperz claimed that her two sons Rudi Jr. and Hansi by her husband Rudolf, were actually fathered by another non-Jewish man and consequently were not Jewish. They wanted above all save their two sons. It is true their sons didn't look Jewish. Rudi Jr. was my age, and we attended the grade school in St. Anton for eight years, always in the same classroom. Nonetheless, within a year Rudolf Gomperz Sr. was taken toward the east, and what is not known for sure, perished in a concentration camp. Eventually, son Rudi volunteered for the S. S. and became a Russian P.O.W.

Their other son Hansi was then conscripted and was killed in France in 1944 after the Allies had landed on June 6th in northwest France.

Mrs. Gomperz lived then a lonely, despondent life in her home, and one day in 1947 a neighbor, who frequently checked on her, found her laying in the hallway, dead. She didn't know that her son Rudi had become a prisoner of the Russians and was still alive, because the Russians didn't let prisoners write to their homes, and none were expected ever to come home. But from 1949 on they started slowly to release some of the prisoners. Three more would return to St. Anton, but Rudi Jr. who was an S. S. soldier, had to wait years more. Finally he returned in the early 1950s, but he could never find peace of mind and within a few years took his own life. The story of the Gomperz family is one of the saddest that ever had happened in my home town.

I remember talking to Franz Klimmer and Herman Ladner about why the Nazis seemed to hate the Jews. One day I watched a couple of our soldiers talking with some Jews and it disgusted me. "Bubi" was the soldier who went up to a Jew and offered to sell him his blanket for some food. The Jewish man agreed and gave Bubi the food then walked away with the blanket. Bubi's accomplice was waiting down the street and stopped the Jew, demanding, "Where did you get that blanket. This is a German army blanket. I suggest you give it to me before I report you." The Jew immediately agreed and without protest gave up the blanket, knowing that the punishment for holding *Wehrmacht* property was the firing squad. I felt sorry for the Jew and felt no animosity toward them or the Poles.

We Austrian's were wearing our *Gebirgsjaeger* hats with a beak and edelweiss patches sewn on the right sleeve and left side of the hat, and more than once I wanted to say, "But we're Austrians, we're not Nazis!"

I was very fortunate at this time to be with Herman Ladner and Franz Klimmer. Franz and Herman were both from St. Jakob, the sister town to St. Anton and only a half mile away from my home. Herman's light-hearted attitude seldom changed and more than anything else lightened the gloom and dread that I felt on this trip east. I respected Franz for his wisdom, his depth of character and his honesty. Because we were Arlberger's, we could share so much: our past experiences, our love for skiing and the mountains, and our hopes for the future. Often I thought, if I have my friends I can bear just about anything ahead of me.

We stayed in Lublin for a week, and we were happy after all of the exhausting marching to be getting back on the train, never mind that it headed east. The training marches were more than an opportunity to condition our bodies; our officers were trying to prepare us as best they could for the coming trials.

"You must fight the inner *Schweinehund* (swine dog)!" they would exhort. It's hard to translate, but it meant that we should expect a battle inside ourselves, a battle that would pit part of us that wanted to quit, to give up, against another part that would push on and keep us going. The heat was stifling and all we had was one liter black coffee a day. On one of these marches, a dozen soldiers dropped unconscious onto the road. They were loaded onto a horse-drawn supply wagon, and when they came to, their pack would be placed back on and off they would march again with an officer yelling at them to keep going.

On October 4, 1941, our *Ersatz* or replacement battalion crossed the border into Russia. My daily diary marks it with this prophetic note: *"Ein trauriger Anblick* (A sad sight)." On October 5th our cattle cars arrived in Fastov, 45 miles west of Kiev, the Ukrainian capital. The next day we marched 27 miles to the town of Wasilkowo. It sounds so simple on paper—27 miles, marching. In early October it was still warm. The roads were very dusty. In four years in Russia I did not come across one paved road, other than in the larger cities. The dirt on the roads was a fine, clay-filled dirt, and when the supply columns, trucks, tanks and motorcycles would roll by, they would raise dust clouds high into the air, into the same air we were trying to breathe as we labored under our 65 pounds of clothing, guns, ammunition and equipment. Actually, part of the time it was over 90 pounds as each squad shared the burden of carrying the machine gun, another 27 pounds added to our sore backs. And there was no water to soothe our dusty throats or to refresh our sweating faces except one liter of black coffee each day. There were ground wells along the way, but no one was allowed to drink from these; no one in his right mind would want to, even when crazed by thirst, knowing they had been poisoned by the retreating Russians.

When we finally got to the town, men were beyond thinking. Some would fall forward on their faces when their packs were removed because they were so accustomed to their center of gravity being so far forward. Many would half crawl to the bathroom. Some would not even get their dinners, they were so exhausted. The conditioning in the mountains at home had helped me, and I was in better shape than most and more accustomed to this kind of endurance. Those summers climbing mountains and swinging the scythe or carrying building materials up to our mountain meadows had done me some good, making me understand what hard work really is and training my mind to go into the realm where pain and exhaustion can't quite reach. I needed every bit of that preparation now. The torment of this was made considerably greater when we saw how the upper ranks lived. Our leaders carried only a small bag attached to their belt, and our battalion commander still wore his immaculate parade uniform with highly polished boots and belt. He of course sat high on his horse with a straight back as if he had swallowed a broomstick.

The next day was only a 18-mile march, and then we were in Kiev. Along the way we saw some early signs of the battles that had gone on just three weeks before we got there. The German advance had been crushing. Combining Goering's *Luftwaffe* with its *Heinkel* bombers, *Messerschmitt 109* fighters, and *Stuka* dive bombers, and the fast moving tanks of the *Panzer* divisions, the Russian resistance had been overwhelmed. Tanks, guns, cannons, wagons, supplies, horses, and much more, littered the roadside where we now walked. As we marched by we were left with our own thoughts about what we were heading toward. It was ugly.

When we arrived in Kiev we had a brief chance to catch our breaths. We were billeted in a ruined chocolate factory, which unfortunately, had been cleaned of any remains of its much-longed for product. I went over four years without a taste of sugar and nearly made myself sick in St. Moritz trying to make up for this after the war. But in our new quarters we didn't even have a stale scent to remind us that there were such things as chocolate in this world.

The front was hundreds of miles to the east now, and as we rested, some foolishly talked about not having the opportunity to earn an iron cross. We all thought the war was pretty well over, and our mood matched this thought. Our only fear was that our building was one of those the Russians had booby-trapped; they would plant time-bombs in their retreat that would go off weeks later. Our mood was not to last because the next day we were on the march again.

On October 7th we marched down from the hills of Kiev, passing the famous *Zitadelle* with it spires, toward the great Dnieper River and crossed it on a pontoon bridge into Kiev East. Here, the road was wide, about the width of a four-lane highway, called *Rollbahn* (main highway) but unpaved and dusty. The Dnieper, one of Russia's many great and historic rivers is at Kiev a half mile wide. Of course, the Russians had blown up the big bridge, but our engineers had constructed a pontoon bridge, and day and night soldiers and supplies crossed this river. Crossing the Dnieper meant far more to me than simply crossing a mighty river. Though I was not yet 20, to a certain degree I passed from naivete to maturity over that river. When I got to the other side, I no longer could have the faith in the goodness of man that I had before; on the other side of the Dnieper I first encountered the unspeakable cruelty of the war I was involved in. In my yellowing diary I wrote the towns and the distances of every day's marches.

The German army had captured some 665,000 Russian prisoners of war in the Kiev pocket, according to Goebel's propaganda; in reality the numbers were far less. It was still early in the day of October 7th when Franz, Herman and I encountered our first columns of Russian prisoners. Our packs had not yet cut deeply into our shoulders, and we were chatting together in a fine mood. "The chocolate factory is still standing," Herman said with a laugh. "*Ja*," said Klimmer. "So we live another day and that means we've got another long march ahead of us."

"How many miles today, you think boys?" I asked. We were guessing as we tramped over the hollow pontoon bridge, and when we got to the other side I ran ahead so I could take a picture with the little camera I had won in the 1936 Austrian youth races in Innsbruck. I could see the citadel of Kiev in the background, and here we were crossing the famous Dnieper. "Hey, Franz!" Klimmer called to me as I snapped the photo. "If it turns out send a copy to my family, OK?" "I'll get you each a copy," I promised my two best buddies.

Several miles past the Dnieper we saw a long column of brown figures in baggy pants walking along the left side on the wide shoulder of the *Rollbahn*. We marched east on the right side of the *Rollbahn*. "Russian prisoners," Bubi, an enthusiastic soldier said with some satisfaction. "Look at those pants; their crotch is way down to their knees." "Pretty sloppy," Herman agreed. But the closer we came and saw their dirty faces and their empty eyes and exhaustion, we felt sorry for them. Ahead of us a short distance we heard the sound of a shot to our left.

"What's that?" I asked and was wondering if there was still shooting going on. Nobody answered. We walked on and then came to the spot where the shot came from. Along side on the shoulder of the *Rollbahn*, one of the baggy-panted Russians lay on his side with his head twisted awkwardly up. He had a brownish complexion, the slightly Mongolian features of so many Russian peasants, and a thin scraggly mustache. His eyes stared emptily straight ahead. Blood oozed from his temple. Herman, Franz and I looked at each other, all with the same thoughts. Is this what they do to prisoners? Are these our comrades-in-arms? Are we part of this army? We marched on, and soon there was another shot. Another Russian in the ditch, this time an older man, skinny, with deep lines of exhaustion. Perhaps he had been too weak or sick to carry on.

The prisoners were marched in columns of about 20,000. This meant that each column was long, and there were several columns. At the end of each column were the stragglers. Some were limping, some stumbling, some clearly sick. If they could no longer keep up, they were simply shot in the side of the head. Franz then said, "We were taught that when we take prisoners to bring them to company headquarters and spare their life, but this is murder." German guards were marching along side the columns on each side about 50 yards apart, and along with them were young Russian boys in Russian uniforms. The 12- to 13-year-old boys, dressed in thin baggy clothes meant for men twice their size were like pet dogs to the guards, talking and gesturing and running along side of them as the guards marched the prisoners swiftly and steadily to an unknown fate. As we marched east we saw huge masses of the light-brown-clad Russian soldiers to the left and right of the *Rollbahn* in the fields sitting in the grass. We heard many rumors about these pitiful souls.

Kiev was captured on the 19th of September, and we assumed these prisoners were in those fields since then. It was now October 7th. Knowing now what we didn't know then was, they most probably didn't get either food or water. One rumor had it, in their hunger they were turning to cannibalism. When one of their own would die, they would cut up the body and roast it and drink their blood, because of thirst. Whatever enthusiasm we had for glory in this war was lost in those few miles past the Dnieper. Only after the war did it get to be known that three million or more of Russian prisoners were purposely left to die. The German Officers, Generals and Fieldmarshalls must have seen this or known of this. That they didn't do something for these prisoners should have been on their consciences until their death. It seems they had only eyes for *Lametta* (decorations). How could they have ignored this calamity? I have wondered often if any of these generals ever saw a church from the inside or knew how to pray.

Now it was just a grim unholy business. Before this march, I held the German army in some esteem; although I had doubts about our enterprise, I was not ashamed of my uniform. Until this moment. Now I felt a sense of shame and disgust that made me feel distant from those I served with.

As we continued our march we heard more shots and encountered more dead Russians. Since we were still new at this war business we discussed the meaning of what was going on. "How can they do this?" Franz asked. "This is against the Geneva convention. When we were recruits in Rum, they told us that when we take prisoners to take away their weapons and spare their life."

"But Russia refused to sign the Geneva convention, so technically we're not violating it." Bubi the Nazi was suddenly a legalist. Herman was trying to find a way to feel good about the uniform we were wearing in light of what we had witnessed. I had given up on that and felt no pride in being part of this army. "Killing in war is not a mortal sin," said Franz Klimmer who was raised a strict Catholic, "but killing a defenseless person is a mortal sin. I'm afraid. There are repercussions for things like this. I was taught to believe in a God who will make things right. I don't like to think what this might mean for our success."

We talked about what this might mean if we were taken prisoners. We knew from our training that by shooting prisoners, our army had forfeited the protection of the Geneva convention. If taken prisoner, the Russians had the right to treat us as they saw fit. Four years later, when I was taken from the hospital in Schoenberg in the State of Mecklenburg on the Baltic Sea to a Russian P.O.W. camp, the worst treatment I saw inflicted on my fellow German soldiers was a kick in the ass for laggards and an occasional exchange of boots—the Russians coveted our German high boots.

We marched on without talking. Every day we marched further east through the fog of choking dust raised by the trucks of our supply columns, marching men, motorcycles and *Panzers*. The thirst was unbearable. We were issued one liter of black coffee every 24 hours. That was all we had to drink. I remember taking our goats up to the mountain meadows with us in the summer, just so we could have fresh milk with our coffee. My God, that sounded good now. Black coffee in our home was a no-no. We were marching ten or more miles per day still carrying our packs and machine gun, ammunition boxes and spare barrels, and every step we had a reminder of the destruction of war for on both sides of the road were scattered remains of trucks, wagons, guns, and horses. One day we walked by a large circle of dead Belgian horses on the side of the *Rollbahn.* These were the handsome, big, muscular light brown animals, a dozen of them, with one dead horse right in the middle of the circle. It looked like a nightmare circus.

Up to this time we had complained about the choking dust. But it was now the middle of October, and there was a chill in the air. If we knew what lay ahead of us when the weather changed, we would have blessed the dust. We left Kiev on October 7th, and we continued a more or less steady march until we came to Sumy, a fair-sized city of about 30,000 people, roughly midway between Kiev and Kursk. We arrived in Sumy on October 25th, and in between we ran full force into Russia's greatest defensive weapon—mud. It was called *Schlammperiode* (mud season). The Russians called it *Rasputitza.* We were not sure if it had anything to do with the mad monk Rasputin, adviser to Czar Nickolaus II.

Mud to most of us in civilized society is what children love to play in, what mothers find annoying when it sticks to boots and shoes, and what happens in our yards and streets when spring is on its way. But I am not talking about this kind of mud. This Russian mud is a most cruel killer of man and beast. It is like a willful monster that sucks the life out of those who dare venture in it. Mud swallowed up trucks and tanks and buried many a giant horse who attacked it with a heart of steel.

Most importantly for Russia, mud saved Stalin. Until mid-October the German army had marched swiftly forward across the flat steppe east to within 200 miles of Moscow, the capitol of Russia and in the south all the way to the Donets basin east of Kharkov, roughly 500 miles as the crow flies due south of Moscow. But in their swift passage, the supplies had been left further and further behind. Now the army was miles ahead, the supplies behind, and in the middle a nearly impassable sea of goo. The Russians had blown up the rail lines; anyway the German trains used a narrower gauge, and it was a giant undertaking to change to the narrower gauge. The roads, even the main highways like the ones we marched on, were unpaved and had turned to the consistency of paste when the October rains came. Every mile became an ungodly struggle. Cold and ice at this time would have been welcomed because the supplies could have moved more quickly to join the troops. That's what I mean when I say the mud was Russia's greatest defensive weapon. We were not the first army to make this sad discovery. We were just the first army to be caught trying to cross it with heavy guns, horse-drawn vehicles, trucks and *Panzers*.

It was so cruel on the horses. Our supply wagons were big and heavy with wooden wheels, a tarpaulin-covered the wagons, where ammunition, food and paraphernalia for officers and sergeants was stored. They looked like the conestogas that carried the American pioneers west in the mid-1850s. Each wagon was pulled by four, big Belgian horses. The roads were not all flat but often led uphill or down into valleys, and frequently fast moving creeks sprang up to carry the heavy rainfall, and these had to be forded because there were no bridges. The heavily loaded wagons needed often four or five pairs of horses to pull a wagon up a hill or out of a creek or ditch. We *Landsers* (G.I.s) would have to get along side the wagon and pull on the big spokes with all our might to help the wagon out of the mud. We stood in the slimy paste up to our ankles and sometimes halfway up to our knees, slipping and sliding and cursing. The packs were still loaded high on our backs because if we sat them down they could easily be swallowed up by the mud. The lead horse had a rider who used the whip viciously to get the animals to pull for all their worth. And pull they did. There were only two outcomes: either the wagon would move forward, or one or more horses would drop, eyes bulging out and with convulsions lay there and die. If one died, another horse would be brought up until the wagon moved. The fit horses were unhitched at the top of the hill and led back to pull another wagon out of the mud until it too died of exhaustion. The orders were "Forward," and nothing could be allowed to stop our progress.

We were now in the vastness of the Ukrainian steppe. It is such an open, empty, windy land. For hundreds of years peasants had struggled to care for their few animals and scratch out their crops in this sometimes rich, sometimes impoverished soil. And very little had changed in those hundreds of years as we were to find out. Industrialization had surely come to this country, but the factories were in the cities. Outside of the cities, little had changed. The Russian peasants lived in small huts called *panje* huts, the same kind of house their ancestors had lived in for hundreds of years. The typical *panje* hut was a one room hut made of logs with mud dabbed into the cracks between the logs to help keep out the Siberian wind. A thick straw roof covered the hut. Near the house was the potato cellar, a hole in the ground about six feet by eight feet with a gabled straw roof just above the ground. On top of the cellar was a small opening where you could climb down into the cellar on a ladder. The centerpiece of a *panje* hut was the *pitchgu* (woodburning fireplace). This was an elevated fireplace, about four feet square with a bench around three sides and another narrow ledge above the *pitchgu* against the wall. It was in the *pitchgu* that the members of the household cooked their meals, and around the *pitchgu* were they sat, conversed and slept. Meals were taken sitting on benches on a regular table with the family dipping their wooden spoons into a single pot. Only once on our march east have I seen a piano in a hut, and I heard that the owner was the local school teacher.

During the long Russian winters peasants would essentially hibernate in their huts. In the attached shed, they kept a cow, a horse and maybe a goat. Small pigs, chicken and other small farm animals lived under the *pitchgu*. It was really comical when the *madka* (Russian housewife) called these animals every morning and evening for feeding, she would imitate a pig with "Oink-oink" and the little pigs would run like mad out from under the *pitchgu* quickly eat and then run back into the hole. The same with chickens, and then all day long you would only hear an occasional sound. But what struck us soldiers the most was that in my four years in Russia, I do not remember seeing one cat. Only once, the end of October 1941, just as it got cold, I saw one dog running like mad from a village into the countryside while some of our soldiers used their guns for target practice.

Each squad from our company was assigned a hut each night. There were no beds, so we just slept on the mud floor. Another thing which we got accustomed to was, as soon as we arrived in a village we would immediately seek out houses which were not occupied by our soldiers and beg for food. We called this *Organisieren*. It was in fact begging. Every German soldier who in the fall of 1941 was in Russia could sing a song about *Organisieren*.

We generally entered a hut, one didn't bother to knock on doors in Russia, and asked in Russian *"Chleba yest* (Do you have bread)?" or *"Molokko yest* Do you have milk)?" or *"Massloo yest* (Do you have butter or lard)?" Many times we would come back with some food. We found the Russian population—it was mostly old men and women and maybe a small child, the ones who didn't have time to flee—very generous. In some towns through the Ukraine people would even come out of their huts and present flowers to our soldiers.

It was absolutely forbidden to take any food at gun point from the Russians as individual soldiers. It would have meant the firing squad. But each unit, like battalion or regimental headquarters, constantly sent out units to requisition food from the farmers to supply our field kitchens with vegetables, meat, flour, and so forth. There was no compensation for it. Hitler's order was that the German army must be supplied with food from Russia, and not expect any from Germany.

After the first few days' marches when the mud period started, we took our boots off when we bedded down at night; it felt so good until we tried to put them on again in the morning. It was nearly impossible, so everyone just left their boots on all the time. They dried out a bit at night through our body heat, although our feet were forever wet and muddy. Our socks just rotted off after a while, but there were no replacements. "Remember those cushy beds and fine furniture heading east?" Klimmer asked when we saw trucks loaded with beds and other furniture driving by us. *"Ja,"* I said bitterly. "For those God-damned higher ups. They get the soft beds and we don't even get socks." It's the same lot for infantryman in every war.

Hitler had made it a part of his plan that the conquered Russian land was to supply the needs of the advancing German army. Before the Russian war started, his generals had pointed out to him that if that were to happen, perhaps several million Russian peasants would die of starvation. I can just imagine the bugger looking at the generals as if to say, "So? What's your point?"

In many villages we passed through there were gallows erected, and men and women hung there like weather vanes, the wind turning them; some looked like they were still alive. Any Russian caught with weapons or discovered to sabotage were automatically hung.

The peasants were especially friendly when we showed them our *Gebirgsjaeger* hats. They were the peaked Austrian hats with the edelweiss symbol sewn onto them. They asked what these hats and the edelweiss meant, and we would try to explain to them we were Austrian. *"Ah! Austrytski karosh!"* they would say with big smiles. *Karosh* means good, so they were saying Austrians are good people. Then they would point to our arm and then to the eagle on the chest of our uniforms, shaking their heads sternly. The eagle patch worn on the sleeve instead on the chest indicated a member of the dreaded S.S. They had heard the S.S. troops were execution-ers. *"Nix karosh!"* they would say emphatically. We, in turn tried to show some measure of kindness to our unwilling hosts.

Their kindness to us was one of the reasons it was so pain-ful to follow the orders that were given me on our way when the *Schlammperiode* was on. "You Gabl and Hummer" the sergeant called us. "See that farmer down there? *Ja*, that one. Tell him we need to borrow his horse and wagon. Tell him we will bring it back after a few days." *"Herr Unter-offizier,"* I asked. "How can we bring it back when we are marching to Sumy?" "Gabl, this is an order! Or do you need to be reminded what an order means to a German soldier?"

His eyes flamed at me, and I was afraid he might report me at once. Sadly, Hummer and I walked down the hill to-ward the farmer in the distance. I understood very well how badly we needed that horse. Our big strong Belgians had dropped dead one after the other from pulling the supply wag-ons through the muck. This village was unusual with its houses built in a circle on the side of a hill. The farmer was down the hill a ways, and I kept hoping that he would catch on to what was coming and would gallop away. I thought quickly how I could get out of this assignment. I knew the sergeant was back in the village up the hill behind us and could watch every move we were making. To this day I wrack my brain trying to figure out how I could have avoided this assignment. We came up to the farmer and spoke to him in

German. With gestures we tried to explain that we needed to
borrow his horse. A look of fear was in his eyes. He sat on
the seat of his wagon holding onto the reins, knowing full
well what was coming. He was looking at the rifles slung
behind our backs. He talked madly in Russian, his hands
waving wildly, no doubt explaining that he needed the wagon
to feed his family and stay alive himself. I went to the head of
the horse and held the harness and finally the old man knew
it was futile and got down. Hummer and I climbed aboard,
and when we turned to look at him he was on his knees and
tears were streaming down his face. We knew very well what
we had done to the poor old man. As we rode back to the
sergeant I thought of my old neighbor Gfall from Rofalt. He
would use his farm horse to plow everybody's field in the neighborhood, haul their wood and produce and hay. The horse
was his pride, his livelihood, his wealth. I pray God forgive
me for what I had to do to that poor Russian. I thought of this
Russian again when I returned home to find out about farmer
Gfall's fate. He had six sons, all of whom went to war. Two
were missing, one got killed, one died within a few months
after coming home and one lost a leg. Only one son returned
in reasonable good health.

When we got back to the village and presented the wagon
to the sergeant he looked at me and said, "Gabl, from now on
leave the thinking to the horses; they've got bigger heads than
you do. A German soldier obeys orders without talking back.
Understand?" *"Jawohl, Herr Unteroffizier,"* I answered.

We arrived in the city of Sumy, southwest of Kursk, on
October 26th and stayed until November 11th. The deserv-
edly infamous Russian winter of 1941–42 was quickly closing
in on us. We still had only our summer uniforms, and they
were rather worn from the marching we had to endure. Had
we known what was in store for us, we would have praised
the dusty highways and then the mud. This cold should have
been only wished on Hitler and all his Nazis. He was the one
who said that if we send winter clothing east, then the soldiers might think that the war wouldn't be over before winter. As we approached Sumy, the cold weather helped us out.
It froze the ground solid within two days; the crust of ice kept
the wagons rolling, but the grooves from the mud left the road
terribly uneven and bumpy.

As we kept on marching, the ones who had diarrhea, had to unload the 65-pound backpack, unbutton jacket and pants, all this in the wide open steppe, do their thing and after that put everything together again. Without the help of one or two comrades one couldn't do it in the 30 degrees below zero, with the wind howling at 30 miles an hour. Here you could see comradeship at its finest. In Sumy we almost froze to death, and everyone had still to walk half a block to a latrine, but at least it had a roof and walls. We were told that roasted bread would alleviate the diarrhea somewhat, so everyone roasted the bread on one of the stoves until it was like charcoal. It didn't alleviate the problem.

The temperatures were already in the nether reaches with the biting Siberian wind in our faces, and the first frostbite cases were sent to the hospital in Kursk. Ours was an *Ersatz* battalion, replacement soldiers meant to fill in for those who had been killed, wounded or captured. We Austrians fondly hung onto the hope that we would stay together and join the mostly Austrian and Bavarian 1st Mountain Division which was part of the 6th Army. Somehow, this army life seemed more bearable if we could share it with our buddies and at least talk to each other in our Tyrolean dialect instead of high German. Our hopes were devastated when our sergeant came back from a meeting and announced that we were to join the 299th Horse Drawn Infantry Division. This division was made up of soldiers from Hessia and Thuringia. Near the cities and towns of Frankfurt am Main, and Erfurt, Eisenach and Weimar in Thuringia. We were told that our battalion would be divided up between infantry companies of Regiments 528, 529 and 530. A company normally held 180 men, with 1,000 men making up a battalion and 18,000 to 20,000 a German infantry division.

"Well, then," said Herman with a resigned laugh, "I guess we shall have to learn to speak high German that they'll understand a word of what we are saying.?" The three of us went to our sergeant and pleaded with him to let us all go to the same company. "I'll see what I can do for you men," he said with little encouragement. "You know they don't want too many men from the same town together. If your unit gets wiped out, we don't want to take all the young men from one village." We kept our hopes up. The idea of parting after all we had already been through was just too much for us.

The sergeant came back from the meeting. "Ladner and Klimmer, you're going to Regiment 528. Gabl, you're going to the 9th Company of the 3rd Battalion of Regiment 530. Now, go to the village square because General Moser, the commander of the 299th Infantry Division, will address the *Ersatz* battalion."

Perhaps it was the fact that we were crushed by this news, or perhaps it was because we had already become jaded to the glory of our German uniform by what we had seen on this march east of the Dnieper. The general was a short man and marched up to the front of the crowd of soldiers after we had waited in the cold for some time. His voice was hoarse and raspy.

"Welcome, men, from the *Marsch Battalion* from the Alps. Side by side we will march on to conquer Russia. This division has already been in combat since June 22nd, and I am proud to say it has earned many citations from the high command of the armed forces, and we will earn many more in the days to come. But," and he paused for effect, "you must not think that the iron cross is the highest decoration for a German soldier. The highest honor earned by any German soldier is the birch cross. The birch cross! Our *Führer* has promised us victory and he has never been wrong! You have seen how Poland in 1939, France, Belgium, Holland, Luxemburg, Norway and Denmark in 1940 was overwhelmed by our *Wehrmacht*. What greater honor can we have than to give our life for our *Vaterland* and *Führer*?" I heard Herman whisper in my ear, "I thought *Führer* came before Fatherland." The general was finished, quickly he hopped into a car and was gone. Herman, ever optimistic, tried to cheer us.

"Well, boys," he said with a laugh, "he did put on a good show. Did you see he didn't even wear ear warmers?" Franz asked to himself as much as to anyone, "I wonder if he really thinks this Russian gamble is almost over?" Then we saw the sergeant come over to speak to us. "Gabl, you go with corporal Konrad over there to Regiment 530. Klimmer and Ladner, go with corporal Hammer to the 528th," he said pointing out the direction.

Then, just like that, I had to say good-bye to my two best comrades in all the world. There was no way I wanted to face

Russia without them. In all my dreadful days in Russia I don't think there was a more painful moment than this. I had heard from uncle Albert and my father and other vets of World War I, what comradeship meant to them, how one would take great risks willingly to save a buddy if it was absolutely necessary. I never really understood it, until this moment. It took every bit of the discipline I had inside me not to run after them and say, "No, we're staying together!" But I couldn't. I watched them walk away. They turned and looked at me without waving.

A letter I wrote to my family a few days after our parting said, "Klimmer and Ladner are now no more with me and I don't think I will ever see them again." These were prophetic words, although, I didn't mean it literally. What I meant was I might not see them again while in Russia. As you will see, I saw Ladner two more times in June 1942, just days before he was missing on a night commando mission.

Within a few months, both Herman and Franz, my two best friends, had received that "highest" of all German honors, the birch cross. Klimmer's was stuck at the head of his grave in the wind blown Russian dirt, and Herman probably had a few shovels of dirt thrown over him by the Russians.

Cold—Lice—Blood

As Herman Ladner, Franz Klimmer and I stood in the village square in Sumy listening to the speech of General Moser, we wondered what lay ahead for us. Would we escape the fighting and just stay behind as an occupation army or would we find ourselves quickly at the front, dodging bullets until our time came to die? On November 9th, the day of the 18th anniversary of the Munich *Putsh*, Hitler spoke in Munich when he said, "The Russians are down and will never recover after the losses this summer." He was thinking that this war was as good as won. Less then a month later, on December 5th, Stalin let the Siberians loose in 40 to 45 degrees below zero, and his *Wehrmacht* in their summer uniforms ran for their lives westward and nearly three-quarter of a million *Landsers* perished or were hospitalized in the month following.

The presence of Herman and Franz had been such a comfort and strength that I felt I could face almost anything with Herman's laughter and Franz's wisdom. That's why it was so disheartening to be so suddenly separated from them after the speech of General Moser was over. They were walking in another direction and I turned to catch one last glimpse of them. Then Ganath, my Austrian comrade, and I reported to Corporal Konrad. As we stood before him he looked us two Austrians slowly over from head to toe. He had a half smile on his face and somehow I

Unteroffizier Konrad in December 1941.

had a feeling that he was a good man. We were still wearing our *Gebirgsjaeger* uniform, and he looked at the edelweiss on the right sleeve and the left side of the mountain cap with beak. These were our signs of identity and pride. I was just separated from my best comrades and wondered about the future of both Herman, Franz and myself. *"Herr Unteroffizier,"* I got up the courage to ask. "Can we keep the *Gebirgsjaeger* hats with edelweiss?" "We will have to wait and see what the regiment regulations have to say about this," he said quietly. I knew then that the way Konrad talked and handled himself I would do anything not to disappoint him. He carried on his chest the iron cross second class, the infantry storm medal in silver and the *Verwundeten Abzeichen* in black, the German equivalent of the purple heart. He had served bravely with Regiment 530 since June 22, 1941, when the Russian campaign began and was wounded in the battle for Kiev in early September. Unfortunately his wound was not serious enough, so like many others, he had been patched up and sent back to the front. Seeing the iron cross on his chest at first made me think that he might be a medal hunter who wouldn't mind jeopardizing the lives of his men easily. I was wrong. When Konrad came back from the meeting he told us Austrians that we could keep our hats and edelweiss. Years later I found out that the deputy to the commander of the regiment, a second lieutenant Franz Gehrig, who was from Frankfurt am Main, was an avid mountain man and he had hiked in the Tyrolean Alps often, and he talked with us as if he was one of ours. Generally German officers let anyone know, who were of lower ranks, that they must not let them get to friendly. Franz Gehrig survived the war, and we would hike together in my home town; he even visited me in America where we hiked in the Canadian Rockies and Washington State.

Konrad soon found out that I was a ski instructor in the world famous Arlberg Region of Austria. He took Ganath and me to the village where the 9th Company, Regiment 530 was located and introduced us to his men. They looked us over from head to toe, and when they heard our dialect they almost laughed. It didn't take long, and Ganath and I fitted in nicely with our new comrades from the *Altreich,* that's, what Germany was called before the *Anschluss.*

Konrad explained to us that we were part of the horse drawn infantry Regiment 530, and with Regiments 529 and 528 made up Division 299. Most men were from the area around Frankfurt in Hessia and in Thueringia from the cities Erfurt, Eisenach and Weimar. During the campaign in Russia, *Ersatz* (replacement) soldiers also came from East Prussia, the Rhineland and Silesia before us Austrians. This division was part of the 6th Army under Fieldmarshall von Reichenau, later under Fieldmarshall von Paulus of Stalingrad fame. Fieldmarshall von Rundstedt headed Army Group South.

It got very, very cold now, and we still had only our summer uniforms from Salzburg. The next morning the company had an inspection, and our company commander Lieutenant Christofzik gave a short speech and then quickly went to his panje hut to get warm. We occupied a hut with an old Russian farmer and his wife, and we assumed their granddaughter. It didn't take long and there was some teasing going on. We told the men that where we came from we had to walk downhill for hours to pluck edelweiss, and the school children had to wear crampons it was so steep. But soon the teasing stopped, and we went on about our business of preparing for the frontline. We spent several hours every day in our hut handling the machine gun, changing barrels and the lock. A German machine gun crew consisted of three men. The No.1 gunner handled the gun, carried a square leather box on his belt with an extra lock and oil can, etc. and a *Luger* pistol. The No. 2 man carried his rifle, two metal boxes, each

Dated November 1941, this photo is labeled "Panje hut, our hosts."

with 300 cartridges on belts and two extra barrels. Barrels had to be exchanged after shooting 400 bullets; they got very hot, and the cartridges stuck in the breach. The No. 3 gunner carried also one or two boxes of ammunition and one extra barrel and his rifle. It took about 15 seconds to change a barrel and lock; the German army record was about 12 seconds to change lock and barrel on the machine gun MG 34.

The worst part was, each man had two hours guard duty and six hours off each day at company headquarters at 30 degrees below zero in our summer uniforms. The first frostbite cases went to the hospital, and by the end of January not a single man was left of our 3rd Battalion, Regiment 530. Most had frostbite, including myself.

In these Russian panje huts we just slept on the floor with the uniform still on the body, but we had the luxury of having straw under us instead of the dirt floor. One day to day scourge with which we had to live with while in Russia was lice. There was no way we could get rid of them. Even in our sleep we would scratch and wiggle our uniform jacket back and forth so that our bodies looked rather red and bloody from the fingernail scratches.

By the end of November we were told to move south about 200 miles to the city of Ahktuerka to settle in for the winter and in spring continue the offensive. Each night on our trek south, we occupied a Russian *panje* hut to rest and sleep. My God, it was so cold. When we arrived in Ahktuerka for our supposed winter quarters, we couldn't find a house which wasn't damaged. All houses which were still intact were occupied by troops already there for sometime, and we had to take what was left. We found a large brick building, but many windows were broken and the Siberian wind blew through the rooms. Konrad then said, "You, Gabl and Herbst, go and see if you can find a stove or something to warm up this joint." Herbst and I left knowing that to find a stove in this cold, God-forsaken city would be more difficult then pull a fart out from a dead body. Off we went. Of course there was nothing we could find. Finally Konrad himself went out; he had the iron cross medal on his chest and was considered a hero and had more of a chance. He came back and had an old stove, though it was better then none, and we started to make a fire. Sleeping was out of question; we just sat there stomping our freezing feet constantly all night long. Finally we got the place warmer and more comfortable.

Now I translate a letter I wrote to my family:

Osten, 9.XII, 1941. Our unit was marching again so we couldn't mail letters. Christmas mail I have not received as yet but it should arrive soon. TODAY EACH OF US RECEIVED A BOTTLE BEER, it was the first since leaving Rum. You can imagine how it tasted.

It meant a bottle of beer war more important than winter clothing. Insanity!

From here many units of infantry were sent out to hunt partisans. Ahktuerka was surrounded by dense forests, and they were an ideal hiding place for them where they could disappear without a trace. Their main job was to disrupt the supply to the frontline troops, blow up railroad tracks, lay mines on the roads, or lie in wait for small army detachments or single soldiers.

One evening we were told that a movie was going to be shown in a hall in town, and it was supposed to be heated. Off we went to see *Rosen in Tirol.* I got very homesick when I saw the beautiful mountains, flower-covered meadows and the cozy Tyrolean villages. The story was about a young woman and a man. They both were stranded in a mountain hut during a snow storm. After days they were rescued and somehow lost each other. After some months, the woman found out that she was pregnant. Then she tried to find this man who would be the father of the child. She returned to this town year after year, frantically to search for this familiar face from that night in the mountains. She would check out every train trying to look for that familiar face. After nine months a baby boy was born, and the woman came back to this village again and again trying to find who this man was. Finally she found the father, after the boy was already several years old. The story ends with tears of joy when mother and father celebrate finding each other and getting married.

As we left the hall, an officer stood up on a chair and called out, "All men go back to your unit now. Germany has declared war on the United States of America, and the Russians have broken through our front on many places." For the first time since the invasion of Russia, Hitler and his generals realized that this might be a long war. They might have miscalculated. The next morning Sergeant Weidman and four men including me were ordered to go fetch a squad of partisan hunters from our company which went into the forests the day before. Weidman our sarge, Herbst, Ganath, Voelker and I were on our way. The sarge explained to us, "We are going single file and keep about ten meters distance between us. If some one hears or sees anything suspicious, we will stop and not move. We will change the lead once in a while, but I don't think we have to worry to much in this God-damn cold." After two hours we arrived near a village. Weidman had us stop, and he looked with his binoculars at the houses. It was so cold, nobody in his right mind would be outside. He then said, "Herbst and Gabl, you go down the hill and check in the first house on the left. We will be ready with our machine pistols." Herbst and I walked slowly down the hill across a frozen creek and up the other side. "Gabl, you wait outside and I will enter," Herbst said. He then pushed the door open with the shaft of the machine pistol. In Russia you didn't knock on doors. There was an old *madka* and *pan* sitting around the *pitchgu*. They were somewhat surprised but not panicky. I then entered and the couple said, "*Germanski Toma*" and pointed to the next house. We knew what they meant. Germans are in that house. We went over, and there were a half dozen of our soldiers sitting around the *pitchgu*. They were eating from a pot of chicken and seemed very surprised to see us. We waved at Weidman and the other two. Weidman explained to their leader that they at once report back to battalion headquarters because the Russians had started an offensive on the whole Eastern front and had broken through on many places, and we were to march to the front as soon the whole company is ready to go. In a way we were glad to leave this God-forsaken, cold place no matter what the future held in store for us. Here we discovered a small railroad which was used for delivering vegetables to the city in the fall. Weidman was a good guy and he said, "We are going to push this car and change the pusher after each kilometer." There were kilometer markers on the track. It was night when we arrived back at Aktuerka.

Within 24 hours we trudged north towards Kursk and maybe death. We marched hard, sleeping squad by squad in *panje* huts at night. One evening when we entered a hut, I saw in a corner a yellowish looking pair of leather boots. I at once inspected them for possible use because mine were rather tight and they had nails on the side which made them colder still. I could use only one pair of socks and maybe a little newspaper for insulation. Sure enough; they not only fit but I could even wear two pairs of socks. The *pan* blabbered something I didn't understand, but I knew what he meant. He would need them in spring during the *Rasputitza*. The boots were very slick on the sole, and quite often I would slip and fall down. It was as if this was the first miracle in Russia I experienced. Without these boots my toes would have had frostbite long before January 27,1942. The weather was always bitterly cold, and we still had the same summer uniform which we were given in Salzburg, September 27th.

It was a few days out of Ahktuerka when we began to hear the distant sound of artillery. Like thunder at first, miles across the steppe, then getting closer and closer. One could hear the thunder for sixty miles on a clear night. Thunder fills one with a certain sense of excitement, a reminder of great powers above our own. But artillery thunder fills you only with dread. It is so anonymous in its destruction, unlike thunder which is so purely human. We were getting closer to the real war, step by step, and I tried not to think of it, still hoping that the war would be over by the time we arrived at the front. Ever since Kiev when I saw our soldiers shooting prisoners who couldn't keep up with the swift marching, I felt distant from this army. I looked at the countryside, now covered with the crystalline blanket of snow, and wherever I saw an embankment I imagined a slalom course. I needed the training, I thought. I have to stay in race condition for after the war and race against my brother Pepi, Pepi Jenewein, Albert Pfeifer, Rudi Moser, Herman Ladner and on and on but all still as friends. But would I have courage to face battle? Would I melt like a coward? Hearing the veterans of the first world war talking how men reacted in battle set my mind a bit at ease. There were cowards, there were heroes and in between, they said. The cowards died just as quickly as the heroes. One needs luck they said, one needs luck. Thinking of it in these terms helped me come to grips with my fears. I felt if it's to be me, then so be it. As we neared Shigry, a small city east of Kursk, we could now hear machine gun fire in the crisp, clear night.

On December 24, 1941, late in the afternoon on Christmas eve we arrived at Shigry, our destination, the Eastern front. Now we would face the enemy at the front. Our Christmas eve present at Shigry was mail call. It was the first mail we had in over a month, and it couldn't have been more welcome. Nearly everyone got letters and many packages from their loved ones. We ripped the parcels open and gorged ourselves like there was no tomorrow. Had we known that there was no tomorrow for some, I don't know what could have been done.

Before nightfall we assembled in the village square and marched in review past our regimental commander Colonel Wittkopf. The colonel was a heavy-set man of gentle nature; he wore the Knights Cross around his bullish neck, and as we marched past him he looked each man in the eyes, his face solemn, almost sad. It was like he was seeing the future, and it was not pleasant. He knew we would be in battle within 24 hours and probably not all would live. He could not have known, even in his darkest fears, what would be our fate; within five weeks the 3rd Battalion of Regiment 530 would cease to exist. Every man would be buried, left in the cold snow unburied or wounded, taken prisoner or in a hospital with frostbite. By march 1945, our company of 180 men, had almost 400 men killed and well over 800 wounded.

After we finished our review in front of the colonel we turned east and marched in the dark toward the front, now only six miles away. We carried our precious, unread letters with us. We could hear constant machine gun fire, and the sky to the east was blood red, lit by the burning villages and serving the same purpose as the column of flame that directed the Israelites in their march across Sinai to safety. This, however, was leading to death, not salvation. Konrad came alongside me. He clearly sensed my apprehension. We had some private talks in the past; he had asked me about skiing and about the *Fraeuleins*. He had never skied but mentioned that he would love to come to my home in the Tyrol and learn to ski when the war was over. He had also shown me pictures of his wife and two children. He wore the iron cross but never talked about how he got it or bragged about the war, which

made me respect him the more. One could feel confident to
have him as leader, which one could not say of many other
corporals, including one from the first world war with the ini-
tials "A.H."

Konrad encouraged me to face my fears straight on and
just do my job. "I'll do my best, *Herr Unteroffizier*," I tried to
assure him. "I know you will, Gabl, that's all any of us can
do," he said. Smoke and stench filled the air as we walked
through a burned-out village. About midnight we arrived in
a village and were told to find quarters in the still remaining
houses. We were directed to a house and told to make ourselves comfortable in there, the *pan* and *madka* still there,
too. Our machine gun was to be set up about 40 yards down
the street in a basement of a ruined brick building. There
was fire in the *pitchgu,* and we could hear chickens under it.
Konrad told us to put guns next to the door in case we would
have to abandon the place in hurry. "Ganath and Voelker,
you stand guard the first hour then you'll be relieved." The
three of them headed out into the dark. It was quiet now
with only a occasional rumble of battle, but all our senses
seemed to be aware of the presence of *Ivan* just a short distance away. When Konrad came back, he suggested that we
might have a taste of the local fare. We quickly grabbed some
of the chickens, who the *madka* coaxed out from under the
pitchgu by imitating them, making them a head shorter and
cleaned them in the attached cow shed. The resident cow had
disappeared, either a refugee or a sacrifice on the altar of
warfare. The chickens were settled comfortably in a pot and
put in the *pitchgu* and an hour later ready to eat. Then Konrad
called to us, "Gabl and Herbst, you are next to relieve Ganath
and Voelker. Now remember, Gabl, Herbst is an *Alter Hase*
(an old rabbit—a soldier with combat experience), so just listen to him and watch him. Use common sense and you'll be
just fine. Don't forget the enemy is just as scared as you are.
The one who has the better nerves in war has the advantage.
They are still thinking about what we did to them in the early
days of this campaign." As Herbst and I got our gear together,
we wrapped potato sacks around our boots, and now finally
we were allowed to put our dear blanket over us.

Then I heard "K" speak up. We should wipe out this
sowfolk altogether he said. No one said anything. It was the

first time and not the last time I heard this remark from "K" and didn't know what to think of it. So far the Russians who had stayed behind in the occupied territories were very generous, and I had no complaints. I only felt sorry for them to have to endure all the hardships we had brought onto their land. Ganath and Voelker were more then pleased to see us and headed for the hut at a run. It was so cold. In no time we were tramping from one foot to the other, trying to keep our toes from freezing and rubbing our uniforms against the body from the constant biting lice which had invaded our bodies like we had invaded Russia. "What do we do if *Ivan* attacks?" I asked, as much for conversation as to ease my frozen mind. I didn't want him to know that I was scared. "I'll shoot the machine gun, and you make sure that the ammo is always ready to be fed into the gun. Just follow your training," he reminded me. A long hour later and our relief clambered down into the ruined basement. Now we would run to a warm *panje* hut, and when we got there the chicken was well done and we ate until we were stuffed. Then I fell asleep. During the night there was little shooting.

At the dawn's early light, *Ivan's* machine guns started up, but it seemed they just wanted to let us know that they are still around. There was no artillery. Then, about noon all hell broke loose. *Ivan* took dead aim at our village with his artillery. Salvo after salvo landed in the village, and while the explosions were not yet close to our hut, we were scared. Konrad looked up as if trying to see through the thatched straw roof. "We better get outside and spread ourselves. If the hut gets a direct hit, we won't all get killed," he said. Konrad headed out the door first, Seidensticker, his deputy, was next and I was last. I was still on the threshold when I heard a massive explosion. I flew backward into the hallway and couldn't move for a few seconds. When I did, I saw the door frame knocked askew. I really didn't know what hit us, though I could imagine it was an artillery shell. It was the first one I experienced in Russia. As I regained my senses I crawled out the doorway and saw Seidensticker and Konrad both down. Seidensticker was laying there in that cold street and was calling *"Sanitaeter, Sanitaeter* (medic, medic)." Quickly I ran over toward him and flattened myself against the icy street as another explosion hit a couple of houses away.

I then ran and reached Seidensticker, but I wasn't trained on how to treat wounds. Fortunately, Wagner, our company medic, came up and relieved me of having to make a decision about how to move the wounded man. I noticed some blood on the snow but not much. Apparently the shrapnel had been small and his wounds were just flesh wounds and in that cold, blood froze instantly. I then ran to Konrad. He lay motionless in the middle of the street, and I stared at his still body; there was no sign of life in him. The thought of Konrad being taken from our squad made me sad. Wagner was still attending to Seidensticker when I called over to him to look at Konrad. Wagner came over and looked if there was still life in him. He rolled his body halfway over and then let his body roll back, and I knew he was dead. Wagner said to me quietly, "Help me get Seidensticker on the sled, then go back and bring Konrad's paybook, wallet, dog tag and ring if he has one." A dog tag is an oval metal, perforated in the middle, about two by three inches and is hung with a string around ones neck. When the soldier gets killed, half of the dog tag is broken off and sent to company headquarters to identify the man if he is mangled beyond recognition. "Bring those to company headquarters when you are done." "*Jawohl,*" I said and pulled Konrad's wallet out and looked at his family photo with wife and two small children. Another German family robbed of a good man. Konrad's body was already getting frozen in the below-zero temperature, and for some reason I took care not to damage his skin when removing the ring. These items were the only reminder of Konrad's life— no good-byes, no I love you's. There was no way we could bury anyone, and we stacked bodies near the houses. By the evening we were ordered to a village further back. Seidensticker was evacuated that night. We found out some months later that he had lost one of his legs, a small price to pay, compared to Konrad. I had lost heart and felt that I would meet the same fate like Konrad before long. We were in a country filled with simple, generous, giving people who meant us no harm and who gave us bread when we begged on our march through the Ukraine.

That night, as I went to sleep in the *panje* hut it slowly occurred to me that it was Christmas. St. Anton was filled with lights, music and gift-giving. The angels would pass through our house with the tinkling of the little bell, telling the occupants that they were on their way to another house to bring joy and toys. The only gift that I could think of that I had received on Christmas day 1941, was my life. I was still living; Konrad was not. I had faced battle and death and had done my best. Konrad would have been proud, and that too was a gift.

In the next village which was located on a ridge above a little valley, each squad occupied a house. During day time we were ordered not to make any fire in the *pitchgu*, because the smoke in the chimney would indicate that *Germanskis* were in there and consequently artillery fire would be expected. I was standing guard at the corner of our hut when I heard yelling "*Hilfe, hilfe* (Help, help)." There was a soldier laying in the snow, wounded and he couldn't run or walk, I thought. It was about 20 yards from our hut and about the same distance from the hut where he came from. A Russian machine gun was shooting at him, and he must have gotten hit, I assumed. I quickly ran into the hut and said to my new squad leader, "There is a man wounded and yelling for help." We all assembled in the back of our hut and discussed the situation. The corporal then said, "Anyone pulling this man to safety would get the iron cross." The bullets were hitting the ground constantly, and no one came forward. We were afraid that the corporal would order one of us to drag this man to safety. It was not long before the man neither moved nor yelled for help. We knew then he was dead. In the evening we were to move back again to another village. There were many dead bodies stacked against the houses, and when an officer came by he said, "Dig a hole in the ground and bury the dead." We thought he was crazy—dig a hole in the ground without tools, the ground was frozen at least three feet deep in the coldest winter in Russia in 150 years. Not only that, he ordered us to dig a hole right on the road. We got picks and one guy had an axe. We started digging, and we were down maybe two inches after some hours. When he came by, we told him the ground was frozen three feet or more. He then yelled at us "go and dig you bastards." It was one of most idiotic order ever given a German soldier. Finally we scraped the mud off the huts and threw it over the bodies in the ditch, but before all dead were buried, we were ordered back to another village.

It was January 1, 1942. In my calender is written, *"Ein schwarzer Tag fuer unsere Gruppe* (A black day for our squad). It was still dark when the artillery started shelling this village like nothing we had experienced up to now. How in hell can anyone survive this, I thought. Our squad was in a hut in the middle of the village. A heavy machine gun was set up next to our hut on top of a potato cellar. The men had cut an opening in the straw roof to see the field towards *Ivan*. Before noon *Ivan* came with little groups from a gully to the left when our machine guns opened up. The commissars could not make them go forward any more, and they retreated with casualties. By noon two tanks appeared on the horizon on a ridge and started to shoot into the houses. We had neither antitank guns nor artillery. We were at their mercy. The tanks started to shoot into the huts from one end and continued on to the other end. When the explosions came near our hut, we quickly went behind it; one was quite safe there, because a tank grenade explodes after hitting the first wall. This went on for a while, then a shell exploded inside our hut. We were six men. After the explosion, Ganath, my Austrian comrade, was yelling, "My fingers, my fingers." The other four didn't move—all dead. I didn't have a scratch, though my hearing is ever since damaged. After the war I was to meet up again with Ganath, whose home was in Feldkirch, in the province of Vorarlberg. He had fingers missing on both hands and was then employed by the Austrian railroad.

There were now only a few men left in this village who could give battle, and we prepared to leave. It was late afternoon, and we had some *akias* (sleds) where we bedded some wounded and left this God-forsaken village. We went out into the open too early, and the Russians shot with machine guns and even tanks. The bullets and two tank shells went past us on the icy crust, like throwing flat stones across a lake.

Since December 24th we had seen so much death and such fierce wounds that I thought it must soon be my turn. Would it be *Heimatschuss* or birch cross? *Heimatschuss* was a wound which was not life threatening but severe enough to be sent back to *Heimat* (home). The less severely wounded were sent a few hundred kilometers behind the front lines and then again into battle. By the middle of January our company had only six men and one corporal left. The temperature was in the nether reaches, and we had not received one single item of winter clothing from our army. Without some of the clothing we took off dead Russians, there would not have been a single soldier left. Our high leadership in Berlin didn't provide us with the most necessary item in all of Russia, the coveted felt boots. They ran around in Berlin and Germany like peacocks, admired by a naive populace. If only God could have arranged that the Nazis would be in the first frontline, and suffered all this misery. They of course paraded in their brown uniforms, talking how our soldiers were bravely fighting for our *Führer and Vaterland.*

Our group of seven was now ordered to march back to regimental headquarters for rest. It was three miles to the rear. Before dawn we left this burnt-out village so *Ivan* couldn't see us and use his artillery, which he sometimes used to shoot at single soldiers. We marched single file along a ridge when we saw in the distance a large column approaching in our direction on a well traveled pathway. "Well, that's reinforcements for our village fortresses," we all thought. We kept on slogging when at once this column of more then sixty men veered to our left towards a forest less than half a mile away. We all stopped for a moment, looking, wondering. We then realized that they were *Ivan's* who operated between our village fortresses at night. They captured or shot cable layers, ammunition and food supply men and took with them what they could carry. We waited until they were in the forest, hoping they would leave us alone. Our fingers were totally numb; there was no way we could have shot the rifles, nor the machine gun. Within minutes of this episode, a group of men came walking from the same direction on the same path. We thought they were our own cable layers or ammunition carriers or our own men chasing this group of *Ivan's* which had attacked the regimental headquarters during that night. As they came closer, within fifty yards, both groups stopped. We felt that there was something wrong. By then our corporal told us to get the rifles ready just in case. The *Ivan's* were not sure if we were Germans or their own men, because we looked like them in our clothing. Finally it dawned on them that we were Germans. Without calling *Rucky-Werch*, they put their arms high up. *Rucky-Werch* means "arms high up or we shoot." Had they known of our predicament that our fingers were totally unusable, one of them could have taken all of us prisoners or shot to death. They must have still thought of us as super soldiers from the previous summer. We took their guns and made them walk ahead of us, first drinking vodka from their flask's. We had to be careful not to get our lips stuck on that cold metal. At headquarters we were received cordially, and our corporal said, "We probably won't be sent to the front again this winter." But one evening Corporal Rein came back and said, "Tomorrow we will be sent to the front again. It is supposed to be a quiet sector." Voelker, the perennial complainer, said *"Alles Scheisse, alles Scheisse* (shit)" again and again. Finally Rein said, " There is nothing we can do, men, we must do our duty. We are not going to question our *Führer* if he sometimes asks for tremendous sacrifices from his soldiers, we don't know the whole picture. Do you understand this?" Early morning we marched off hearing the thunder of artillery like we had heard every day since Christmas. It was near the end of January 1942 when we ended up in one of those villages. We were joining remnants of other units unknown to us, also mauled, like every unit from Leningrad down to the Black Sea. Our company was ordered to defend a village. It was above a gully and the houses lined the street on both sides. Our squad was assigned the last house at the end on the road. At once two men had to stand guard and keep an eye on the wooded gully beyond. We were lucky. We found lamb meat in the house and at once got started to cook on the big frying pan the meat and some potatoes. Just as the food was ready, the two guards came running and yelling into the house, *"Ivan* is coming from the bushes." Instantly we all grabbed our rifles which were always put next to the entrance and ran down the street full tilt. In Russia many of our soldiers paid with their lives if they didn't move within a second when the call was uttered, *"Ivan* is in the village."

Halfway down the road we were stopped by Lieutenant Lindner, our company leader, and he gave us hell. He then gathered other squads and told us to take back the houses at once. He told us, "One squad will move on this side of the road, the other squad across the street. I will move with my men about twenty yards, then we stop and you on the other side move past us twenty yards and so on." As we neared the last house which we left, we all roared "Hurrah, Hurrah." Sure enough, we saw some dark forms running down the gully into the bushes. As we entered our house again, our lamb chops and potatoes were neatly eaten. It seemed they even licked the frying pan clean.

By January 27th, there were only twelve men left of our battalion, from our company only three, and all three of us were Austrians: Baumgartner from Schwaz, Budik from Innsbruck and me. We had no leader anymore and fended for ourselves as we saw fit. I was looking for something to eat in one of the *panje* huts when I saw across the street an anti-tank gun crew hitch their gun onto a truck so fast I couldn't believe my eyes, and take off towards our rear. Those bastards must have heard the *panzers*. I was just walking onto the street when I heard calling out to me *Panzer*. I couldn't hear them myself as my hearing had been damaged on January 1st when the tank shot into our hut. I then looked in the direction towards where the tanks were sighted. I was in the middle of the road when I saw the two monsters coming down the road at a good clip and was not sure to which side of the street I should run to. I was afraid they were going to shoot with machine guns, and I wouldn't have time to run to one of the houses, so I threw my rifle into the deep snow and quickly dived into the ditch. Thank God the snow was quite deep, and with my hands quickly dusted myself and waited. The biggest fear was that the tanks might have seen me diving into the ditch and run over my body. The noise grew louder as they approached. I held my breath until they were finally past. I then got up and went to the hut which the antitank men had left to look for food, but I was not hungry anymore. Now I worked my way along the rows of huts towards our rear and waited in the last hut for the two tanks to return from their foray. Within an hour I could hear their clatter of the tracks again. It seemed they were scared as they drove at a high speed back towards their own end of the village.

It was now late afternoon, and I ventured onto the highway towards Shigry, about three miles away. What I saw I shall never forget. The soldiers who left the village on the road to Shigry before the tanks came, were caught in the open, treeless countryside. Corpses were lying all about. Some were run over by the tanks, some only parts of the bodies. It was a ghastly sight. I was walking on the road for a few hundred yards when a machine gun opened up to my left. It seemed it came from a farm house, a half kilometer away. There were some men ahead of me, some behind me, but I was alone. I moved by instinct, knowing the lesser a crowd, the lesser one gets attention, because the enemy tries to hit into a crowd rather than single men. The machine gun shot constantly. The time between hearing the shot and hearing the echo determines the nearness of the bullet. If the time is longer between shot and echo, then the bullet is farther away. I played dead, got up and ran, played dead again, this went on for sometime. I wanted so badly to lie on this God-forsaken, cold, icy road until nightfall, but I just couldn't. Finally the gun went silent. I was sure the gunner ran out of ammunition. Thank God. Like another miracle, I had survived. When I finally arrived in Shigry, I felt like kneeling on the cold ground to thank the Maker. I still don't know why I didn't do it. In the first house which I entered, I heard familiar dialects, as if they were men from Vienna. These soldiers told me they had just arrived from southern France. They were the 44th Infantry Division, called *Hoch und Deutschmeister*. All were from Vienna and vicinity. They all still looked like German soldiers, whereas we looked like *Ivans*. They told me to go to a big red brick building in the middle of town; that's where the main first aid station was.

When it was my turn to be treated, a doctor came by and asked me my name. *"Gefreiter Franz Gabl,"* I answered. He then asked if I was related to Pepi Gabl? "Yes, he is my brother." He knew my brother from skiing. The doctor then ordered one of the helpers to put a black salve on the toes of both my feet and bandage them and have me move to one of the huts. It seemed the whole city was full of wounded and frostbite cases. I was moved to a hut where the Vienna men were staying. They were telling me they would show the Russians what combat is and make them run all the way to Siberia. They didn't use the epithet *Ivan* like we *Alte Hasen*. I then said, "Wait and see, maybe in a few days you will speak another language if you are still alive or out of a hospital, and you still might get to see Siberia, but, to shovel coal in the mines." Ironically, the 44th Vienna Division was captured in Stalingrad, though a few would see Siberia, but to shovel coal in the mines. Almost none would see their *Steffel* or *Riesenrad* (Saint Stephens Cathedral and Giant Wheel) again or drink the *Heurigen* (wine) in Grinzing.

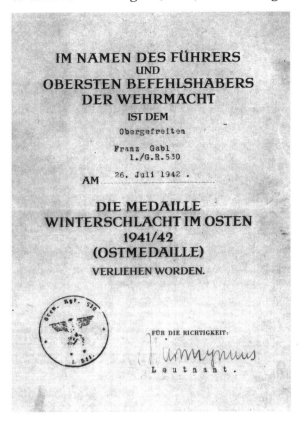

IM NAMEN DES FÜHRERS
UND
OBERSTEN BEFEHLSHABERS
DER WEHRMACHT

IST DEM

Obergefreiten

Franz Gabl
1./G.R.530

AM   26. Juli 1942 .

DIE MEDAILLE
WINTERSCHLACHT IM OSTEN
1941/42
(OSTMEDAILLE)

VERLIEHEN WORDEN.

FÜR DIE RICHTIGKEIT:

L e u t n a n t .

Certification for Gabl's "frozen flesh" medal awarded for participation in the winter campaign on the Eastern Front, 1941–42.

For two nights I could sleep in a warm hut. My God, it felt so good, not to worry about being shot at with tanks, artillery, mortars or guns and above all stand guard in this unbelievable cold. After two days, about ten of us frostbite cases were loaded onto a flatbed truck with the sides a yard high. Our feet were wrapped in rags for warmth. The more serious cases, third degree, were sitting against the cab, others against the sides. I myself lay flat on my stomach in the middle of the flatbed, my feet in the air and the upper arms on the floor. The roads were very bumpy; after the mud period the roads froze and left huge grooves and bumps. It was a rough ride to Kursk, thirty miles or so to the west. The third-degree cases were crying like I had never heard before. German soldiers are not supposed to cry. They must have felt unbelievable pain. In Kursk they unloaded us quickly in a large hospital. Day and night one could hear moaning. There was little or no pain killing medication. When the bandages were taken off, the black toes often came off too.

This was Hitler's war, and when his generals told him in October to have winter clothing and winterizing materials for tanks and trucks ordered at once, he told them: if we order winter clothing now the soldiers would think that the war would not be over this year. It was Hitler's fault that hundred's of thousands of soldiers went to hospitals with frost-bite—a sure way to lose this war.

From 6th Army to Army Group Centre

While I was in the hospital in Kursk recovering from frostbitten toes, my battalion didn't have one man left. Most, like Konrad, were laying in a ditch covered with mud scraped from *panje* huts or just on the cold, open ground of the frozen Russian farmland. Some were taken prisoner and faced years of hard labor in the coal mines in Siberia; few of these would survive long enough to return to Germany or Austria.   A few lucky ones received *Heimatschuss* in battle (the disabling wound that meant the war was over for them but not their lives) or frostbite, loosing toes or fingers. And the rest, like me, were recovering from frostbite or wounds only to return to the hopeless fight as soon as we were fit again.

In early February 1942, when I was discharged from the hospital in Kursk, my greatest fear was that I would be ordered to join another infantry unit and find myself right back in the thick of it at the front lines. To my great joy and relief, I was ordered to join our company's supply column. The supply column! The guys with the cushy jobs who took care of everything we needed at the front and we seldom got. I walked a few miles to the outskirts of Kursk to find our supply column. Schneeman, Bauman, Mieger and several others who had been wounded or with frostbite hospitalized earlier were now returning to our company. I filled them in on what had happened to our company. Frequently I found eager young faces listening in to our conversations. They were *Ersatz* (replacements) fresh from Germany and about to join the fighting at the front. Just like me a few months earlier, they were eager to hear as much as they could about what to expect. I noticed how young even the sergeants looked. I could tell by the way they looked into the eyes of the survivors that they saw something in them that was different and frightening. How soon that would change. I was just 20 years old but felt much older. It slowly dawned on me what it felt like to be an *Alter Hase*, a soldier who had lots of front experience.

I remember a particularly beautiful early spring day, in mid-March. There was still lots of snow, but the sun was shining so brightly that you had to walk around with your eyes in a tight squint. It was still cold outside, but the sun had just that faintest of hints of warmth in it, the first clue that spring was indeed coming, and that finally we would be through with this horrid winter—the coldest winter in Russia in a hundred and fifty years, and we had survived it, not to mention the fighting, with just our light uniforms!

Voelker, my companion in many of the battles of the previous months, had also been in the hospital with frostbite. He and I were walking down the village road toward the supply house, enjoying that first precious feeling of spring sun. All I had on my mind was skiing. I must have been filling his ears with endless talk about skiing the Galzig. Once again, thoughts of actually surviving this madness were beginning to creep back into my nearly frozen brain. We noticed a number of sleds pulled up in front of the supply house. And then we noticed that the supply personnel were sporting beautiful, and very warm looking long suede coats lined with clean, white fur. The winter clothing for the front line soldiers had finally arrived. These were donated by the population of Germany. In mid-March 1942. Just in time for the spring thaw. So much for German organization. But Voelker was furious.

"Look at those God-damned swine," he said, referring to the supply men who were already dressed with the big long fur coats. "They grab all the best stuff for themselves. They're not even at the front taking the bullets, but they got to have the best." "If you were in supply, what would you do?" I asked him gently. Voelker marched over to Schneeman. He had been a supply driver since the beginning of the Russian campaign, missing out in the heavy fighting Voelker and I had faced. Schneeman was never known for his brains. "What's left?" we asked the half-wit.

"There's some short coats. All the long coats are gone, but the short coats are better for you guys because you can run faster in them." Schneeman was perfectly serious, and he was quite right, but I thought Voelker was going to smack him right in the face. "I see you took good care of yourself pretty well, Schneeman," Voelker said as I grabbed the short coats and then pulled Voelker away.

"Shit, shit, shit!" he murmured as we walked away. It was what he always said when frustrated, and that was often. Voelker had a right to be angry. But at least we finally got the coveted felt boots. Since we were both recovering from frostbite, we were first in line for these valuable items—right after the *Etappenhengste* (the supply "studs"). Other winter items we were issued included heavy quilted mitts, connected together with a string that hung across our shoulders. The German army had so many people in the *Hinterland*, every time you came back from the frontline, there were masses of soldiers keeping busy with trying to stay back and avoid the real front, like the plague. When it happened that some of the *Etappenhengste* were to be sent to the front, one could hear: we are not meant to be on the front, we are supply personnel. We, who were on the front constantly, had fun with these guys and teased them.

While Voelker and I managed to get these items, along with the short fur coats, many of the fighting men in our company, the ones who just came from Germany, still didn't get their winter clothing. The more I thought about it, the more I boiled just like Voelker. It did our army's morale no good when the soldiers facing hell at the front realized that no one was looking out for them and that everyone in the whole chain of command, from the peacock generals to the greedy supply clerks could get anything long before the poor guys at the front. When we returned to our quarters Voelker was still grumbling.

"We have no right to be here in this God-damned land," he said with deep passion. "We're gonna die here just like Napoleon's army. Just wait and see." Deep down, I believed he was right. We had no business to invade this country and destroy everything in our way. Why was I here when all I really wanted was to be skiing the Galzig? Hitler. *Heil* butter, we have too much Hitler. Way too God-damned much Hitler. My disgust at the memory of those stupid villagers in St. Anton stabbing that good clean air with their right arm held high was growing.

A few days after we received our long-awaited winter uniforms, we received orders to head south. We were going to Karkhov. This was the second largest city in the Ukraine, after Kiev, and quite modern by Russian standards. It was the key center for our sixth army which was now led by Colonel General Paulus. Field Marshall von Reichenau had died of a heart attack in January. The Russians were on the offensive, and we heard they were at the gates of Karkhov. Karkhov was about 200 miles south of Kursk, and we gathered at the train station to catch the train that would carry us once more into battle. For two days we waited in unheated cattle cars while the train stood still in the station. As bad luck would have it one of the cattle cars was hit by an artillery shell, and all 25-30 men were killed. Even though it was March, that ever-so-slightly warm sun had disappeared, and the Siberian cold roared back with a vengeance, intent it seemed on blowing as many of our soldiers out of this country as it could while winter still hung on. It was colder than ever, with the temperature at 35 degrees below zero and the wind whipping at 30 miles per hour. Instead of heading to the front, many in our company headed to the hospital with new cases of frostbite. After two days of riding the clacking rails, we arrived, half-frozen, in Karkhov.

We got off the train and immediately headed east to make contact with *Ivan*. The Russians had broken through the German lines in several places, so we were not sure where we would find them. We were crossing a large snowfield heading toward a forest when we saw seven of our soldiers laying in the snow outside of a *panje* hut. As we came close to them we saw they had met a brutal death the night before. Some had their jackets, boots and mitts removed, and we could see that all of them had been bayoneted to death. Their faces in particular had received blow after blow and were mutilated beyond recognition. We figured they had been staying in the hut when they were surprised at night by a Russian commando unit and were trying to flee, or so it seemed. I vowed then and there that I would never allow myself to fall into Russian hands alive. I would do myself in without hesitation if I thought *Ivan* was going to get me. Such brutality feeds the hatred of war. I later realized how the horrible treatment of the Russians by the S.S. and the *Einsatz Kommandos* who exploited Russia in the occupation areas helped strengthen the resolve of the population to fight until death.

Stalin was no dummy when it came to propaganda, and he made sure to make the invaders look like the worst kind and have his army fight to the death. We had still not made contact with the Russians when we were ordered to Pestjanoje, a little village above the banks of the Donez river.

During the war years in Russia I said more often than I care to remember that once I got out of this God-damned land I would never want to return to it. But I would very much like to see Pestjanoje again. For almost two months this little village was a battlefield and my home. I experienced much fear, bravery and death in this little village in these two months than I care to remember. Yes, I would like to return to Pestjanoje and see these people again in very different circumstances.

Pestjanoje is a fairly large, picturesque Russian village, on the west bank above the Donez river. Laid out like most of the other villages, the houses line both sides of the road that runs parallel to the Donez. The road through town runs uphill making the south eastern end of the village a hundred fifty or so feet higher than the north western end. The river flows peacefully below the town in a southerly direction then the land stretches out into the endless steppe for thousands of kilometers.

When we arrived in the early morning, it was just in time for the routine Russian attack. *Ivan* occupied the high southeastern end, and we Germans occupied the lower northwestern half of the village. The middle was a battleground that had changed hands as often as three times a day before our unit came.

Here we received the new machine guns 42. They shot 1,300 bullets per minute where as the machine gun 34 shot only 800 rounds per minute. The number of the MG's indicated the year they were issued. I was the first one to receive the MG 42, and I remember the number stamped on it very well. It was 8815.

The attacks came always with the expected and murderous artillery barrage, followed by several rumbling tanks. Our battalion, along with the existing battalion still in place, went to work to repel the attack. Thanks largely to the use of our antitank guns, the Russian attack faltered, and they never made it into our half of the battered village. Before we came to this village *Ivan* must have overrun the houses we were quartered in. There were two knocked-out tanks in front and three Russian soldiers laying on the ground nearby, all of them burnt black like the darkest people in Africa. One of the tanks could still shoot, and one of our guys got into one and shot two rounds towards *Ivan*.

Every house in the village wore battle scars; the ones in the middle were little more than smoking shells. But what was most surprising was that the village was still occupied by some of the civilian population. The Russians are not like western European civilians who flee from the path of battle. Russian villagers and peasants stay with their homes and meager possessions, facing the same hunger and horrors as the soldiers. The stoicism of the Russian people is incomprehensible. They seem almost rooted to the land and getting out of the way of danger makes as little sense to them as a tree moving out of the way of a *Panzer*.

It was now the end of March, and we could at last feel the real promise of spring. After enduring the most bitter winter in a hundred and fifty years, in addition to the near constant bloody warfare, the idea of spring and warmth was like a glimmer of light in our dark night. We could be outside now without constantly stamping our feet and moving about to keep warm.

One night I was on patrol with one of my fellow *Landser*; this one never gave me a lot of pride to be wearing the same uniform. We were on night watch as listening posts near the village center, in no-man's land that was certain to be the focus of tomorrow's battle just like it was earlier that day. Suddenly we heard voices whispering. They were close, and we peered into the dark nervously. We were trying to find the source of the voices.

My partner "K" motioned me toward him, waving at a potato cellar. "I think they're in there," he mouthed quietly. We moved closer and suddenly shone our flashlights into that cellar. There were eight frightened women all sitting on the floor along the walls. I breathed a huge sigh of relief and was about to turn away when I saw my partner "K" reach for a hand grenade in his belt. "What are you doing?" I demanded. "What do you think? I'm going to wipe out this *sowfolk*," he said. "Are you out of your mind? These are civilians, women, not soldiers," I said, my anger growing rapidly. "What difference does that make. They're a *sowfolk*." And he started to pull the hand grenade from his belt. I grabbed his arm, trying to take the hand grenade from him. I couldn't believe that a human being could think of doing such a thing to a cellar full of innocent women. With frustration and a good deal of confusion he put the grenade back on his belt, and we marched away. If I hadn't stopped him, not only would eight innocent lives be lost or badly mauled, but something valuable would have been taken from me as well. I know I would have been tortured to this day by the thought of that senseless and cruel action. As it was, I'm just glad that I was there that day and that I thought and moved as quickly as I did. Maybe it is one small reason why my life was spared in so many miraculous ways during this war.

After our two hour listening post duty was up, we were relieved and returned to our huts to catch a couple of hours sleep. The next morning, it started all over again with another artillery barrage and another Russian attack. More dead on both sides and nothing gained.

By now it was early April, the snow was melting. The middle of the village was strewn with hundreds and hundreds of dead still unburied, lying in the melting snow and cold mud. As senseless as it all seemed the commissars would push the Russian foot soldiers on, now directly into the withering fire of our new MG 42 machine guns. Russian prisoners would gesticulate and say *"Germanski mashinka blocha!* (German machine guns terrible!)" Sometimes it seemed just a burst from one of these guns was enough to send the attackers scattering. At those times anyway they preferred to face the pistols of their angry commissars than the *blocha* German guns.

Finally in early April general winter retreated and *Ivan* seemed to retreat with it. At least the attacks came less frequently and then finally stopped altogether. We thought that we would have a rest as we were near exhaustion. No such luck. On April 8th our orders from Regimental HQ came: attack and capture the southeastern half of Pestjanoje tomorrow in the early morning of April 9th. *Ivan* had been trying for weeks to capture our side, the lower half, the easier side to attack. Now we were supposed to take them out? In war you do not question the decisions made by the commanders.

Actually, there was good reason. The Russian part of the village held a commanding view of our *Hinterland,* and *Ivan* was using it to good advantage to direct artillery fire against our supply columns. We needed to take the high ground. The good news was that for the first time we would have *Stuka* dive bomber support, and six tanks to lead the attack. It would be a classic *Blitzkrieg*-style attack, executed with vaunted German precision. I could feel the mood of the men changing. For the true *Alte Hasen* (the old rabbits) who had been in Russia since the incredibly successful attacks of the summer of 1941; this was to be like the old days. For me who had only fought a defensive war, this would be a new experience.

At dawn on April 9th, the artillery shook the ground behind us. Then, precisely fifteen minutes after they started we heard a devilish whine of sirens and watched in awe as nine *Stukas* dove nearly straight down from the sky, raining their bombs onto the Russian positions. The pieces of smashed Russian houses and bunkers were still dropping from the sky when our tanks went on the move and us foot soldiers running behind them. Our company, the 9th, was on the right and the 10th on the left of the road. We were just past no man's land, the killing field of the village center, when machine gun fire opened up on us. Our soldiers were dropping right and left, some silently, some screaming *Sanitaeter! Sanitaeter!* They were brave Russian machine gunners who stayed behind as a suicide crew. They swore to their commissars that they would not retreat, rather give their lives for "Mother Russia and Papa Stalin." They didn't last long. Soon their MG nest was reached and the vicious gun went silent.

I remembered the veterans of World War I telling stories of how lieutenants and sergeants yelled at their men while attacking fortified enemy positions in withering machine gun fire: *Vorwaerts ihr Schweinehunde, wollt ihr ewig leben?* (Forward you swinedogs, do you want to live forever?) I have never heard these words myself during World War II.

From here on it was just a walk through the village. We got all the way up the hill without encountering any more fire. When we got to the end we saw the Russians were escaping by scrambling down the bank and diving into the Donez River below. The water was near freezing with chunks of ice floating down the river. When our soldiers saw them escaping they stood upright at the top of the bank and shot down at them in the river or the ones running down the bank. It was literally like shooting rabbits in an open field. I stood there with my rifle at my shoulder, looking down my sight at a fleeing soldier. I saw a man running towards the river. A inner voice told me which said, "Franz, why don't you let this guy go?" I am sure he wanted desperately to go home and see his family again, or maybe just to work the fields and care for the animals. Just maybe I might find myself in a situation like this man and someone would do the same to me. I didn't pull the trigger. It made no difference. He was also in someone else's sight, and soon he tumbled face first into the dirt and did his dying quiver near the edge of the Donez River. Very few Russians escaped across the Donez.

It was a great victory. We counted 200 prisoners and four tanks. But there was no victory parade for us, no cheering crowds, no bright martial music. Just the grim task of burying 2,000 young men who were still laying all over in this village and had no business at all being there and certainly no business dying in this otherwise quiet and pretty village.

Yes, I would like to return to Pestjanoje, maybe more so then any other place in Russia. Because I am grateful for the peace. And perhaps, if I sat in the village square in the spring sunshine I might watch a young child play, a granddaughter perhaps of one of those eight terror-stricken women in that dirty potato cellar in the spring of 1942.

After the dead of Pestjanoje had been buried, one of the quietest periods of my four years in Russia began. I could feel the hope of life begin to creep back into my frozen bones and spirit as the spring sun warmed the land. Both the Russians and we Germans were exhausted from the endless fighting and the cold. We could walk outside without worry of either frostbite or a bullet smashing into us. It was an unbelievable feeling of peace, even in the middle of a war zone. Instead of attacking the Russians, we found ourselves occupied by attacking the Russian lice who had invaded our bodies like we had invaded the Russian homeland. But unlike the Russians, we fought a losing battle against the lice.

For the first time since I came to Russia I saw birds and a single butterfly which was unconcerned hopping from flower to flower pollinating new life, whereas we soldiers tried to wipe out our enemy's life. My thought was, my God, how wonderful it would be to fly away from all those massacres.

How I wanted to be one of those creatures. It seemed to me that in Russia there was no wildlife, deer, elk, chamois, none. Even birds one might see only very seldom.

Since there were very few houses left standing in the village area we made ourselves at home in a potato cellar. Our host was an elderly *madka* who welcomed us in and seemed to try to make us feel comfortable. Still, after a day or two we wondered why she didn't move on to one of the houses left standing in the less damaged part of the village. We also noticed she spent a lot of time staring at one particular spot on the floor. While sitting there one of our guys suddenly put two and two together and started to dig at the spot. The old woman's expression turned to fear and disappointment. Sure enough, there were six cans of meat buried in the dirt floor of the cellar. We gave her two cans and she promptly left.

Even though our leaders left us pretty much alone in these quiet days, there wasn't a Russian in sight for weeks. We were ordered after a few days to dig defensive positions. First, we dug machine gun nests, then we dug holes about eight or nine feet square and about six feet deep for our bunkers to live in. Across the top we would lay wood beams from the ruins of the houses or logs from fallen trees, and on top of that we would place straw or grass to prevent dirt from trickling down when artillery was shelling. These were mortar proof but would not stand up against a direct artillery hit. Still, they were far better defensive positions than we had had before.

Rumors were flying now, and like all rumors we tended to believe almost anything. One rumor had our division being sent to southern France; it was wishful thinking, but it was what 99% of us wanted desperately. Another rumor had us advancing on the Caucasus, meeting up with a German army coming up through Iran. And, we also heard there was a huge German army assembling behind us that would attack the Caspian oil fields and Stalingrad to disrupt traffic on the Volga River. This turned out to be the truth. We were still part of the 6th army, that ill-fated group of 330,000 German soldiers who would attack this essentially meaningless target. Not many would return. Another rumor that turned out to be true was that *Ivan*, under Marshall Timoshenko, was aiming a giant offensive at our area. The objective was

Karkhov, 15 miles behind our position. We received orders to redouble our efforts to build defensive positions.

By the 11th of May we knew it was no rumor; now the only question was when the attack would come. All night we could hear the Russians barking orders and men and equipment on the move. The Russians were given vodka liberally before attacking German positions; it was to steel their nerves. They knew to attack a German fortified position was akin to death.

Every morning before dawn we would peer anxiously toward the east, not looking for sunrise but looking for when the sky would in an instant turn blood red with the Russian artillery having been fired. We could see the firing before we could hear it, and we knew that it was only a matter of seconds before more than the sky would be bloody. The only confidence we had was that we faced the Donez River which by now was free of ice. The Russian tanks could not cross it in front of us. We were as ready as we could be.

5:00 a.m. on May 12th, 1942, the skyline in the east turned blood red. The Russian *Trommelfeuer* had started. Death would reap a rich harvest. This was it. But nothing could have prepared us for the artillery barrage we received that day. The devil in all his fury couldn't create a hell more terrifying, more cruel, more sickening in its devastation. To us Germans it felt like *Götterdaemmerung* (Twilight of the gods), the end of the world. Once it started I couldn't imagine living to hear it ever stop. The dust was so thick from all the artillery explosions that you could hardly see your hand in front of your face, let alone your buddies. Except for the choking, the dust made you feel that you couldn't tell if you were dead or alive.

By the time I shook myself off, my ears ringing painfully from the noise, and realized that I was actually still alive and unhurt, how in hell can anyone live through this? Then a new terror struck us. It was the *Schlachtflieger* (twin-engine *Illushyn* ground attack planes) the Russians used to strafe ground troops and targets. As they swooped down raining bullets from their wings, I hugged the walls of my nest, grateful for the extra digging I had done to make it safer.

Finally the Russian infantry appeared. We Germans attacked in swarm order: you shoot, I run, then I shoot and you run. But not the Russians. They attacked in columns like the old set piece battles of Napoleons era. Three columns, marching calmly, side by side. It was insanity, and to prepare them for battle the infantry was given vodka the night before the battle to help them steel their nerves. Our artillery, positioned behind our village, had not shot yet. When they were within 600 yards, I opened fire with my machine gun because the tracer bullets that showed where my fire was going extinguished after 700 yards. I saw men drop, then suddenly my gun stopped. I pulled the trigger and a few more rounds sputtered out and it stopped again. By now the Russians had seen my position and mortar and rifle fire began to be trained on me. I changed the lock and barrel and shot a few more rounds and then the gun quit for good. The dust from the hellish artillery bombardment had fouled the mechanism of the MG 42.

I was alone in the nest and called for my buddies but no one answered. Where were they? I couldn't possibly get out of the nest as shrapnel and bullets were zinging by at a furious rate. I had recovered a rifle from a wounded man, and now I fired single shots at *Ivan* across the river. Looking out, I saw that *Ivan's* tanks had broken through our lines about two miles north at the village of Nepocrytaya, and now the Russian columns were veering north to surge into this breech. It was good news for me. About noon I started getting very worried. Not a single man of my company was anywhere to be found, not in the holes, nowhere. Usually, when there is a break in the fighting someone comes around and tells you what is going on, but no one came. I felt I was the last German soldier left to face the entire Russian army on a hillside of Pestjanoie. Finally, I decided to leave. A soldier is not to leave his post, but what could I do? I couldn't fight this war alone, I had a machine gun which didn't work. I dismantled my gun and took it with me, slowly working my way from crater to crater toward Battalion HQ near the top of the village. The firing was coming now from the north, so I was keeping myself hidden as much as possible.

Finally I worked my way into the battalion command bunker and expected to get chewed out for leaving my post. Instead, I found what was left of my outfit, and after I explained that I couldn't find a single soldier left of the 9th Company, they gave me some food to eat and expressed amazement at my surviving the awesome hell of that bombardment. Many of my company did not survive, however.

After about an hour in the bunker, we were ordered to move back to another village, two miles west. Retreat again. After spending a memorable time, I would be leaving Pestjanoje. About six of us ran to the top of the village then began working our way west along a ridge towards the artillery emplacements. I saw a twin-engine plane appearing on the horizon, coming from the west thinking it was one of ours to be attacking the Russian tanks or infantry. Then it turned directly toward us and noticed fire on its wings. I thought, "This boy is in trouble!" Then I noticed the explosions on the ground heading straight toward us. *Schlachtflieger!* I dove onto the ground, but there was no cover. As the exploding bullets approached I put my hands over my head waiting for the bullets to slam into my exposed body. Suddenly, not five feet in front of me, they stopped. Why? Another miracle? I have no answer. I picked myself up, my heart in my throat, and we ran down the ridge into a depression where there at least were some bushes. Anything seemed to give us more protection than the open ground.

We made it back to the next village without further incident. There we were organized into smaller fighting units. Our battalion had been reduced in half that day. We dug holes with our bayonets, knowing that *Ivan* would not pause but come at us with a vengeance. The order came down: "Not one step back." We were to make our stand here and fight to the death. To our good fortune we did not receive an infantry attack. Instead, at night the sewing machines circled above us—so called, they were old single engine crates which sounded like a sewing machine—and threw everything they could out of their doors or windows. Small bombs, mortar shells, nails and even small pieces of metal; anything they could put their hands on that they thought could damage us. We didn't understand why we were getting so much attention from the Russian pilots until the next morning when we noticed that we had been placed right next to our heavy artillery, the 21-cm *Mörsers*, eight-inch caliber guns.

Because of this we were also given the attention of the Russian infantry the next morning. The columns advanced until they were about a quarter of a mile away, and then our artillery opened up shooting direct into their midst. The Russians scattered in panic, running for their lives. Then we heard noise of tanks on our right. Oh no, we thought how did the Russians get over there? The tanks broke into view, there were about forty of them, and we saw they were ours chasing the Russian foot soldiers. We followed after the tanks to help mop up but there was little to do, besides by now there were only about two dozen left of our company. Many Russians were shot or taken prisoner.

The last couple of days I had felt a growing rawness in my throat, but when your life is constantly threatened by bullets, artillery shrapnel and strafing planes you don't pay a lot of attention to a sore throat. By May 17th, I was feverish and weak, and the medic sent me to the doctor.

"Angina," (strep throat) he said, and just like that I was sent to the hospital in Karkhov. I had never felt so grateful for a minor illness. While I was convalescing, our soldiers were fighting off a heavy-handed Russian attack led by Marshall Timoshenko aimed at retaking Karkhov. The hospital was clean and the only noise was familiar tunes such as *Lilly Marlene* playing on the sound system. "Underneath the lamp-

post--by the garden gate." I couldn't believe the clean white linen and the meals; best of all, the battle against the lice was temporarily won. Thank goodness it was a pretty serious infection, made worse no doubt by a weakened condition brought on by nearly constant warfare and little sleep, and I was in the hospital for a month. Finally I was discharged and sent to Division HQ northeast of Kursk in a dirty little place called Malo Archangelsk.

In another of the many quirks of fate or providence, I found that our division, 299, was no longer part of the 6th Army. This was the army that was to attack Stalingrad in a highly questionable strategic move a few weeks later. In spite of the most bitter fighting in all the war and heroic street by street defense of Stalingrad by *Ivan*, Hitler demanded that the fight be continued until the entire army was surrounded and destroyed. Only 5,000 of the 90,000 men of the 6th Army who were taken prisoner on February 2, 1943, were to see their home again. That was not to be our fate, however. We had been so decimated by the defensive fighting around Karkhov that we were considered unfit for the offensive and assigned to *Heeresgruppe Mitte* (Army Group Center) during the rest of the war.

Our battalion settled into a hut in the countryside outside of Malo Archangelsk east of Kursk. Here I found out that Regiment 528 was just south of us, only a quarter of a mile away. That was Franz and Herman's regiment. I asked for permission to see if I could find them. I had not heard from them since early November when we parted and hardly dared to hope that they were still alive. But I thought if I can survive this there's no reason those tough Arlbergers could survive it as well. After asking around I found their unit and in a few minutes I found myself surrounded by the hearty laugh and giant arms of my friend Herman. What an incredible great joy to find this good friend. I think it takes someone who has faced bitter battle to really know what comradeship means in war; discovering real comradeship is such an important and heartwarming experience that in retrospect you may realize you wouldn't want to have lost that joy even if it came at the cost of the kind of misery we were facing. Certainly Herman was that kind of man. He thrived in the camaraderie of warfare; he had lost little if any of his warmth, laughter, optimism and sheer delight in living. If anyone deserved to live on through this to experience all that life had to offer, it was Herman.

Our reunion was dimmed by the news that Herman gave me about Franz Klimmer. Franz was the serious one of our little St. Anton squad, the philosopher, the thinker. But now he was dead. He had survived the winter but in early April a mortar burst hit him and filled his body with shrapnel. He was taken back behind the lines but he lived in agony for two days before he finally died. Earlier in the war I felt that my spirit had died within me and that I was too numb from the cold and the suffering and dying to feel anything anymore. But the news about Franz hit me hard, and I felt my heart slump. I knew when I heard those vet's talking in the *Weinstube* of the *Gasthof* Post, that we were headed for this kind of fate. Why didn't I run then? But, what could be done, then or now? One does what one has to do and tries to make the best of it at the time.

Franz Klimmer was buried unceremoniously in Russian soil with the birch cross stuck above his grave. At home the band would have played the song: *"Ich hat einen Kam-e-ra-den, einen bes-sern findst-du - nicht.* (I had a good comrade, a better one you don't find.)"

> "A bullet came flying,
> is it meant for you,
> or is it meant for me?"

At least I was with Herman again, and I took greater delight in his ribaldry, his laughter, his mocking the arrogance of the military system than I ever had before. I was surprised how little the war experience had changed him. He seemed untouched by it while I felt that it had turned me from an optimistic and hopeful young man into a withered and bitter *Alter Hase.*

The fighting was taking place in other sectors at this time in late June, 1942. The big offensive of the 6th Army toward Stalingrad had not started yet, but on June 28th that would change. Field Marshall von Bock would head the IV *Panzer* Army toward Voronezh, about 100 miles to the east, and Colonel General von Paulus would head the 6th Army driving south along the Don river, then head east and reach the Volga at Stalingrad. To help the offensive get off to a good start, those units that were to stay behind and not taking part in the offensive, were ordered to create commando squads to mount fake attacks on the morning of June 28th all along the Russian front. This was designed to confuse the enemy, hiding where the main thrust was occurring and creating the impression that the attack was coming along the entire eastern front from Leningrad all the way down to the Crimea. The Russians were fooled somewhat as they expected the main thrust to be in the direction of Moscow. Herman told me that he was selected for one of these special fake attack squads. They were called *Himmelfahrtskommandos* which is literally and ominously translated as Journey to Heaven Commandos. I had an awful feeling in my stomach and had enough experience with these feelings to know that they should be taken seriously. I also could tell from Herman's rather forced laughter and nervousness that he, too, must have had a premonition about this assignment.

About noon on June 28th, I went over to Herman's squad to inquire how they had fared. Herman's sergeant was there, although wounded, he had been shot in the cheek, though not seriously. Herman was not there. The sarge told me the story. Of the four in the fake attack squad, only the sergeant had returned. In the early morning darkness they were in the middle of no man's land between the lines when they were surprised by a Russian patrol. *Ivan* opened fire with their sub machine guns. Herman went down, shot in the chest. The other two men were either dead or badly wounded, the sergeant was wounded as well but able to move, and he started back toward the German lines. "Take me with you, please, take me with you!" Herman cried at him pitifully, his lungs rattling with blood.

But the sergeant had no choice. It would have been certain death for both of them if he had tried to carry Herman back, and he knew that Herman's wounds were likely to be mortal. He left, knowing that Herman faced a Russian bullet in the head at best. Now both my best comrades were dead. My heart and spirit had returned by finding my friend again, my thoughts returning to good times and even the future back on the Galzig with Herman. His laughter and jokes were

now silenced. He didn't even have a birch cross over his head.
I felt I had no fight left in me and was certain that I was not
far from the same fate as Herman and Franz. And I really
didn't care.

Ironically, the summer of 1942 was the most peaceful time
of my four years in Russia. The weather was sunny, the mud
period in the spring had been mercifully short. The fighting
was now going on in the east and south, and it was going well
for the German 6th Army as it marched quickly toward
Stalingrad. It was almost like June 1941, with one great difference: now the Russians were in orderly retreat, meaning
they were saving themselves for the best possible defensive
positions, luring the Germans and their satellites as far east
as possible so that their supply lines would be stretched to
the limit and then wait for the greatest ally of the Russians,
"Marshall Winter." Still, from the news we received it was
tempting to think that the Russian army was truly nearly
finished. Because of the good news—and the good weather—
our spirits were buoyed, and we allowed ourselves to hope
that the war could possibly be over soon. Not that we didn't
think about going home. One day some of us saw a dead cow
rotting in a stream below our trenches, in the Kunatsch River.
We looked at each other, the thought occurring to us at the
same time. We went down stream a few yards and eagerly
lapped up the water then went to our bunkers to await the
illness that surely would send us to a hospital or even home.
We waited for days but, unfortunately, our health remained.

Here in this quiet sector of the front *Ivan* was at least half
a mile from our trenches, and there were days when we didn't
see a single Russian. Every day we dug more trenches and
eventually bunkers, all during daylight. There wasn't a shot
fired from a rifle or artillery for weeks. An order was given
also that during the darkness every soldier had to be awake
because there were big gaps between platoons, and it would
have been easy for Russian patrols to sneak behind our lines.
One night as I stood guard at the MG nest I saw two figures
approaching; I was not sure if they were our own men. Then
I yelled: "*Parole?*" Each evening the company commander
gave instructions to every squad what word would be used as
the password. If anyone came from the enemy's, side this
parole word would have to be uttered, or the soldier on duty

had the right to shoot. As I yelled parole, I thought these two figures had skirts on, and I was a bit nervous. There was no answer, but I saw that they held their arms high up into the air. Sure enough they were two Russian women. At once I escorted them to my sergeant's bunker who took them to company headquarters. Some of the guys teased me after that and asked why I didn't rape them. A few days later we were told that the two women were to spy how much war material was being ferried between Kursk and Kharkov. Both women were then shot.

While we were enjoying a relatively quiet summer and fall, the news went from good to worse with the 6th Army. By November 22nd *Ivan* had surrounded the 6th Army, trapping it in Stalingrad. Hitler's stubbornness and stupidity had forced them into this position, and Stalin's orders were: "Stand fast and die if necessary, there is no more land beyond the Volga." Both armies had been told to fight to the last man, and they practically did. The spirits of our elite troops were broken; they felt betrayed and did not understand why the Fieldmarshalls and Generals didn't stop this mentally sick man. They probably were still thinking, that if the war could be won, they knew that anyone who was decorated with the Knights Cross with oak leaves would get an estate from the *Führer*.

On November 28th our regiment was marched about 15 miles north to replace the 17th *Panzer* Division which was to be shipped by rail toward Stalingrad for a relief operation. We went from heaven to hell. Not only had the weather turned cold but we found the defensive line laid out by the tank troops to be terribly inadequate. The trenches were too shallow and poorly arranged, unlike the fine defenses we had built in our sector near Malo Archangelsk. At least we now had warmer winter clothing, the treasured felt boots and quilted, reversible uniforms, white on one side and gray on the other. But unlike the summer and fall, we again found ourselves skirmishing with *Ivan* almost constantly. We were not trained in trench warfare as our training was primarily for attacking, but we learned quickly. We called the sector we were defending *Sudetenland*. Many of our men, myself included, earned the bronze *Nahkampfspange*, a medal given to soldiers who had been in hand-to-hand combat 15 times or more.

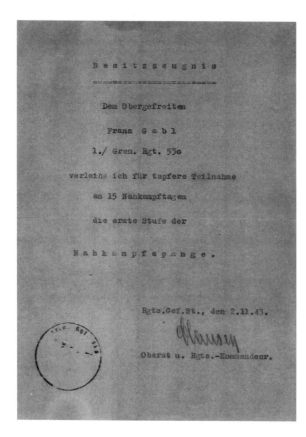

```
B e s i t z z e u g n i s
========================

Dem Obergefreiten

Franz  G a b l

1./ Gren. Rgt. 53o

verleihe ich für tapfere Teilnahme

an 15 Nahkampftagen

die erste Stufe der

N a h k a m p f s p a n g e .



Rgts.Gef.St., den 2.11.43.


Oberst u. Rgts.-Kommandeur.
```

Certification for Gabl's bronze medal awarded for having engaged in hand-to-hand combat fifteen times or more.

Herbst was an East Prussian who had been a good friend and comrade since the earliest days of combat. We were in the *Sudetenland* in early December 1942 which was becoming the graveyard for many in our company. Herbst was just finishing his two hours on guard duty in the machine gun nest, and I was coming out of the bunker to relieve him when there was the bone rattling explosion of a mortar shell near the bunker. Everyone scrambled out quickly expecting *Ivan* to attack again when another mortar hit nearby. But this one came down directly on our machine gun nest. Herbst's head received the full impact of the blast, and he became just another one of the near-daily casualties we suffered.

Here, east of Malo Archangelsk in December 1942 I engaged in the heaviest hand-to-hand combat of the war. The battle lines changed back and forth, and *Ivan* was now not a distant enemy; we saw his many faces daily. One time when we recovered a bunker that had been taken over by the Russians, we used their dead as steps to get in and out of the bunker. This was not to show any disrespect; in fact if we had pushed the bodies out of the bunker onto the top of the trenches they would have been blown to bits.

We were now becoming experts in this kind of trench warfare and hand-to-hand combat. To move forward we would throw hand grenades ahead of us, shoot the sub machine gun, yell like mad "Hurrah-Hurrah," then run like hell for maybe 20 yards, duck low, throw more grenades and run again and shoot. We had two types of hand grenades: one had a wooden handle, was about ten inches long and at the end had a metal container with the charge. At the end of the handle was a ring attached to a string which when pulled started the fuse which within seven seconds would explode the charge. We had to count: twenty-one, twenty-two, twenty-three and then throw the thing quickly at where we expected *Ivan* to be. It was not uncommon that the enemy would have time to throw the hand grenade back if we threw it quickly after pulling the activator ring. Besides the hand grenades with handles we also had "egg" hand grenades. They looked like a large egg and also had a ring attached to the string.

We also tried to remember that *Ivan* was just as scared as we were. Still, we took casualties constantly, and in spite of the better clothing there were again the painful cases of frostbite. After the deaths of Herman, Franz and now Herbst, more and more often I found myself wondering, when will it be me? What will it be: *Heimatschuss* or the birch cross? But I also remembered what Konrad said before my first day of combat: Cowards die just as quickly. One needs luck, one needs luck.

December 29, 1942, was my 21st birthday. There are no birthday parties on the Russian front, just guard duty as usual. Two hours on duty in the machine gun nest, four hours off, then two hours on, 24 hours a day, day in and day out. It was snowing lightly but not severely cold. My *chef* our company commander came through the trenches just as he did every evening. His name was Franz Gehrig, and he was one of the few officers I trusted and respected. Perhaps it was because he liked us mountain boys and talked often about the hikes he took in the Tyrolean Alps. He had been the one responsible for influencing the regimental commander that we Austrians could keep our mountain hats and edelweiss patches after Herman and Franz and I were separated in November 1941. He stayed with his men during any and all conditions, unlike many officers who seemed to stay away from the trouble spots and stay in the bunkers and send a messenger to check on his men in a fight. Gehrig would come himself. As a result, he had suffered many wounds during the war. He was a conscientious German officer. When he came by one evening and spotted my machine gun uncovered while it was snowing I felt there was trouble for me. Regulations called for the gun to remain covered with a tent poncho when not in use.

"Franzl," he said, calling me by the familiar name he always used. "How come the machine gun is not covered with a tent poncho?" I thought as quickly as I could. "This way I am ready to shoot quicker," I said without a lot of conviction. He also knew that I was one of the best machine gunners, and good marksman and did not have the fear like some of the others had being the No. 1 machine gunner. It is true, the enemy tries first of all to silence the machine gun before any of the other weapons. But I always remembered the words of Konrad: one needs luck, one needs luck.

It seemed to satisfy him because he didn't chew me out, although I could tell he was somewhat disappointed with me and that bothered me worse than a good tongue lashing. Near my MG 42 I had a captured Russian light machine gun. This one I used to shoot harassing fire at the enemy. It stopped sporadically, and I got mad at this gun. Finally I took it apart and found the lock had one part missing. The lock had only three parts; the problem with this one was one of the three parts was missing. The Russian guns were very primitive compared to ours, but because of this they usually kept firing despite mud, snow or dust. I could speak from experience that our delicate MGs did not always fare so well in these conditions.

About midnight, still on my birthday, I was off duty and back in my bunker when the big loudmouth East Prussian named Mollenhauer came looking for me. "The *chef* wants to see you, right now." He seemed to enjoy my look of concern. On the way over to *Chef* Gehrig's bunker, I wondered what punishment he would give me for leaving the gun uncovered. When I got to his bunker, I thought I saw a slight grin on his face; he must have seen the worry in mine.

"Franzl, do you know why I have called you?" "Because my gun wasn't covered, *Herr Oberleutnant,*" I said with certainty. "No," he said, a smile spreading across his face. "In two days you can go home on leave. This is your birthday present. Happy birthday." I was stunned. There was no way I expected it. The thought had never even crossed my mind. I knew that several men were ahead of me for leave. After a few seconds of silence I said the first thing that came to my mind. *"Danke, Herr Oberleutnant."* In my mind I wished he had waited two days to tell me. I saluted and left the bunker.

He understood what I meant. The day before our badly mauled company had seven men killed when the Russians attacked our trenches. I had been in the thick of this fight and was lucky to have survived to see this birthday. The thought of dying a day or two before I could leave for home was almost unbearable. As I headed back to my bunker I crept down as low as I could, suddenly more aware than I had been in months of the constant danger—a mortar shell, a stray machine gun bullet, a Russian commando stumbling around in the night, anything and my chance to see my family and my beloved mountains again would be lost forever.

I was just settling back into my bunker, and in my thoughts storming the Galzig, when another messenger burst in. "Gabl," he said breathlessly. "Get your belongings. You're leaving right now!" Within an hour I was ducking down through the trenches heading west. Sergeant Kiefer from the Black Forest was with me, and we would travel home together. After we got out of the trenches we ran for a while, still hunkering down low, wanting desperately to avoid an unlucky bullet that could come from the Russians nearly constant harassing machine gun fire. When we felt safely out of bullet range we settled to a walk, then caught a ride on a *panje* sled and finally hitched a ride with a truck to the railway station at Kursk, 25 miles southwest. In Kursk we spent two frustrating days waiting for a train. We passed the time and in the evenings went to the theater provided for the soldiers in every major city near the front.

When we finally boarded the train we knew we were still not out of danger. The partisans were getting bolder blowing up railroad tracks and bridges. Here it was easy for them to melt into the immense forests of White Russia. After passing through Russia and getting deloused in Wolkowisc on the old Russian-Polish border, I said my good-byes to Sergeant Kiefer, and he took a train in a different direction home to the Black Forest. I passed through Prague, Vienna and then Innsbruck. As I got closer and closer to St. Anton I seemed to be going through a kind of life-dimension change: the horrors of war in the east were being left farther and farther behind and in the process took on a feeling of unreality. And while going home had seemed so foreign and unrealistic to me before, now as I approached familiar territory, it all seemed to make sense. My excitement was unbounded as I thought for hours on the train about storming the Galzig—this was our term for non-stop skiing on our favorite ski terrain.

Finally the train pulled into St. Anton and stepping onto the station, I felt much of the weight of grief fall off me. I walked the few blocks toward house number 14. Nothing had changed here it seemed. The Nazi symbols were still visible but not flying with the celebration they did in 1938. The flags and banners seemed tired and worn, many of the local people you met on the street wore a black arm band or a black ribbon on the lapels. Their faces somber and earnest. The greetings on the street was no more *"Heil Hitler."* Even the right arm didn't go up anymore, except for the fanatical Nazis.

Then I came to the familiar wooden door, hesitated for just a moment before entering, then pulled the handle and walked in. My mother was in the kitchen. My face was beaming with a smile. She looked at me blankly. I know I looked familiar to her, but I saw her mind race to put the pieces of the puzzle together. Then she cried out, "Franz! Franz is home!" In a moment I was surrounded with the love and comfort that only a family can give. They treated me as if I had returned from the dead. For all practical purposes, I had. It was January 6, 1943, and as hard as it was to believe, I was home.

The next three weeks were the closest I have ever had to experiencing heaven. I had returned at the peak of skiing season. As soon as I could tear myself from my family I strapped on my skis and headed for the Galzig. I drank in the sight, the sounds, the feeling of crisp snow rushing beneath my feet, the wind blowing in my face.

There were other soldiers on leave but we did not talk about the war. It was dangerous to say anything negative about what was happening in Russia or our attitudes about the war. There were still too many Nazis about who would be happy to report on soldiers who didn't show the proper enthusiasm for Hitler's *Wahnsinn* (idiocy). Still, I could tell in subtle ways that I was not the only soldier who didn't give a damn if this Third Reich, this from Satan sent Nazi regime fell straight into hell right now with all those who thought that Hitler and his cohorts were great men.

I found out about my brothers who were also in the war. Karl was in Finland where he was serving as a regimental motorbike messenger. It sounded like his job was not quite as dangerous; he even wrote to me at one time and mentioned that he would gladly change with me for a time. It was very generous of him. Pepi was in the *Luftwaffe*, stationed in Russia along with friend and fellow skier Pepi Jenewein.

As the three weeks began to come to an end, my mood began to darken. I had put all thought of return out of my mind as I was coming home and said over and over in letters to my family that, "If I ever get out of this God-damned land nobody in the world will ever get me to go back.'" I was certain I would find a way to avoid getting back to the Russian front. But as the day for my return grew nearer I could think of no way out. A deserter not only faced the firing squad or being detailed to a penalty battalion, whose men were sent in front of an attacking infantry unit to explode the mines. His family would suffer, too. I almost went crazy with the thought of returning. I knew there was no way that we could win the war and also knew that I had cheated death too many times to think I could go on forever. I felt certain that if I did go back I would never return to my St. Anton. But there was simply no way out. With a heart as heavy as a wet log I embraced my family once more and boarded the train on January 27, 1943, after my 21 days leave was up, and headed back to the Russian front.

It was the end of January 1943, and all that was left of the 6th Army in Stalingrad were a few pockets of resistance. On the train to Karkhov we heard persistent rumors that returning soldiers were being formed into emergency units and sent directly to Stalingrad for relief operations. We also heard that these units took very high casualties because they did not have the cohesiveness of units that had been fighting together for awhile. On the western outskirts of Karkhov I got off the train and started walking in a northeasterly direction avoiding the main railroad station, wanting to get back to my unit near Kursk, avoiding being sent to Stalingrad if that indeed was happening. I found a train heading toward Kursk and helped out the engineer by shoveling coal. Actually, it was the only warm place on the train; the Siberian cold had returned again.

When I arrived at HQ in Kursk I was very relieved to find that our company had been sent back to defend the sector we had during the summer and fall of 1942. No going back to *"Fortress Sudetenland."* Our old sector had far better defensive structures in place and far better memories. *Ivan* was also farther away. Not for long, unfortunately.

I arrived back at my 9th Company, Regiment 530, on February 5, 1943, in the evening. In the early morning light of February 4th, the day before I arrived, the Russians had attacked in droves with wave after wave trying to overrun our lines. The MG 42s and their 1,300 rounds-per-minute speed proved devastating. *Ivan* had been driven on by commissars with drawn pistols, yelling and screaming at them and shooting those who hesitated. Their own artillery was poorly aimed and fell short, killing many of their own soldiers. The Spanish wire in front of our trenches was filled with over 100 dead *Ivans*. In this fierce fight our company suffered only three wounded. During the night of February 4th, a commando unit from our company was formed to look for weapons among the dead Russians. While they were searching among the bodies, one *Ivan*, badly wounded and unable to walk, managed to kill two of our men with a sub machine gun before he was gunned down.

I reported to *Chef* Gehrig when I arrived February 5th in the evening. Eagerly he asked me about skiing and all about home. He had the heart of a mountain man and could enjoy my return by just listening to my stories. Then he asked if I wanted to go with him and Corporal Guensche to search the dead bodies in no man's land and try to bring back some weapons. It was a common procedure since the Russian machine pistol was a treasured item; it shot 72 rounds from one magazine and was superior to our *Schmeisser* sub-machine gun which had only 30 rounds per magazine. I didn't relish the thought of searching the dead in the best of conditions, but after what happened the night before I was a little skittish. But I reminded myself that the Russians had been laying there for two days and a night in the freezing wind and snow and it was extremely unlikely that any of them could have lived that long. In deference to me, no doubt, *Chef* Gehrig choose "Tyrol" as the password for our venture that night. The password had to be uttered if you come from the enemy's side. If not known, then the guard had the right to shoot.

We had been walking about the bodies for some time when we heard a faint groan. All of us felt our fingers tighten on the triggers of our machine pistols. After searching with our flashlights we came across a Russian soldier twisting, moving slowly about in great agony. He was not conscious, and we saw frozen blood that had come from his stomach. In his uneven breathing we could hear the death rattle in his lungs. There we held court, discussing what to do with this man. *Chef* Gehrig was a humane, honorable man and did not want to just shoot him, even though that is exactly what many Russians did when they came upon a wounded German, and it didn't matter how badly wounded. He respected the enemy. We discussed what could be done, even possibly to take him to one of our bunkers. We also knew clearly he would not last long in this world. His groaning pierced us, and we could not leave him in the agony he had already endured far too long. In the end we did what we thought was the humanitarian thing to do. With a pistol shot he was sent to Valhalla, the home of warriors.

Although many Russians died, we could also see from the bloody tracks across the snow, that many wounded Russians had crawled back to their lines. They, too, no doubt, were patched up and thrown back into the battle. On this outing we brought back several weapons, a few PPSH sub machine guns, rifles with scopes and pistols. Two scopes from the rifles I packed up and sent to my home; they never arrived.

Though this seemed a bloody spot, we would soon look back on our secure defensive line with nostalgia. We had only a few days left here before being driven back, and once the backward movement began it would not end until the end of the war. Even though it was only on February 2nd, 1943, (while I was on the train coming back from my three weeks leave at home) that the last Germans surrendered at Stalingrad, even before that *Ivan* had been pushing our lines back in many places. Our army had been driven out of the Caucasus, barely escaping entrapment there. And now they attacked furiously just south of us. When they attacked now it was usually with a numerical superiority of four *Ivans* to one German. We gave up our secure trenches and went back from village to village fighting. My regiment was retreating to the northwest while the Russians converged on and captured Kursk. The night after we began our backward movement, my machine gun was set up in a hedgerow. I shot for a long while at *Ivan* who had learned by now that when the enemy retreats that is the time to move fast and pursue. Pursuing he was; on skis, on horseback, but mostly on foot. The snow was deep, and it was a chore to trudge through it. I set up my machine gun on a hedgerow and started to shoot in the direction of the pursuing *Ivans*.

After a while I got very tired and called for Sergeant Werner Kehr, to relieve me. I moved a few feet away from the gun and promptly slept. By now we could sleep in the most awkward positions, even under heavy fire. In my sleep I sensed that something was wrong. The machine gun was not firing. I moved over to investigate and found Sergeant Kehr laying next to the gun. He didn't move. I saw a single bullet hole in the middle of his forehead. There was very little blood, a quick and painless death. After what I had seen, I thought the sergeant was lucky. Of course, it could have been me. Kehr was a good soldier and a good man. There was no time to mourn. I shoved him aside and resumed firing. Before next morning we would pack up and move back to the next village, and now there was one less man to help carry the ammo. I wanted to get rid of ammunition as much as possible. That night I shot over 20,000 rounds. Before morning we were moving back. *Ivan* responded with a deadly artillery barrage on the village we were crossing through. *Ivan* had learned much; we were paying the price. The snow was three feet deep, and the artillery men had to destroy all the heavy equipment. Conditions had deteriorated again to the point where we could not and did not stop to bury our dead.

Wensky was my number two gunner, and he wasn't much of a soldier. One day during that languid summer of 1942 we were in a training drill, and Wensky was lying behind a big mound of dirt. It was too tall for him to see over. The sergeant yelled at him, "Wensky, do you have *Schussfeld?*" He was asking him if he could see where to shoot. Without raising his head, Wensky yelled back, *"Jawohl, Herr Unteroffizier!"* The sergeant just laughed knowing that Wensky was not the brightest the German army had produced. Wensky, ran the back of his gloved hand over his runny nose constantly, like a little kid.

One day near this time Wensky and I were deployed in front of a village. We were exhausted from trudging through the deep snow and lay down behind a mound of snow we had built. Then we covered ourselves with a tent poncho to protect us from the heavily falling snow. It was not very cold. We slept for a while and suddenly were awakened by one of our men accidently stumbling on us. He had been sent to find out what happened to us. We had become completely covered with snow and if he hadn't stepped on us we might not have been found in time. The danger wasn't freezing to death, but *Ivan* had worked his way dangerously close to our position. I picked up my MG and started to move back when suddenly a Russian machine gun opened up. Wensky took a bullet in the hip and went down. I moved toward him and found he could still walk by leaning on me. When it dawned on him that he was all right and was probably going to make it back to safety, it suddenly occurred to him that he had just received the greatest gift then given a German soldier: *Heimatschuss*—million- dollar wound—an injury serious enough to be send home for recovery, but in this case, probably not serious enough to permanently cripple. He became almost ecstatic as he approached our buddies in the village.

"Heimatschuss!" he yelled. *"Ich habe Heimatschuss!"* Just then another shot ripped through him, this time in his stomach, tearing him out of my arms. This wound was mortal.

The next day we were on the move again, *Ivans* chasing us. I was laying along a hedgerow when a good sized group of *Ivans* approached our village. I waited until they were close and grouped together. Then I pulled the trigger and let my MG 42 do its deadly work. Later, I went with my *Chef,* Captain Gehrig, to look over the dead. In the midst of the riddled bodies we came across a commissar. Checking his documentation we could tell he was a high ranking political officer. It was February 20, 1943. For this action I received the iron cross second class to add to my growing collection of tainted German metal. I had already received the *Ostmedaille* (frozen flesh order) and the silver Infantry Storm medal. I take no pride in these trinkets; never in those four years of war did I put myself out for the purpose of gaining recognition or awards. I did what I had to do to survive and hopefully go home again, see all of my family and ski the Galzig.

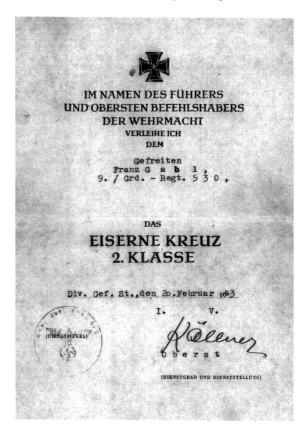

Certification for Gabl's Iron Cross awarded for his participation in the battle at Kursk.

By coincidence February 20 is also the celebration date of the great Tyrolean hero of 1809, Andreas Hofer. When the Austrian *Kaiser* (emporer), had made peace with the French Emporer Napoleon Bonaparte in 1809, who had invaded Tyrol a few years earlier, Hofer and his Tyrolean citizen soldiers kept on battling the French on the now famous *Berg Isel* in Innsbruck where the Olympic ski jump stands and where Birger Ruud had flown to such fame. The Tyroleans were badly outnumbered and outgunned and fought with everything they had: pitchforks, scythes and some rifles. Eventually the French forces overwhelmed the Tyroleans, and Hofer fled into the mountains and hid there in one of the mountain huts which farmers use during the summer. The French put a high price on his head. An Austrian Judas then told the French the location of his hideaway, and Hofer was captured. When the French escorted him down the mountain to their commander, Hofer asked them, "Why did you invade our beautiful mountain country of the Tyrol, where we only want to live in peace and work hard to wring a sparse living out of the fields and worship the Almighty?" The French officer seemed to take pity on Hofer and with chivalry asked him to plead his case to his superiors by saying he did not know about the armistice between France and Austria.

"A Tyrolean does not buy his life with a lie," was his now famous reply. On February 20, 1810, the French led him out of the prison in Mantua, in the part of Tyrol that belongs now to Italy, and as he passed the barracks where other Tyrolese were confined, all who were there fell to their knees and wept aloud. He then said to his people, *"Landsleut,* (fellow Tyroleans), please forgive me for having you caused all these hardships and miseries!"

When the *Manifesti* (priest) came to hear Hofer's confession, he gave to him all his possessions to be distributed among his country men. It consisted of 500 *Florins* in Austrian bank notes, his silver snuff box and his beautiful rosary. The French soldiers then stood him up before a firing squad. They formed a square, open in the rear. Twelve men stepped forward while Hofer remained standing in the centre of the square. The drummer offered him a white handkerchief to bind his eyes, and told him that it was necessary for him to kneel, but Hofer declined the handkerchief and refused to kneel, observing, "I am used to stand upright before my creator, and in that posture I shall deliver my spirit up to Him." He cautioned the corporal of the firing squad to do his duty well, and offered him 20 *Kreutzers* (Austrian change). Hofer then gave the order "Fire" with a clear voice. The blast of guns echoed through the streets of the old town Mantua. When the smoke cleared, Andreas sank only to his knees.

"Frenchmen! Shoot better," he yelled. They did.

In Innsbruck one should see the famous *Rundgemaelde* of the paintings inside a dome like building where a German artist portrayed the fighting of the Tyroleans against the French on the *Berg Isel* and around Innsbruck in 1809. It is a must see!

Certification for Gabl's Silver Infantry Storm medal awarded May 30, 1942.

Troyer and Gabl in Russia in June 1942.

The Battle of Kursk

While Ivan continued to pressure us in late February and early March 1943, he was reaching the end of his supply lines and growing weak and weary from the constant attack. As the Russian pressure petered out we had the opportunity to dig in and build some reasonable defenses. The *Rasputitza* was mercifully short, and the ground was much less frozen than the year before. Our winter clothing was adequate, compared to the winter of 1941–42.

We dug holes eight feet by eight into the ground for bunkers first, covering them with logs or wood, then filling the grooves with straw to prevent dirt from dropping down on us when *Ivan* was shelling around our bunkers. After that we piled dirt on top. Jagged trenches were then built between our machine gun nests which were placed at strategic spots to provide withering crossfire.

Even though the fighting had died down, word reached us by way of the rumor mill that our leaders were not satisfied with the Kursk salient. It represented more than a bulge in our lines; it was like a dangerous boil that could serve as a forward base for future attacks. At the same time, since it was a salient with exposed flanks, it represented an attackable target. Our training—inclination in the German army—was always for attack, and Hitler in turn was not easily contented with lost ground. So Hitler told his Fieldmarshalls to cut off the Kursk salient which extended into the German front for a hundred miles. The Russians expected it and dug tremendous fortifications: thousands of miles of trenches, machine gun nests, anti tank nests, millions of mines laid, even tanks dug in up to the turret. And *Ivan* was also so much more adept at camouflage then we Germans were. Guderian and some Fieldmarshalls tried to convince Hitler that it would be a mistake to try to attack the Kursk salient, because of the tremendous fortifications *Ivan* had constructed, and they expected the German army to take Kursk back.

Hitler, the corporal who never before had commanded even a squad, said "Attack." The Fieldmarshalls clicked their heels

and said *"Jawohl mein Führer."* Before any plans for the
armies were undertaken, Hitler had to give his OK. Later on
in the war, he even ordered battalions shifting from one the-
atre of front to another.

Our armies could not conceal the preparations which were
made, and *Ivan* knew that something was up. When either
side wanted to get a better picture of what was happening on
the other side, the best way was to interrogate some captured
soldiers. When the heat of battle didn't create the required
captives, then one had to be more creative. That meant entering the enemy camp at night to take prisoners. When we
Germans were given this assignment it was definitely considered a *Himmelfahrtskommando* job. The chances of returning were never good. The Russians seemed to excel at
this sort of night fighting. It was a dark night in mid-June
1943, when Wagner, our first aid man, and a sergeant were
walking through the trenches to inspect the posted guards on
duty. They didn't notice a small group of *Ivans* perched on
top of the trench waiting for them. Wagner was hit on the
head with something hard and went down in a heap; the sergeant ducked at once under to avoid being hit and ran like
hell back to the bunkers.

"*Ivan* is in the trench! *Ivan* is in the trench!" he yelled
when he got back to the bunkers. "They've got Wagner."
Wagner was one of the very few men who had been with me
most of the time I was on the front. It was he who was with
me, telling me what to do when I took my first artillery hit
that stunned me, killed *Unteroffizier* Konrad and wounded
Seidensticker. Immediately a group of us scrambled out with
machine pistols drawn to try to find the Russians and hopefully get Wagner back alive.

It was amazing that *Ivan* was so cunning at night. We
felt so safe in our defenses. We had time to establish a good
defensive perimeter that included razor sharp Spanish wire,
antitank mines, infantry mines, and mines which hung from
the Spanish wire so that when they were cut they would fall
to the ground and explode. We even had run *Stolper Draht*
which was a thin wire tightly stretched a few inches off the
ground that would trip up anyone running into it. Now we
ran through our own defenses in the pitch darkness. We
hardly gave it a thought; we had become accustomed to this

night fighting that we began to feel as if we had the instincts of cats. We searched desperately and with sinking hearts. We went as close to the Russian lines as we dared but could not find a trace of Wagner. We never saw him again, and I do not like to think about what he had to endure that night. A quick bullet to the head would have been a great mercy, I am certain.

The next evening we had to listen to the loudspeakers from *Ivan's* lines brag to us about capturing Wagner. "Last night," the Russian-accented, German-speaking voice said, "in spite of mines and Spanish wire, we hauled *Obergefreiter* Wagner right out from underneath your noses." Of course, they told us that Wagner had willingly cooperated and told them all about our plans and everything they wanted to know about the coming offensive. The voice went on. "Wagner is being treated very well, we wish to assure you. Because our supreme commander, *Generalissimo* Stalin, has ordered that German or Allied soldiers who are captured or willingly come over and cooperate with the Russian army will get the same food and medical treatment as our own soldiers." This went on frequently back and forth. Our loudspeakers were set up right at the trenches the next night, and our speakers would trade lie for lie that few if any believed.

After the Wagner incident we had a few days of peace. Like always, we would begin to let our guard down just a bit. I was on guard duty in the machine gun nest one night, slouching against the back wall, when there was the awful racket of a Russian machine gun and exploding bullets. I immediately dropped, but if it were not for the strangest miracle of the war it would have been too late. After the dust had cleared and I had a chance to throw a flashlight beam on the back wall where the bullets hit, I saw something I will never understand. The exploding bullets tore good sized holes in the dirt wall, crossing about chest high. There were about 10 holes all together and they were spaced an even four inches apart, except for one spot where there was about a two foot gap. No bullets in that space. On the other side, the bullet holes continued, again about four inches apart. The space the bullets skipped, of course, was where I was standing. I say this is a miracle because I have no possible explanation for why the bullets stopped in a space just big enough for my

body to fit. But I am here to tell this story because they did stop. Why? I have asked myself that many times and still do not have an answer and can only say that a power from above must have been the reason.

Exploding bullets are wicked inventions. They explode on contact creating horrendous noises and causing ugly wounds when they hit soft flesh. They created many a sickening sight on my comrades. We were also using exploding bullets, and in the ammunition belt for the MG 42 we inserted one in every fourth position; in every third one was a tracer bullet.

I had often wondered why the Russians liked the exploding bullets so well, especially at night. After I picked myself up and got ready to shoot my machine gun, it suddenly dawned on me what their fascination was with these things. A group of *Ivans* night commando were busy working on our Spanish wire and the bullets would hide the sound cutting wires and of removing mines. It was a sound cover for their work of getting through our defenses.

It was just starting to get light when I was surprised to see a squad of about seven or eight *Ivans* rushing my machine gun nest. They were spread out in front of me and suddenly very, very close, so using the machine gun effectively against all of them was out of the question. There just wasn't time. By pure instinct and speed that was created by an adrenaline burst coming from the knowledge that my life was definitely on the line, I scrambled out of the nest and ran back toward our bunker for all I was worth. The bunker was about 50 feet back, and it was an excruciatingly long 50 feet. When I got near the bunker I screamed, "*Ivan* is in the trench! *Ivan's* in the trench!"

There was a stairway leading down to the bunker and another one to the top of the trench. I scrambled up the stairs and dropped behind the dirt mound of the bunker. I pulled out a couple of hand grenades and threw them into the trench to my right, just where I thought *Ivan* would have had enough time to run up the trench. I was right, but Russian hand grenades were also being thrown at us, and one of our men— I think it was Hans Bucher, who beat me out of the silver medal in ski jumping at the races in Kitzbuehel in 1934— was wounded by one as he tried to scramble up the stairs and join me behind the dirt mound. I was lucky to have escaped in time. The machine gunner in the next nest over to the right, about a hundred yards away, was not so lucky. *Ivan* got him and shot him dead.

To this day I wonder if Wagner was telling the Russians the exact location of my machine gun and telling them that this Austrian was one of the best machine gunners in the company. It was true, I never shirked to be the No. 1 machine gunner like so many others who thought machine gunners are the first to die. I always thought of Konrad who said to me on my first march to the front, December 24, 1941—one needs luck, one needs luck..

After this things quieted down while final preparations were being made for the German army to go on the offensive again. A sergeant friend of mine Herbert Baumgartner and I decided to take advantage of the brief quiet before the storm to visit our company *Chef* Franz Gehrig, who was wounded again and in a hospital in Orel. Orel was a good sized city about 30 miles northwest. In addition to visiting Captain

Gehrig, I also had the chance to get together with my brother Pepi. We had a lot of catching up to do to talk about our experiences. He seemed to be still optimistic about the war, whereas I hated every minute to be in Russia and never ever thought we could win this war.

My brother Pepi and his buddy Pepi Jenewein were both fighter pilots in the *Luftwaffe* and stationed at an airport near Orel. Pepi asked if my friend and I were interested in an airplane ride. I had never flown before and had been fascinated with planes since I saw my first airplane during the youth races in Kitzbühel in 1934. Even the terrifying experience of watching the Russian *Schlachtflieger* swoop out of the sky, spitting bullets at me on May 12, 1942, at Kharkov did nothing to dim my enthusiasm for a plane ride. Pepi's plane, the famous *Focke Wulf 190*, was a single-seat fighter, so there was no ride for us in that. Instead he took me and my buddy Baumgartner up in a *Fieseler Storch*, a gangly, long-legged, high wing, spotter plane used to carry officers around and sometimes for reconnaissance or hauling mail. He landed on a small airfield in Orel, and we visited Franz Gehrig, our company commander, in the hospital. It was an enlightening experience seeing the endless Russian steppe from a height of a few thousand feet. I looked down at the drab landscape thinking that down there men are fighting and dying, but from here the conflict seem distant and even unimportant. There is something about getting above the scene to gain a sense of God's perspective on our futile human battles.

Herbert Baumgartner, Franz Gabl, Luftwaffe *pilots Pepi Jenewein and Pepi Gabl, near Orel in 1943.*

Pepi had shot down over 20 Russian planes by this time and had built a solid record. But it was not comparable with his friend and comrade Pepi Jenewein. The two Pepis were in the same outfit, and so I also had the chance to visit with this old friend who had so inspired my competitive spirit on the steep hill of the *Schlosskopf* and had gone on to win the alpine combined at the world ski championship in 1939 in Zakopane, Poland. About eight months later Hitler invaded that innocent country, and Pepi Jenewein along with my brother, volunteered to become fighter pilots. Pepi Jenewein's courage and competitiveness came out in the cockpit like it had on the ski slopes. When I visited him in June 1943, he had 80 kills and would eventually end up with 86. He was one of Germany's most dashing and well known fighter pilots.

The newspapers in neutral Sweden referred to him as the *Russenschreck* (Russian terror). After the war, his sister Steffi told me that when he was on his last visit home, he said to his family that he would not come home again. He, like so many other German soldiers, must have had a premonition— like Herman Ladner had the day before he was to go on a night commando mission on June 28, 1942, and many, many others. What surprised me somewhat was the fighter pilots had for their living quarters only a large hole in the ground with some logs covering it and a thin cover of earth. It wouldn't stand up to a mortar grenade. They were on either side of the runways, so that they could quickly board their planes and intercept *Ivan's* planes. Our bunkers for the infantry were much larger and more comfortable and had much more protection against mortars.

With a heavy heart, all too familiar in this time of good-byes, I said farewell to Captain Gehrig, my brother Pepi and Pepi Jenewein. Who knows if I would see any of them again. Luckily my brother and Franz Gehrig survived the war, and we would together be hiking in my home town. We headed back to our unit knowing that we were about to enter a huge battle that very well could determine the outcome of the war.

On July 5, 1943 Hitler struck. From the north Field-marshall von Kluge with 18 divisions and from the south Fieldmarshall von Manstein with 23 divisions. Many of them *Panzer* divisions. Germany with over 900,000 men, 10,000 artillery pieces, 2,700 *Panzers* and 2,500 airplanes. The Red army countered with 1,377,000 men, over 20,000 artillery pieces, 3,300 tanks, 2,650 airplanes. The Russians were well informed about the plan and prepared a defensive perimeter over 100 miles deep. Millions of mines were laid, trenches by the thousands of miles, antitank gun emplacements by the thousands, even tanks buried up to the turrets.

This was the mammoth battle in history of warfare. It would decide the outcome of the war, and it did. My Division 299 was on the northern salient, and we were not to be on the attacking line. We could hear the sound of the battle ever since July 5th. By July 13th Hitler ordered the battle to stop and go over to the defensive. The allies were landing in Sicily, Italy, and he sent several divisions there to save Italy. By the middle of July, Shukov, the Russian Commander of all the forces involved in the battle of Kursk, gave the order "Attack." And from then on the German army and the satellites moved only in one direction—west—and they never stopped until the war's end on May 8, 1945.

We were already out of our trenches for a few days and retreating toward Orel when we were ordered to stop and dig foxholes. My No. 2 machine gunner was none other then "K," the one who called the Russians *sowfolk*. We were standing at the gun, looking for *Ivans* to appear when a single shot rung out and "K." collapsed without a sound in the hole. The single bullet went directly into his heart. I thought to myself, "It all comes back." I then laid "K" on top behind the wall of dirt. It was July 26, 1943. Later that day I heard the sound of fighter planes overhead. There were two of our fighters, *Focke Wulf 190's*, in hot pursuit of two Russian fighter planes just above tree top level, disappearing to the east. I waited and waited, but I saw only one German plane return. Not long after that I received a letter from my family that Pepi Jenewein had not returned from a mission and was missing on July 26, 1943. The thought occurred to me that in this strange war, it was possible that I observed the disappearance of a good friend and one of the world's best skiers, without even knowing it. After the war my brother told me the story. Pepi was the *Katschmarek* of his superior, which means, he was supposed to be behind him and watch that the back is protected from enemy fighters. Pepi Jenewein was already boss and had his wingman to protect him. They flew in twos. Then my brother heard on the intercom, "*Pepi, ich habe Motorschaden.* (Pepi, I have motor defect)." My brother then immediately asked, "*Welches Plan Quadrat bist Du* (Which square are you in)?" There was no answer. The chance of Pepi Jenewein to survive, if he was brought down behind Russian lines was nil.

In 1942 Stalin ordered that any German pilot who was brought down behind Russian lines was to be shot on the spot. The reason was that many German pilots were rescued behind Russian lines by their comrades and were able to inflict again a terrible toll on the Russians. Major Rudel, the most famous of German warriors, was shot down three times behind Soviet lines and each time he was rescued. Once he was already captured by two soldiers, but escaped again after hitting one of the soldiers and then jumping down a steep embankment and swimming across a river. Major Rudel once sunk a battleship alone with his *Stuka*, a slow moving dive bomber, besides destroying 504 tanks and thousands of trucks, etc. He also received the highest decoration in the second world war from Adolf Hitler, a medal made especially for Rudel. Many years after the war, I met Rudel, then minus one leg, in Innsbruck and he autographed for me his book; *Stuka Pilot.* It said, "*Verloren ist nur der, der sich selbst aufgibt* (Lost is only he, who gives himself up)."

The battle of Kursk in those early days was primarily a battle of the big weapons: tanks, planes, artillery and rockets. With only the tall grain to hide us, we watched in amazement as tank battles rolled on in front of us, tanks destroying tanks with huge explosions as their ammo erupted from direct hits. It was hard to tell which tanks belonged to which side. In those first few days literally thousands of tanks were destroyed. Sometimes we found ourselves right in the middle of these tank battles in the grain fields only a few hundred yards away and we couldn't tell if they were German *Tiger Panzers* or the Russian T-34s. The *Tigers* were fearsome, but the famous T-34 was a good weapon and now outnumbered our *Panzers.*

The Russians employed now another weapon, mine dogs. These were dobermans and German shepherd dogs. They were trained to run under tanks and trucks and would get their food only under them because they weren't fed for several days. Each had a mine strapped onto their back with a antenna sticking straight up, which was to be the trigger. These handlers used whips to drive herds of these unfortunate animals towards the enemy vehicles. The first time the mine dogs were used was in the battle for Moscow in December 1941. Now in the battle of Kursk the Russians finally realized that it was not worth it, because these dogs were shot up with machine guns which spewed 1300 bullets per minute out of the barrel. They then abandoned this experiment during the rest of the war.

The Russians were now extensively using the Stalin Organ, a rocket launcher mounted on a truck that threw dozens of whooshing rockets into the air. Their distance was limited to about three miles. They made an unmistakable sound, like a large electric motor starting up, three dozen times within a span of a few seconds. When we heard the electric motors starting up, we ducked at once into the next hole or depression we could find. The rockets were only a few seconds slower then sound. These explosions are probably the most nerve-wrecking experience an infantry soldier can have.

On July 27th we were still in the same location when we heard "Urraeh--Urraeh," the Russian battle cry. *Ivans* came over a hill and ran towards our foxholes. I looked out from the nest and saw more then twenty of them heading straight towards my MG nest. "Out! Now!" yelled Captain Gehrig. He was in a foxhole a few yards from mine. He could tell we were about to be overrun, but instead of ordering us back, he wanted us to attack! I left my machine gun, grabbed my *Luger* pistol and scrambled out of the hole, running with my squad, Captain Gehrig right with us, waving his sub-machine gun with his right arm, like you see in movies. Immediately the surprised *Ivans* laid down in the grass, dropped their weapons and covered their heads with their hands. They expected to be shot on the spot. There was practically no shooting, and we had to kick them and yell at them to get moving toward our lines, leaving their weapons in the field. This was a lesson I learned: show more courage then the enemy. Then their artillery opened up. Russians and Germans alike darted from crater to crater, trying to avoid the explosions and shrapnel. Generally the Russians were very glad when captured.

I got back to the foxhole and caught my breath. But I was concerned about another wave of *Ivans* coming over the hill, and I wanted to stand up high to get a better look so we wouldn't be caught by surprise again. "BAM!" A Russian exploding bullet smashed into my helmet. Although the bullet didn't penetrate, the explosion drove pieces of steel from the helmet into my left temple and my ear. Blood was streaming down, and I thought, this is no *Heimatschuss*, this time I'm really done for and called "*Sanitaeter! Sanitaeter* (medic)!" And here he came , braving the intense shelling so he could bandage my bleeding head. A *Sanitaeter* would never hesitate to come to the aid of a wounded comrade, no matter of shelling or rifle fire. They were all heroes.

I had gone through most of the war without wearing a helmet. I hated the heavy, cumbersome thing. We, of the horse-drawn infantry, were never reprimanded for not wearing a helmet, but God help you if you didn't have a gas mask on you; then all hell broke loose.

The day before I had picked up a helmet, thinking it really wasn't a bad idea to wear one of them with all the heavy fighting going on. It was like a voice from heaven. Without that helmet, half my left temple would have been blown to smitherines. It was the first time in Russia I was wounded. It would be five more times before the massacres were over.

An hour or two later things quieted down, and I worked my way cautiously to the rear, darting from crater to crater. Not long after that I was in a horse-drawn field ambulance being taken to the airport at Orel where I had visited Pepi, and from there I was loaded with 25 other wounded into a glider that was pulled into the air by a *Junkers 88*. We landed about 300 km northwest in the city of Orsha, and I found myself back in the hospital.

Most people in normal life hate the thought of the hospital. For us it was heaven, at least if we were conscious enough to enjoy it. Sure, there was the pain, but there was pain plus all kinds of other forms of discomfort at the front. In the hospital beds we had white sheets on beds, showers, lack of lice, cleanliness, the access to toilets, meals—more than one every 24 hours. And the mere presence of that gentler, nurturing side of the human race: women. Not that they were all pretty or even kind. But they were women.

My stay this time in the hospital at Orsha lasted four brief weeks, but during that time my buddies in Regiment 530 were fighting and dying in a near continuous backward movement. By the time I rejoined them they were 150 miles west of where I had left them—and there were considerably fewer men.

A few days of this, and I realized that I wasn't feeling well. It was early morning and we were keeping a careful eye out on a forest of young trees from where we expected *Ivan* to appear at any moment. Suddenly I found myself on my knees in the full grip of violent vomiting.

"Franz, get to the doctor right now," the company medic said when he came by. He had a pretty good idea from the color of my skin what the problem was. The doctor confirmed it. *Gelbsucht* (yellow jaundice) he said matter of factly. "I'm sending you to the hospital in Bobruisk."

Back to the hospital! What a treat, even though I had no idea what this disease was all about. All I knew is that I was going farther west (toward Austria), away from the fighting and back to clean, white sheets. This time it was for about three weeks. Yellow jaundice was just about the ideal wartime sickness as far as I was concerned. And it couldn't have come at a better time: the fighting was continuing its vicious pace, and our unit seemed to be continually moving west, nearer home. In order to be cured of yellow jaundice, we were given some kind of a sweet rice and told to absolutely avoid anything fatty. Given that our diet normally consisted of chunks of fat or lard for our bread, or heavy sausage or cheese, the change was quite delightful. There were several other soldiers in the hospital with yellow jaundice at the same time, and I was tempted to do as they did: trade precious cigarettes for fatty food in the hopes of prolonging this heaven-sent illness.

Finally, my reprieve was over. I had spent nearly two consecutive months in the hospital, and the thought of returning again to the front was incredibly depressing. Again, I thought desperately of any way I might be able to avoid it. Before heading back to my unit I was told I needed to get a final examination by the doctor. I went in for the exam and at the end of it the doctor looked me in the eye. "Gabl," he said with a kind of fatherly concern, "I'm sending you home to Austria for three weeks of recuperation leave."

"To Austria? For three weeks leave?" I couldn't believe it. Soldiers weren't entitled to three weeks leave until they had served two years on the front. Twice now I had gotten an early, and according to regulations, an undeserved ticket home. Either the doctor felt sorry for me, or he honestly felt that my physical condition was such that if I went back to the front it wouldn't be long before I'd be back in the hospital with another disease. I think it was the latter.

For whatever reason, I was going back home. This time I was somewhat more prepared for all the emotions involved. And I also realized how painful the reality would be of having to return once again to this senseless slaughter, a struggle that made less and less sense as the days, months and years wore on. We all knew now that it was hopeless. We no longer believed in the rumors of a super weapon which Hitler's co-horts spread constantly to make the soldiers fight another day and maybe turn the tide. We could see every day that our enemy was growing in strength, resources and confidence, while our strength, resources and confidence diminished almost daily. In spite of all this, at the end of those precious 21 days in St. Anton, I would once again board the train and return to hell. I also knew that I had already cheated death too many times and had every reason, in the world to believe that I would not return home again.

It was in this mood that I once again greeted my astonished family. There was greater pain in this greeting than before because, no doubt I looked considerably older than I had before, and they too knew that I would have to return. My sister Kathi told me many years later that when I left she believed to her bones that they would never see me again. Hitler and his God-damned war had managed to take the joy out of even being with my family.

I don't recall a tremendous amount about that time at home in early October 1943 but remember one incident very well. My school friend Heinrich Kössler and I traveled to the town of Flirsch, about six miles east of St. Anton. There we climbed up to the rocky crags and carefully dug up some of the most beautiful edelweiss I had ever seen and wanted them to grow on the *Weisser Schrofen* high above St. Anton and to come back after the war and find that this mountain flower, the symbol of Austria, and a symbol of my love for these mountains, would be flourishing throughout my favorite alpine meadows. After we planted the edelweiss in the mountain dirt, I took a picture so that I could remember by looking at the landmarks, exactly where we had them planted. As we headed down back towards our little village, I wanted so very badly just to stay up here, to hold on to these sights and smells, to just enjoy friendship, and family, and life as it was meant to be.

In late October I was back on the Russian front just in time to be nearly caught in a giant pincer movement that *Ivan* had been working on for some time. By careful attacks, the Russians had squeezed a large German force into a salient or pocket. Now they were on the move to seal off the western end of the pocket and capture a hundred thousand of our soldiers, this time including Regiment 530 and a reluctant soldier from St. Anton who had just returned to hell after leaving heaven.

We marched three days and two nights with few stops, trying to escape the trap. It was just a matter of timing. If *Ivan* could close the gap, we were headed to Siberia; if we could escape, we would live to set up more defensive lines and continue the fight. I discovered it was possible to fall asleep and dream even while continuing to march. A pothole or uneven part of the road would usually wake us. When we would have a few minutes rest then we would roll into a ditch and immediately be asleep. Before long, we were tramping down the road again, trying desperately to avoid *Ivan's* trap.

The way out was a four-mile gap in the Russian lines to the west. We were even told that there would be no talking or making any unnecessary noise. It was during this time that my old "Max the horse" injury acted up—when just a youngster I was kicked into the wheels of a gravel truck and suffered a serious injury to my right knee and hip. Now, when I needed my legs the most, the knee gave out. It stiffened and froze with the cartilage jammed so that I had to walk with a bent knee. I went to an officer asking, practically begging, to be allowed to ride in a horse drawn wagon. "If you can't keep up then you can just stay here until *Ivan* comes," he yelled at me. I'll never forget or forgive him for this cruelty. I had to carry on. I had decided long ago that I would put a bullet in my head before I'd allow myself to become a prisoner of the

Russians. There simply was no choice; if I could crawl, I would try to escape the Russians. I carried on in excruciating pain, eventually finding a way to get my rifle onto a wagon, and then locating a big stick to use as a sort of crutch to help me along.

So after a little rest even my knee began to feel better, and finally I had again full movement of the knee and then we were out of the cauldron. Now it was back to the routine of build defenses, fight off *Ivan*, and start the process all over again.

Our orders during this withdrawal had been to pursue a scorched earth policy. This meant blowing up or burning all the houses, barns and earthly belongings of the long suffering Russian peasants. The idea was simple: repeat what Russia had done to Napoleon in 1813, 130 years earlier; take away from the enemy everything that might be used to carry on the war against you. While it made some sense strategically, the effect on the poor Russian farm families was totally devastating. I'll never forget them looking at us while some of our soldiers went about this grim task.

"Why are you doing this to us?" their eyes would ask. "We have so little to begin with, and you take even that away from us. Why have you come to our land and burn down our homes? What is the cause of this evil that you have brought?" In their eyes I saw my own mother, and my uncle Albert, the farmer and our family home. I remember very well one of our *Feldwebels*. He was a very short man, but he had lots of decorations on his chest. He even had the *Deutsche Kreuz in Gold* (German cross in gold), a decoration just below the knights cross. He took this business very seriously. He went inside the hut to throw a hand grenade into the still burning *pitchgu* while we waited outside. There was an explosion, and the *Feldwebel* became another *Gefallen für Führer und Vaterland.*

As winter began closing in, the Russian push decreased. The front stabilized, and we had a chance to build some reasonable defenses. Life returned to something more acceptable, and even though it was again bitter cold, it was nothing like the winter of 1941–42. By now we were prepared with adequate winter clothing, and we moved into prepared trenches which the local population was ordered to dig.

The night of December 29, 1943, I was standing guard in a trench at the machine gun. It would be my 22nd birthday. Again I wondered what my birthday present would be? Last year I had been surprised by Captain Gehrig with a leave home. I knew I couldn't expect that again, as I had just returned from my second leave. Perhaps this birthday a stray bullet would find me, perhaps it would be *Heimatschuss* or I'd get lucky and get another case of yellow jaundice. I heard a series of heavy thuds as objects landed into our trench. They were two five-cm mortar shells, but, miraculously, they didn't explode. I stared at them without believing.

What is this, I thought, a new kind of *Ivan* weapon that clunks into our lines and then explodes like a time bomb at a later time when we're not expecting it? I didn't dare touch them, thinking they might blow up if I tried to throw them out of the trench. Finally I got up my courage and tossed them out. They were duds, plain and simple duds. As I contemplated that, I came to the conclusion that perhaps I would have a good birthday after all.

This section of the front was where the heaviest fighting took place on the eastern front, and we would get a *Führer* pack every few days. This was a special gift, courtesy of our much beloved leader, given to men on the front who are in the thick of things. That the monster thought he could buy our morale with a few cookies, candies, a chocolate bar and six cigarettes seemed a testimony to his lack of contact with reality. Nevertheless, we gratefully accepted our *Führer* packs, and within a few minutes the cookies and candies were completely devoured. It was the way most of us did things on the front. There seemed no point in stretching anything out because we had no assurance that we would be alive five minutes from now. It was a simple way of thinking we had adopted. Eat, drink and be merry, for in a minute or two you may be dead. Before midnight another five-cm mortar shell landed, but this one wasn't a dud. It landed a few yards behind me, and the flying shrapnel found my unhelmeted-head. Immediately I was covered in blood, which looked spectacular, but actually the damage was rather slight. Shrapnel had entered my head, but it did not enter my skull or touch anything vital. I carry it with me to this day, having fun with my dentist when he does X-rays. Unfortunately, it wasn't even

Heimatschuss. I was bandaged up and spent the rest of my birthday in the forward hospital.

In a letter to my family at home I wrote, "29-12-43. Dear Parents! Today is my 22nd birthday and as a present—don't be frightened—*Ivan* sent me two shrapnel into my head. It is not bad. Am only in the battalion's sickbay. On December 5th I also got three shrapnel in my leg, (three above the left ankle), I had bad luck that I didn't get back to Germany. Don't worry. Mail I get little. Your son, Franz".

A week or so later I returned to my company. Our division had been moved to the area near Vitebsk which was now the real hot spot on the eastern front. The main weapon seemed to be artillery, and we heard that the artillery battles were like the famous barrages from the first world war at the fortress Verdun and the River Marne in France. Entire forests were laid waste by endless shelling. The Russians were trying very hard to capture the critical Vitebsk-Orsha rail line, and we were trying to keep them from getting it. For my part, my luck seemed to have changed for the better. I was now assigned duty as a sled driver which meant, it was my job to deliver the meals and ammunition to the men at the front every evening instead of being one of those eagerly waiting for the delivery. The supply unit was stationed three miles behind the front line in a small village. Every afternoon I would get my pony and sled ready and an hour before dark would head toward the front line. My pony must have had premonitions heading to the front, and I had to use my whip to coax him on. If my timing was right I would arrive just after dark when *Ivan* couldn't see our men gathering for their meal and their ration of ammunition. It was not all fun being a supply driver. On most trips back from the front I carried dead or wounded men and took them to a first aid station. The dead were buried and the birch cross fixed at the head of their grave.

It was kind of funny, as soon as I headed back towards the supply base, the pony would gallop as fast as it could, knowing full well it was going further and further away from explosions.

I could sleep peacefully in a house without the fear of a shell exploding next to me. It was very cold but, our clothing was adequate and the *pitchgu* would warm us. I still had to take my turn standing guard every night. One night while standing guard I saw a curious sight. One of the buildings in the village contained a sauna, and as I stood guard I saw a steady stream of single soldiers going into the sauna, then after a few minutes, coming back out again. Before my replacement came I watched more than a dozen soldiers come and go. Later I found out what the attraction was, a Russian *madka* was entertaining the soldiers.

During this time the German propaganda reported that the Russians had enormous casualties and predicted that they would not be able to keep up the offensive push for much longer. What we saw was a steady increase in Russian confidence that seemed to coincide with the continued arrival of new American trucks, tanks and other war materials. Our generals outdid themselves with reports of Russian casualties. They wanted to look good in the *Führer's* eyes. The trucks gave the Russians the speed and mobility they lacked early in the war and enabled them to keep on the offensive, pushing into the soft spots, making steady if uneven advances.

Then my time was up. Our company was down to just a few men, and I was ordered into the trenches. It was March 21, 1944, and I had spent three months on light duty. I was more than aware of the fact that I had already survived three winters on the Russian front, most of that time in nearly continual fighting, and had managed to survive. So I headed back into the trenches with that deadly feeling creeping into my soul, the feeling that said, "Let no joy, no fear, touch my heart." The way to living in this constant hell of war was to give up the feeling of living. When you are alive and you knowingly go into that abyss of total apathy about living, it is a dread and pain that cannot be described.

They made me squad leader. I was now a corporal. My new-found leadership position would be short-lived, as in just a few days I would be back in the hospital with my most serious war wound yet. But in the meantime I had the opportunity to find what being a leader was all about. Squads normally contained 12 men, but our unit size was generally four to six men. I found six men in my squad. We were assigned a bunker near a main highway. Highway of course meant a gravel road that was a little wider than the normal dirt tracks that would go from village to village. It was spring 1944, and the snow was melting which meant we were also in the *Schlammperiode—Rasputitsa*—the mud period. Our white winter uniforms were coated with the reddish gray yuck. I was standing at the bottom of the steps leading into our bunker when I heard one of my men yelling, "I am dead! I am dead!" he screamed with a funny sound. My God, I thought, what carrying on is this?

As he came down the steps I saw he was in serious trouble. There was blood spurting from the right side of his throat like it came from a squirt gun. It would have looked humorous had it not been for the fact that the man's life was very much in danger. I thought quickly. What was I to do now? The medic was nowhere around. If we went to look for him the man would be dead before he got here. Before I could count on my squad leader to take care of such things. I became aware of the others looking at me and realized they were expecting me to fix things. I remembered from watching Wagner work that you need to put something hard onto the spot of the main artery that is bleeding and hold it there. I pulled a coin out of my pocket and held it firmly against the fountain in the man's throat and quickly wrapped a few layers of bandage around the coin and his throat and saw with relief that the bleeding had slowed to a trickle. That night the supply man took him back on his pony-powered wagon to the relative safety of the forward hospital. We heard later that he rejoined the fighting that summer.

The next day we were ordered to move to a different sector of the front. We marched during the day and stopped at a village about noon for some rest. I was standing next to a house when four 76.2-mm shells hit right around me. These were the *ratsch-bumm* shells that gave us no warning they were coming. These four were all duds. Sure, there were plenty of duds in the war. But four of them right together? By now I was almost accustomed to such miracles and decided either I had someone looking out for me or I would just plain go when my number was up. It didn't seem to make a bit of difference what I did or didn't do. Some, no doubt, thought I was bold or courageous. I don't think that was it. I felt I was walking around in a protective bubble just waiting for my time, or else was really protected. The words from Konrad always came back to me—one needs luck, one needs luck.

The next morning *Ivan* really let us have it. It was again like at Kharkov on May 12 1942. *Goetterdaemmerung* (Twilights of the Gods). The salvos were landing practically on top of our trench, and we knew that it was likely that an outburst like this would be followed by an all-out infantry attack. Whenever we could we stuck our heads above the trench to see if *Ivan* was coming yet. No sign of him. Something else was bothering me. A messenger was supposed to come from HQ telling us what was going on and if we were to pull back. No messenger. Were we abandoned again? A little before noon, the suspense got to be too great, and I told my men to move back to the second line of defense, another trench. There we discovered the likely reason why *Ivan* didn't attack us directly: three of our *Tiger* tanks were in a gully directly behind us. *Ivan* no doubt had them spotted.

This second line had a long, continuous trench. Unfortunately it had about a foot of water in it, and the wet muddy loam from the side walls covered our clothes. A couple of hours later, early afternoon, we saw *Ivans* heading cautiously, one by one, toward in our direction. There were three of us in the trench with one machine gun, one sub-machine gun and one rifle, but hardly any ammunition. We all wanted to shoot, so we passed the rifle between us, taking turns firing. The one rifle was enough for the Russians. They turned and went back. Unfortunately, it seemed they went back to tell their artillery gunners where we were because now the shells began to home in on us. After dark we managed to collect what was left of our unit. My squad now had only four men now.

That night we were told to retake our defensive lines. Shit! We knew *Ivan* had followed us when we abandoned our trenches. They were now safely settled in, and the confident *Ivan* was getting very difficult to dislodge once he had claimed his own territory. Orders were orders, and we prepared to attack.

It was now 1:45 a.m., March 24, 1944. In my little calender I wrote: "*24. Maerz, 1:45 Angriff auf unsere alte Stellung* (Attack on our old trench). The plan was for our artillery to shoot for half an hour into the muddy trenches we had abandoned. Then the Very lights, (flares), would go off and we were to run toward the trenches with a loud "Hurrah!' Unlike *Ivan*, we used the "H" and *Ivan* yelled "Urraeh." Russians don't use the letter "H," like in Hitler they say *Gitler*. The artillery started as planned, then suddenly stopped. How often did they leave us in the lurch!.

"Of course," we laughed bitterly to ourselves. "Those sons of bitches of artillery men want to keep a reserve. They'll just have to blow it up when we're retreating again so as not to fall to the enemy which happened many times.

The Very lights (flares) lit up the darkness, casting eerie shadows. We ran from behind our cover, me with the sub-machine gun, leading the charge shooting from the hip just as we trained in practice. The trenches were in sight. With a frightening groan one of my men, a man from Vienna, went down with a bullet in the stomach. He was dead almost at once. He had been hit by a burning tracer bullet in the stomach, and his uniform was on fire. I grabbed the hand grenades from his belt, threw them toward the trench, all of us yelling "Hurrah, Hurrah" and kept moving toward the trench. I looked around and couldn't see any of my men. Damn, abandoned again?

"There is no way in hell I'm going to jump into *Ivan's* trench all by myself!" I said to myself and turned to run back to the big hay barn which was clearly lit by the flares.

Brummmp! I heard a burst from a Russian sub-machine gun and felt my leg give out under me. I jumped into a shell hole. It was half filled with water but, I got down in as flat as I could and was sitting in water up to my belly. I was glad for the cover, though, because now I could hear *Ivan's* bullets flying over my head. The Russians had recovered from the surprise of the initial rush and were now clearly in control of the battle. Then I heard the advancing explosions of hand grenades coming closer to my hole. I still could remember the stories, soldiers of the first world war were telling us. They often threw hand grenades back to the enemy. I kept my eyes peeled, waiting for one to land in the hole with me and getting prepared to toss it out. Suddenly, the Very lights went out, and I dragged myself out of the shell hole. To my amazement I found I could still run even with quite some pain. The bullet went through my thigh, leaving the bones untouched and allowing me to run. Then the lights illuminated the scene again, and I had to dive into another shell hole. A couple more times like this and I made it back to the big barn. Behind the barn field ambulances were waiting. Wasn't it nice of HQ to prepare for the wounded they knew they would get when they sent their men into missions like this.

They lifted me on a stretcher into an ambulance and found that in this ill-fated attack our company had lost every one of its leaders. Most had *Heimatschuss* like I did. Then it occurred to me. I have *Heimatschuss*. Then I thought of Wensky. He was celebrating his wound that would send him home when he was hit with a second, fatal bullet. No, I would hold my celebration until I got out of the danger of Russian bullets and artillery shells.

By the time I got into the hospital in Minsk, White Russia, my leg wound had become infected and gangrene had set in. Waiting that while in the mud of the shell hole had no doubt not been the best first aid for it. I became very sick and weak. Still, I was in the hospital. Clean white sheets. No lice. Good food. And I even was visited by my brother-in-law Franz Rofner, who was stationed in Minsk with the railway engineers. It was just a taste of home and family but it whetted my appetite for more. Again, I found that once away from the front, the desire to survive and think about a future began to blossom. As I lay on this bed for a few days my thigh started to turn yellowish. Then the doctor came and inserted a plastic tube through the hole and the sister (nurse) put a glass char on a low chair to catch the puss which ran day and night from the wound. One day the nurse came, she looked at the thigh and said with a frown, "Gabl, your leg does not look good."

I knew the way she said it that in her opinion it was going to have to be taken off. I had seen war invalids with one leg from the first world war. But I had never seen one of them ski. "No!' I said firmly. "It's getting better. I can feel it." The thought of coming this far and not being able to go home again and ski was just too much. The leg stayed.

In May I was transferred several hundred miles west to a hospital in Sokolov, about 60 miles northeast of Warsaw in Poland. Sokolov was a pretty little city, quite modern by eastern standards, and I knew from my time in occupied Poland in 1941 that the Poles were friendly toward us Austrians.

At the end of May, I was well enough that I could go out into the city and walk around. We were warned not to go alone for fear of what the Poles could do to solitary German soldiers. Infrequently one would disappear without a trace. I felt that as long as I wore my edelweiss on hat and arm, the Poles would look past my German uniform. As May turned into a delightfully warm June, we were given further warnings and even issued rifles to us in the hospital and ordered us off the streets. Rumors were flying of an allied invasion of the French coast, and our higher ups expected a Polish uprising when that happened. As it turned out, on June 6th Eisenhower did indeed land on the French coast, but we saw no Polish uprising. Not even a whisper of one.

So it was safe again to go into town and *Gefreiter* Raeder, a fellow patient, and I were invited to a Polish family's house for a party. There were two blond girls and two older *madkas* and a few men. Raeder was a real joker; he came from the area of Thuringia. He was also a real party guy and helped me get in the mood for some revelry. We were in no time deep into the Polish *Samigonka*, a kind of moonshine. Raeder and I had our eyes on the two girls and made our plans to steal away with them for a little hanky-panky. For one reason or another they didn't cooperate with our plans, so we carried on with our drinking. Soon we were deep into conversation about our feelings about the war we hated. They seemed to feel kind of sorry for us German soldiers, knowing what we had to endure these last three years. I remember only getting up in the morning from under the table and slowly walking back to the hospital. Raeder told me the story. As we tasted more and more of the *samigonka,* we both must have passed out. But Raeder remembered that two military police came by, saw us on the floor and kind of laughed seeing us down. The reason they didn't take us with them, I am sure, was, we both had all kinds of decorations on our chest, including the *Nahkampfspange*, the iron cross, the purple heart in silver, the infantry storm medal in silver and the frozen flesh order. What could they have done with us?

One of the saddest sights in this hospital were two of our soldiers who were totally blind. I remember them so well; one was not more than 18 years old. He walked along the corridors like he could see, and he could stop at any door of his choice. He had a stick and hardly ever missed his choice of doors. The other blind man, he was a bit older, sat most of the time on his bed, hardly talking. I thought to myself, dear God, don't let me go blind. Please, rather let the bullet go into my heart, to stop this kind of fate.

The doctor determined that my leg had not healed sufficiently to require me to return to the battle, which was coming ever closer to us in Poland. Instead I was sent to a hospital in Goslar, Germany, in the Harz Mountains. I had to pinch myself to make sure I hadn't actually died either of gangrene or too much partying.

Back in Germany! In the Harz Mountains. It was spectacularly beautiful and peaceful there. Oh, how I wanted to spend the rest of the war here! It reminded me of St. Anton and home, though the mountains were more like rolling hills rather than the jagged peaks and knife-edged ridges we called mountains. For the first time in my life I heard that here they skied on a hill on needles from spruce and fir trees.

About a month later on July 20, 1944, a buddy and I were wandering around the town of Goslar to have a beer at the Hotel Achtermann, a castle-like building, when we heard a woman yelling something out from her second floor apartment window. "They've tried to kill the *Führer*!" She said it with fright in her voice, but my heart nearly jumped for joy. Could it be true? How I wanted that insane maniac dead. The one I held personally responsible for Herman's death, Franz's death, Konrad's death, Wensky's death and many, many millions more. For having been four times wounded up to now, for taking me away from the only things that really mattered to me, and far worse, taking my heart and soul away. "Please, dear God, let it be true. Let this bastard be dead." When one thinks back to those days, it is incomprehensible that the Fieldmarshalls and Generals didn't see that this man was totally insane.

That night I heard his voice on the radio. Shaken, but determined, he promised that those who were involved in this *Attentat* would be punished and that this would not deter him from bringing glory to Germany. Punished they certainly were. The men who were involved were hung with piano wire to the *Führer's* entertainment, who ordered the hangings filmed and after that shown to him on a large movie screen. A great many more innocents lost their lives in that monster's attempt to destroy the conspiracy. I lost a little more of my hope and quite a bit of what little was left in my faith in a God who cared about what was going on in this sick world.

What really sickened me after this was how much loyalty and faith so many in Germany and Austria still had in this man after everything that had happened. No doubt, the failed assassination disappointed millions in Germany, but most seemed as convinced as ever that Hitler was the one to bring Germany out of the disaster it now faced. A few weeks after the assassination attempt, I was told I could leave the hospital and was ordered to report to the Division 299 home base in Büdingen, near Frankfurt. But once again, instead of sending me there, they sent me home where I could complete my recuperation with a three-week leave.

Back in St. Anton I hiked up to the *Weisser Schrofen* in search of the edelweiss I had planted the year before. On the way up, sucking in that precious air and that beautiful view, I marveled again at the fate that had once more brought me home. Now, rather than allowing the sense of dread of knowing I would have to return to the front overcome me and take away my joy, I was glad to be walking with both legs and to be alive. Life was good. But the edelweiss had died.

The mood in St. Anton was despondent and fearful. Everyone had on their mind the unspoken question. What would happen if Germany lost the war? Except they were beginning to realize that it wasn't if, it was when.

I knew the war was over as far as the issue of winning or losing was concerned. I knew from first hand experience that the Russians were not going to be content to reclaim their land and let us return to Germany with our tail between our legs. I also knew from personal experience that our wise leaders were too prideful, stubborn and careless of human lives; they also knew that many of their own heads would roll once the atrocities came to light which they knew were committed in the name of Nazism and that there would be a reckoning. Knowing all this, at the end of October I once again said my farewell to my family and went to the railroad station in St. Anton, boarded the train and trudged back to the Russian front.

Defeat and Prisoner of War

From now until the war ended, I lived in a particular kind of agony. I experienced it when Lieutenant Gehrig told me I was going home for my first leave in two days December 29th, 1942. When the goal is so near at hand, the possibility of missing it is uniquely agonizing. It was now late 1944, and the outcome of the war was all too clear to us. The issue was very much settled. We just weren't at all certain that we would be able to go back to our homes and resume any kind of life after the war or end up in Siberia to endure many years of cruel hardships.

When I located my unit, Company 9 of Regiment 530, they were Northeast of Warsaw on the Narev River. There were hardly any men left. On June 22nd, 1944, the 3rd anniversary of *Barbarossa*, the Russian juggernaut pushed our *Heeresgruppe Mitte* (Army group center) back with huge losses of some thirty divisions. When I arrived I didn't recognize a single familiar face. In fact, just about everyone in our entire Division 299 had been wiped out.

So I found myself back in the trenches. At least from now on we had trenches already prepared for us which the local population was ordered to dig. There would be many times in the coming days and weeks when having a trench would be considered a stroke of good fortune. And the weather was still warm and dry. The warmth was great—we knew it would be ending soon and we would once again face winter, our fourth one—but the dryness wasn't good news. Our German machine guns still had a tendency to jam in dusty conditions.

Soon after I arrived back in the trench in early morning, *Ivan's* artillery started in earnest to pound our positions with artillery, mortars and the nerve wrecking Stalin Organ, the rocket launcher, then there would be a tentative infantry attack, perhaps a few hundred or maybe a thousand. A few sharp bursts from our MG 42s and they'd be scampering for cover, even if their commissars were screaming at them with pistols drawn. Now it was very different. The artillery and mortars would lay an indescribable barrage into our trenches, then the infantry would come in endless hordes of brown-clad soldiers, thousands of them, more than I had ever seen before, and they were not so easily dissuaded from their attack. They attacked now not with great fear but with the confidence of knowing that they had their enemy on the run.

"Brrrrp!" I fired my machine gun and saw little effect. How in hell was this horde going to be stopped. Then my gun jammed. Quickly I tore it down, replacing the barrel and the bolt. "Brrp!" It shot a few more rounds and stopped again. The dust from the artillery bombardment had fouled the delicate machinery. I had to get back; *Ivan* was pressing forward and now getting uncomfortably close. I looked to my left and to my right and called for my comrades. I found I was all alone once again. Everyone had apparently pulled back, and here I was trying to hold off the whole Russian army with a fouled machine gun. Move Gabl! I said to myself.

I jumped out of the trench leaving my gun and ammunition behind and darted up a hill. I knew that to leave the machine gun behind could lead to court martial. But I also knew to take the machine gun with me would be suicide because there were 3,000 *Ivans* chasing me at full tilt. The hill led down into a small depression, and I ran through that expecting a machine gun bullet in my back at any moment. Finally I reached some houses with most destroyed. I wondered why *Ivan* didn't attack like we Germans did, shooting while our buddies ran, then moving while the other buddies were shooting. Of course they couldn't shoot as there were 3,000 of them running full tilt and without stop. When *Ivan* attacked now it seemed they expected us to put up no defense and we would just keep on running back toward Berlin nonstop. More and more often they were right.

In this little village I found a few of our men and asked about my unit. Finally I found them holed up in a forest— actually the woods were a shambles with few trees left standing. Still, the stumps and broken limbs provided some cover, and here is where my unit of what was left was hiding. The order came down to move out from the forest into an open field. Of course, right out in the open where we were sitting ducks. But they were orders.

We were laying on our bellies trying to hide behind dry grass when we heard the unmistakable sound of the Stalin

Organ. I looked around desperately and found a shell hole and flattened myself in it as best I could. I covered my head with my hands since I had once again abandoned the idea of a helmet. As I lay there listening to the explosions and shrapnel whistling through the air above me, I became aware of the fact that my butt was sticking quite prominently out in the open. At first I tried to figure out what I could do; then I realized a bit of shrapnel in my ass would be a gift of God. Sure, it wouldn't feel good, but I'd be heading back to the hospital and that sounded a hell of a lot better than getting killed in this ridiculous situation we were calling a war. But, no such luck, and I survived another attack in one piece.

I noticed something else that changed in this later stage of the war. Before, *Ivan* would stay a good distance away from our lines, usually about 400 to 600 yards. Now, when we dug in, we found *Ivan* would dig in as close as 100 yards away. This was very unnerving, not to mention dangerous. On guard duty at night we'd peer into the darkness knowing that *Ivan* was in easy earshot and a good hand grenade throw away. It just about drove me nuts. One night I kept thinking I was hearing *Ivan* moving up toward our trenches in the night. I fired my machine gun almost continually through the night and kept throwing hand grenades at the sounds I was hearing. It was the only time I ever wished I had taken up another sport other than skiing. I thought if I had the arm of a shot putter or discus thrower I could get those grenades right into their foxholes or trenches and get them to move back a little bit.

It was near the end of November when a commander gave the order to capture a Russian soldier for interrogation. It wasn't that their plans or strategies were a great secret at this point. But, orders were orders. A *Himmelfahrtskommando* squad was selected. It consisted of one seasoned sergeant and four corporals, including Corporal Gabl. The Russian trenches were about a football field length away from ours, and we spotted a machine gun nest that stuck out a bit from the rest of the line. That would be our target and if we were successful, an unlucky Russian soldier would be treated to less than gentle interrogation by German officers. During the day we were given binoculars so we could study the situation and get a good idea of the lay of the land. The Russian nest was uphill from our trench and the terrain was pretty open. This was clearly the 1944 version of Russian roulette, but our odds were worse. As you know, in Russian roulette, you put one bullet in one of the six chambers of a revolver, rotate a few times, then point the gun on your temple and pull the trigger. It means, one in six chances to be killed. In our situation the odds were reversed.

As darkness approached, the five of us were assembled in the company bunker to discuss our final plans and preparations. Darkness and stealth were our only hope, so the order was given: under no circumstances would anyone send up a Very light. We gave our I.D's., watches, medals and other personal effects to the company *chef.* He would send these back to our families if we didn't return, along with a nice letter about how we died bravely doing something really important for our *Führer*.

Finally, with fear, we climbed out of the trench and headed for the Russian nest on all fours. The sergeant led the way, and I was right behind him with the other three behind me and the sergeant's deputy last. We were about twenty five yards from our trench when there was a loud explosion and then a painful cry. The sergeant had crawled onto one of our own personnel mines. We had no time to lose. *Ivan* would no doubt know something was up and train all kinds of fire in our direction. Without knowing the extent of his wounds, we grabbed the sergeant, dragging him as quickly as we could back to our trench. His legs were badly wounded, and he was quickly attended to by a medic. Even though I was right behind him, I was untouched other than being thoroughly covered by a layer of dirt. We went back to our bunkers to report what happened. Remarkably there had been no response from *Ivan*. Were they sleeping? It was eerie.

Suddenly, artillery, mortars and machine guns all were fired at our trenches and the field in between. They must have concluded there was an attack underway, and they were shooting with every weapon at their disposal. I made my way back to my machine gun nest. The tension was too great for one of our men, and suddenly he started running through the trenches yelling, "*Ivan* is in the trench! *Ivan* is in the trench." He became insane, then someone grabbed him and held him down. I remember him well; he wore very thick eye glasses, and I wondered why he somehow did not break or ruin them, so he could go back to the supply unit and get new ones and maybe have a few day's rest.

It was pitch dark when suddenly a Very light went off, lighting the surroundings with an eerie, white bouncing light that seemed to make all the shadows come alive. Through the darkness, I looked to see if *Ivan* was trying to come across the field. "Bamm!' A mortar shell exploded right in front of me. A shrapnel had penetrated through the main artery into my throat. I cleared my throat and felt something hard in my mouth. I spit it into my hand. Along with blood, I found a piece of shrapnel about the size of a small fingernail. I looked at it in amazement. I kept this shrapnel and the steel helmet splinter from the Kursk wound in 1943 for years in my home, even the meniscus from my right knee I kept. Eventually I lost all three.

"This I have to keep," I said to myself and put it in my pocket. I headed back to the bunker to get some first aid. There wasn't a lot of pain except a tremendous amount of powder smell, but the bleeding continued and I knew without stopping the flow of blood I could well bleed to death. The medic bound my throat with some bandages. My boot made a squishy noise when I stood up. My foot was warm and wet like I had pissed down my leg. I looked down and saw a stream of red. Blood running down my chest, into my pants and into my boot. It flowed like a river and I thought of that poor guy near Vitebsk in March 1944 who had yelled, "I'm dead! I'm dead." Now, I thought, I'm dead. This is just too much blood. The shrapnel had punctured the main artery. I felt some of the men grab me by the arms and start rushing me through the trenches to the doctor. Then it started getting darker and I didn't remember anymore.

I spent the next four weeks in a hospital in Graudenz on the Vistula River in Poland. In a letter home I wrote: *November 28.- 44, from: Obergefreiter Gabl, Kriegslazarett, II—D Graudenz, Polen.* Dear Hilda, (my sister) please do me a favor, send me a razor, comb, wrist watch with the silver band, also hair lotion. I am OK, the shrapnel gives me not too much pain. Hearty greetings, Franz.

When I returned to my unit it was nearly Christmas. The men I returned to, those who were left, were shocked to see me. They were certain I could not have survived the loss of so much blood.

I celebrated my 23rd birthday on December 29, 1944. It was a time of complete despair. The life was being sapped from us daily, and we watched as our enemy became stronger and bolder. A birthday present of sorts came a few days into the new year when we were told our unit was being removed from the front line and assigned duty as a corps reserve. How wonderful, we thought. At last, a break from the constant battle and constant danger. Perhaps we can get a little rest and recover maybe even a little of our spirit and will to live. But then some damned, arrogant officer decided that we needed some training. He was yelling at us as if we were first day recruits. At this time there was a big danger that mouthing off would land you quick on a tree or in an earth hole. There we were, in the middle of another frozen winter, crawling around in the snow. It was a ridiculous sight to see *Alte Hasen,* including grizzled sergeants who had seen years of warfare and sporting iron crosses first and second class and other assorted medals on their chests, crawling through the snow on their bellies and following the orders of a snot-nosed officer who didn't have any medals on his chest and had not seen anything of the war, except from a staff desk. Like many others in my unit, I wore the *Nahkampfspange.* The bronze bangle said to anyone who cared to notice that I had been through hand-to-hand combat fifteen or more times. Perhaps seeing some of these medals on the chests of some of us veterans was what drove the Johnny-come-lately officers to do such idiotic things in these late days of the war. As for me, I would have traded every last one of them for a few days storming the Galzig, and would have done just about anything to avoid the foolishness that could get me killed at this late date.

We were now behind the line as a corps reserve unit when I started getting some pain behind my right knee. It soon developed into a full fledged boil, and I was ordered to the battalion sickbay. There, a splint was fitted to keep from bending my knee and assigned a *panje bude* or one room shack. It turned out to be another stroke of miraculous good luck for without the knee boil I could never have survived what was to come on the front lines. It has made me wonder if it is possible that Someone was looking out for me.

Rumors were flying now that *Ivan* was assembling a huge army just across from our lines on the other side of the Narev river, northeast of Warsaw. This army, the rumor mill reported, was getting ready for the final big push to drive us back to Berlin. We knew that if this great offensive came, it would be the biggest attack we had faced the entire war. Every morning at dawn we watched the eastern sky for the telltale blood color that meant the artillery shells were on their way.

On January 14, 1945, the sky turned the fearsome red. Two days earlier, on January 12, Marshalls Shukov and Konev had started their offensives further south, and now Marshall Rokossovsky joined the attack to drive the enemy once and for all out of their homeland and then go on to Berlin, their goal. These three giant Russian armies joined together, would be the largest concentration of fighting men and armor in history. Thirty-five thousand artillery pieces of all calibers were now shelling the German and their satellites' trenches. Eight thousand tanks spearheaded the infantry and the Red air force bombed any moving object. When the German attack on the Soviet Union got underway June 22, 1941, Hitler had about 3,000 pieces of artillery, 3,000 planes and about the same number of tanks. Hitler then told his generals before the attack of Russia on June 22, 1941, "All we have to do is push in the front door and the Russian army will crumble like a deck of cards!"

If I had been in the front line with the rest of the brave but demoralized *Landsers*, the chances of surviving would have been essentially nil. Instead, I was about three miles behind the front line and all this carnage, nursing an infected knee boil. This was the last great offensive of the war, and all I and everyone else around me wanted to do was get the hell out of the way and leave the Russians alone.

Immediately on seeing the red glare, I took the splint off my leg, quickly packed my few belongings and waited for the horse drawn wagons of our supply column to start moving westward. Time was slipping by. We knew *Ivan's* emboldened tanks leading the infantry would be on the move, and there was little left of our front line to slow them up. I hopped onto a wagon and headed west. Within a few hours, my little shack was blown up like all the others around. Later I talked to a survivor of that first artillery barrage, and he said it was unlike anything anyone had ever experienced. The shells poured on them like a cloudburst.

Our supply column kept moving to the northwest. Day after day we kept on the move. There was no stopping now to set up defenses and try to slow the oncoming horde. The German soldier finally saw the total futility, and all what he wanted was to get the hell out of Russia and the hell with this from Satan-sent Nazism.

One day we were told we were on German soil. We were in the province of East Prussia, a part of Germany for hundreds of years, now part of Russia. It was a great feeling, but perhaps anticlimactic, because we had always thought and been told that once we reached German soil the German army would stop and fight until death with the motivation of protecting our homes, women and children. But there was no place to set up a defense. We of the supply unit kept moving northwest in the direction of Danzig. The houses now were getting neater and the towns cleaner, and every day it felt more like home and less like a foreign country. In the mass of humanity fleeing were not only civilian refugees and party officials, also many stragglers of military units who got lost, some of course on purpose . If they were caught without the right papers or excuses they were hung on a nearby tree or telephone post to remind other stragglers of the fate which awaited them.

The refugee treks, a long-familiar sight on the Eastern Front, for the first time were composed of Germans. For the first time, too, the treks did not need to be urged onward; they were propelled by sheer terror. The Russian vengeance on German civilians was swift, personal, merciless and more often then not, brutal.

The population was scared out of their wits. They had been told endless stories of the cruelty of the Russian soldiers, and if they expected much out of us in stopping them, one look into our war-weary eyes left little doubt that we were in no condition to stop the onrush. The highways and village roads were now choked with refugees; many millions of the German villagers were trying to escape the inevitable Russian occupation. History had seen such movements of frightened and desperate human beings many times in the past hundreds of years. The Russian peasants stoically stayed on their land and accepted whatever happened to them with little expression or comment. Germans are not made the same way. They left behind what they couldn't take with them and fought desperately to avoid the horror they believed would soon fall on them. We heard stories that their fears were well founded. The Russian soldiers were told, that in their first three days after occupying a German village, they could "do anything," take "anything," behave in "any" way they wanted. For three and a half years we had been occupying their villages and farms, killing their cows, chickens, men, women, children, burning their homes, destroying their lives. What cruelty man is capable of committing is beyond any comprehension. Those who do not believe in such a thing as evil are very poor students of history and fools.

When all was over, more then eight million Germans, who lived east of the Oder-Neisse River in the provinces of East Prussia, Pommerania and Silesia who left their homes and were lucky enough to escape the Russians, were settled in what became West and East Germany. Others emigrated overseas, most of them to North America. Many were captured and were sent to Russian labor camps; not many would return to their homes. Some Germans who failed to escape were integrated into the now Polish or Russian peasant towns, though there were not many.

The mad rush to escape had its own dangers. For one thing there was now the cold of the deep of winter. The end of January the temperature dropped to 20 and some days to 30 below zero, though it was a far cry from the winter of 1941-42. Almost all refugees were caught unprepared, except some of the Nazi big wigs who fled with loaded cars or wagons just before the Russians came. They didn't want the civilians to know that it was time to move, so they waited to the last moment. There was no shelter for those millions; many froze to death. Children, needing to be stilled, would die in their mothers' arms. All they could do then was, wrap them in a blanket, lay them gently in a ditch, say a quiet prayer and shed tears. Another danger was created by all the traffic. The mixture of horse drawn wagons and modern motorized weapons could be a deadly one. The Russian tanks didn't bother to order the horse-drawn wagons to move off the highway; they just run over them or pushed them into the ditch.

I was still with the supply column and was on a wagon when we drove down a steep, icy hill one night. Suddenly, I heard a crashing sound behind me and I stood up on the wagon to see an 18-ton, tracked vehicle pulling a cannon sliding helplessly down the icy road toward our wagon. It hit several wagons just behind ours. Men and horses were screaming and yelling in warning and pain. I jumped from the wagon as hard as I could down the embankment and narrowly escaped being one of those unfortunates caught in the mangled chaos. Those of us who had managed to get away in time had to help with the grisly rescue.

After everything was untangled, we headed northwest again in the general direction of the Polish port city of Danzig, also known as Gdansk. We were part of a human river flooding this famous port city, the gateway to escape *Ivan*. Included in this human flood were western prisoners of war. Though prisoners of Germany they seemed more afraid of their supposed allies the Russians than they were of their German captors. I was walking side by side with a French prisoner; he spoke some German and gesticulated with his hands, when he motioned with forefinger held on the temple and said, "*Russki boom, boom.*" What he meant was, that the Russians shoot all German prisoners.

It was near the end of February, and there was less and less snow on the ground as the climate became tempered by the Baltic Sea. I began to realize that my time with Regiment 530, Company 9 was nearing an end. It pained me in a strange way. I spent four years of my young life living nearly every minute with a desperate prayer that I could be away from all this and back to my family and skiing. Now I knew that part of my life was almost gone, the camaraderie and even the misery would start to become a memory. What was ahead was still very much unknown. I did know this: against all odds I had survived—so far.

It struck me powerfully when I was talking to Lieutenant Fries, our company supply officer on the road to Danzig. He addressed me with *Du* (you); this was unheard of that a German officer addressed a *Obergefreiter* with *Du* instead of the formal Sie (you). He knew that when a prisoner of the Russians you did not have to address an officer with the formal *Sie*. He had the numbers on our unit. Our company at full strength was 180 men. But Company 9, Regiment 530 had seen almost 400 men killed and over 800 wounded, sick or frostbitten or prisoners of the Russians. It was amazing. The numbers were very much against me, but somehow I had managed to survive—so far. I knew the danger was far from over and the future was scary, to say the least. Lieutenant Fries said to me then, "*Du Gabl*, in our company records you have had 29 *Nahkampf Tage* (hand-to-hand combat days), and we want to recommend you for the Iron Cross first class and also for the *Nahkampfspange in Silber* even though your record says you had 29 days, not 30, which are required for the silver spangle." I then said to Lt. Fries, "*Herr Leutnant*, look, the Russians are already 200 miles to the west of us, and we will soon become prisoners of the Russians, and with all these decorations I would be a prime candidate for Siberia." He realized this, and we never talked again about the two decorations. When the time came to become a prisoner of the Russians, the first thing a German soldier did, was throw all decorations and paybook fast and far from the road and lie to the Russians as much as you can in what units you served.

There were now only three possibilities: become a P.O.W., escape by ship from Danzig to the west, or get killed. To escape by ship you needed a pass from a ranking officer, and only wounded soldiers, women, old men or high ranking Nazis got passes which they made out for themselves and their families. One has to realize that the leading Nazis knew perfectly well that the war in the east could not be won. Now all they wanted was to have a few more weeks or months to live before they became prisoners of the Russians

About 130 miles before Danzig we passed by the great Hindenburg Memorial at Tannenberg. For some, this brought great hope. After all, it was here that Germany during World War I had defeated a much larger Russian army and won an astounding victory. To the German military mind, this monument stood as a reminder of German invincibility. To me, it was another symbol of military ambition, ego and humiliation. Sure, Germany won this battle, but who won the war? And who got the credit for this great battle? The aging, bumbling Field Marshall Hindenburg? It was said that he was a dullard and had slept through the whole thing while his brave foot soldiers were dying in the trenches.

When we were about 30 miles from Danzig, an officer stopped our column and tried to gather up as many fighting men as he could. None of us knew the others. After he lined us up he counted less than 70 men, the remnants of three different infantry divisions. We were told by an officer to defend a small village and a sergeant was placed in charge. "See that hill over there?" He pointed to a grassy knoll facing the enemy in front of the village. "Defend that hill." We looked at him like he was crazy. *Ivan* was expected to show up any moment in a forest 350 yards away. There was hardly any snow on the ground, no fox holes, no trees to hide behind, not even shell holes to hide in. We just knelt on the ground and waited for them to shoot at us. "Now!" he yelled, and off we went.

In four years, I've outlived almost 400 men, and now some damned stupid officer is out to get us killed. Within an hour or so the Russians appeared at the edge of the forest and immediately spotted us. Soon little geysers of dirt around us marked where their rifle shots were hitting. We fired back, but the *Ivans* were on the edge of a forest and standing near trees and hard to see. We then heard the first one of our men, then another groan, and yell *"Sanitaeter."* We were getting slaughtered. Someone got smart and yelled to get to the houses. We grabbed the men who were wounded and dragged them toward safety, taking fire all the time. Finally we made it to the safety of the houses and breathed a quick sigh of relief thinking we had escaped. The same officer came over. "Who gave you the order to leave your position? Back on that hill now!"

It was all I could do to keep from shooting that bastard in his back. In four years of warfare, it was the most insane and inhumane order I had ever been part of to receive. But, we also knew then that to disobey an order was akin to being shot on the spot or hung on a tree by the Nazi zealots. All that the higher ups wanted was, to get as much distance between *Ivan* and themselves; they also knew that their decorations on their chest wouldn't mean a thing when coming home after loosing the war. Back we went. Once again men around me were getting hit. It was only a matter of time before one of those little puffs of dirt would find my exposed body. I looked over and saw one of our men assisting a wounded soldier toward the houses. I, at once, joined him using it as an excuse. The brave officer who had ordered us out, had already abandoned his house; he was supposed to have notified our group, but he was marching west! About four of us survivors then went to a nearby farm house and one of the men said, "I am surrendering here to the Russians, this is totally insane." So we all sat with a farmer family on chairs to consider really giving up; we waited for the Russians to take us prisoner. The rifles we hid outside the house in a shed in case a Russian soldier would come to this place, so he wouldn't see German rifles and get panicky. But within an hour we all got up and almost ran towards where our unit went.

We finally came to the outskirts of Danzig, but *Ivan* was still right on our tail. An officer made me squad leader. I wanted to tell him the last time that happened I lasted for three days in March 1944.

It was now March 16, 1945, just as it got dark, we once again found ourselves in a flat meadow. There were foxholes dug already, and as we occupied them we saw arms, legs and pieces of clothing and human bodies lying all over the place. An artillery shell fell directly into a foxhole. Even for us hardened veterans of the Russian campaign, it was a sickening sight. We were there only half an hour when we were ordered a few hundred yards further north. Here we stopped and were ordered to dig our own foxholes. We were glad to leave this grisly place behind.

Twenty yards behind us was a steep embankment and behind that our command bunkers. I noted the distance with some satisfaction thinking if we were wounded or had to drag wounded back under fire, at least we wouldn't have too far to go. We dug foxholes furiously during the remaining night for some cover when daylight came. Fortunately there was no snow and the ground wasn't frozen. The hole was deep enough so that we could keep the machine gun hidden without being seen by the time daylight came, so I instructed my gunner to keep it down until *Ivan* was attacking and quite close. My gunner was just 16 and scared to death. "Keep down and listen to what I say and we'll be all right," I tried to reassure him. "I'll do all the shooting." By now I had been through enough battles to know a thing or two about staying hidden

and keeping some element of surprise. I wasn't about to let
Ivan know where our machine gun was placed until I absolutely had to.

Dawn came, and we saw *Ivans* digging foxholes at the front
edge of a forest about 600 to 700 yards away, just on the edge
of machine gun range. Two tanks were positioned between
the forest and the men digging in front. An officer came by to
inspect our positions. "Why aren't you shooting?" he demanded. "Can't you see these digging Russians in plain sight?"

"Jawohl, Herr Leutnant," I answered, dumbfounded. "But
if I shoot now I will give away my position and they'll just
direct all their fire at us. We will shoot when they attack;
that way we will make sure we get some of them before they
get us." The Russians hated our machine guns more than
ever. By now they had plenty of reserves, and they would
expend vast amounts of ammo just to knock out one hated
German machine gun. "You may have a chest full of medals,
but you are a coward," he yelled at me. "Shoot at them now!"
Just at that time the artillery started to shoot again, and the
coward quickly turned and run back to the safety of his bunker behind the embankment knowing full well that the tanks
would try to knock out my machine gun. I wanted very badly
to train that MG 42 on his retreating back.

I put the gun into its exposed position, trained the sight
on two Russians busy digging and fired a couple of quick
bursts. Both of them crumpled and didn't move. The ground
was dry, and the gun, positioned close to the dirt, raised a
cloud of dust above our hole which now served as a signal to
the Russians as much as if we had waved a red flag in front of
a bull. Quickly I pulled the gun back into the hole and told
my gunner to lay down on the bottom of the shallow hole, and
I laid directly on top of him knowing that the two tanks would
now train their guns on the spot where they saw the cloud of
dust. We waited and waited. It was a terribly uncomfortable
silence. I knew in my bones what was coming. How many
times did I have premonitions before. When Herman didn't
return from a night commando raid. When I picked up the
helmet on July 26, 1943, near Kursk. Now I waited for the
blasts. It must have been 15 minutes or more.

Just when I started to think that maybe for some reason
they had decided we weren't worth the effort, we got the full

force of *Ivan's* anger. The two tanks I had spotted trained their cannons on where they saw the puffs of dust. Blam! Blam! Blam! I counted twelve shots. The explosions hit around us, but mostly in front or behind us. A mortar or artillery shell can drop into a foxhole, but a tank shell has a very flat trajectory, so getting into our hole wasn't easy. It wasn't for lack of trying. I had my hands up covering my head and was still laying on top of my gunner when a shell finally hit the back of the hole. I felt a tremendous blow on the right side of my rib cage and my shoulder. I almost blacked out and thought for a minute that someone had hit me in the side with a sledgehammer. I couldn't breathe anymore. I tried to suck in air but couldn't, and for an agonizing 20 seconds I thought: four long years of hell and now five minutes before the end of the war this is what happens. I opened my eyes, straining to open them wider because now my vision was graying. I was passing out. Then, all of a sudden, I caught my breath. I became aware of my gunner moaning beneath me.

"My legs, my legs," he was yelling. I moved off him so I could see what was wrong. His legs were bleeding from many shrapnel splinters. How could this be? I was protecting his whole body with mine and his legs are full of shrapnel and mine had none. I knew, though, that I had been hit in the right side of the rib cage and shoulder. Why my legs or back didn't get hit is still a mystery to me. The miracles weren't finished yet, as I was still to discover.

The tank shelling had stopped, but artillery continued to fire into the area behind the embankment. By now I knew from experience what was next. The infantry would attack, accompanied by the two tanks, and we'd be found. We were both wounded. Russian policy hadn't changed even though their fortunes in war had; wounded soldiers were shot on sight. They didn't want the burden of caring for them. I didn't want to be killed by the Russians—that much hadn't changed in these years of misery.

"Woerner," I asked my wounded gunner. "Give me your *Luger*." German machine gunners were issued the *Luger* pistol instead of rifles. He gave me his gun, and I rolled over so I could see the Russians approaching at the edge of the hole. I readied the gun, so a quick bullet in the temple would end the suspense. But the infantry didn't come. After a while I decided we would be better off taking our chances with the artillery fire than just laying here waiting for *Ivan* to finish us off. Besides, since the tanks stopped shelling, they may have figured that our hated *Germansky Machinka* was *kaputt.*

My buddy said he thought he could run, and even though I was breathing with some difficulty, I knew the 20 yards would be no problem. I handed him his *Luger,* and we scrambled out of the hole, up and over the embankment. In a moment we were in a bunker, and it wasn't long before a medic was tending to our wounds.

The war was over for me. This was definitely *Heimatschuss.* But there was one problem. How does one get to a hospital when the entire world is collapsing around? The fighting may have been over, but the worry wasn't. First of all, with shrapnel in my lung and shoulder, I knew the wound was serious and with the deterioration of the whole German system, including medical care, I couldn't be assured of getting adequate treatment. And it was getting more and more clear that as the danger of being killed in warfare subsided, the danger of being caught in the confusion of defeat was even greater. The Russians were already 200 miles to the west of us on the Oder River, and there was only one escape route possible—by ship out of Danzig.

We were taken first to an emergency hospital; in reality it was a big villa on the outskirts of the city of Danzig. I remember it being in a beautiful parklike setting. It's stunning to see beauty while the world is collapsing in explosions and terror. The war was closing in on the hospitals by now as well. The next day, just when we thought we might be safe and could start to recuperate from our wounds, the bombers came and sent glass flying about our beds. Russian bombers were coming over Danzig day and night, and because the city was crawling with millions of refugees and soldiers every bomb seemed to fall on a crowd. The hospitals couldn't keep up, not even close. Thinking back now to these times, I am glad that the U.S. and British air forces were not bombarding Danzig. The Russian air force couldn't compare with the Allied air force in the west.

The next night I was moved to a large hospital, a four-story brick building right in Danzig and not too far from the harbor where I was hoping to find an escape by ship from the war. We knew that on land escape was no longer possible. So there were only three possibilities: either escape by ship, become a P.O.W. or die. I was definitely feeling the effects of my lung wound and knew I needed rest and care. But that was not to be. The day after I arrived the Russian artillery shot into the city, and shells landed in the hospital. Even though I felt myself getting weaker I couldn't feel sorry for myself; the guy in the next bed had been shot in the testicles and was enduring unbearable pain. He knelt in his bed, his face yellow and contorted and his crying never stopped.

In the morning the order came, "*Rette sich wir kann* (Every man for himself)." We were freed to survive on our own. The discipline of the German army was finally relinquished, and we were left to our own devices to live, die or be captured. I had become so weak that I didn't think I would have the strength to even go to the bathroom without help from the nurses. But the thought of being left to the Russians put such fear in my heart that I crawled out of bed, got into a uniform that a nurse scrounged for me, and stumbled down the halls of the hospital. When I got outside I saw a city in flames. The smoke was thick, and my lungs were struggling with a splinter stuck in the edge of one lung so the smoke was causing me much discomfort. I headed toward the port which was about a mile away, following a stream of refugees. It seemed like it might have been across the continent. It was either get to the harbor and find a ship to crawl on, or stay behind and face the Russians in my uniform.

Here, I want to mention, many years later, I read reports by German soldiers who were in hospitals and unable to escape when the Russians entered Danzig. They said that the Russians let the German nurses care for them and didn't do them any harm. So much for the Nazi propaganda. The Russians are *Untermenschen.*

What I saw on the way to the harbor was like a vision of hell. If you want a picture of the world gone insane, picture Danzig in late March 1945. I walked along a tree-lined boulevard, surely one of the most beautiful in Danzig in better days. But now it held one of the ugliest sights imaginable, for from nearly every tree hung a German soldier. On most of them had signs hung from their broken necks with the words,

"I was a traitor," or "I was a coward," or "I didn't fight to the death." How many of them, like me, were young men who had survived weeks, months, years of battle, giving everything they had to their country only to face this bitter conclusion in the name of preserving some semblance of discipline in a hopeless and unworthy cause. My bitterness and anger at the officers, generals and especially the political leaders, the only ones I could blame this on, might have been so great to cause me to do something truly stupid.

Streams of humanity kept moving toward the harbor. My strength was failing, but my determination was not. I knew as long as I could crawl I would find a way to get away from the Russians. Finally I arrived at the waterfront. There were ships of all sizes moored. Smaller ships were tied up at the wharves, bigger ships were at anchor in the harbor with tenders running back and forth. It looked like all of them were being loaded with the endless stream of humanity trying to escape. I watched with some bitterness, certain that many of the healthy non-uniformed men that were being loaded with all kinds of boxes and suitcases were sure to be Nazi bigwigs. They, of all people, deserved to stay behind and face the fury of the enraged Russians. Of course, they were the first to escape.

The *Gauleiter* of the district, when asked why he didn't stay with his people answered, "The *Führer* needs me in Berlin." This swine got his reward after the war. Death by hanging. Colonel General Guderian said in his book *Panzer Leader*, "My wife had to stay in their home to the last day before she could be driven by car west to escape the Russian occupation forces. If she had left several days earlier people would have known and would have packed their bags and left too." This is only one of many occasions to see how the Nazi bigwigs behaved.

We all waited there, looking for an opportunity to get on board any ship, as long as it went west. Russian torpedo bombers constantly attacked the large ships anchored in the Danzig bay. Several of these precious escape routes were sent to the bottom.

Finally I found my way onto an old merchant ship. It was so crowded the only place I could find was sitting on the floor below deck against a wall. The ship, now totally overloaded with about 1,000 people, waited until dark and slowly started to slip out of the dangerous harbor heading for Copenhagen, Denmark. I sat down against a bulkhead in the pitch dark stuffy hold, sharing limited air with a thousand other frightened souls as we sailed through mine infested water with the constant danger of attack from the air and submarines. Hardly a restful experience. I was getting weaker and weaker, my wounds were oozing pus constantly; it ran down the side of the body like lava, and there was no one there who could help me. For two days we sailed toward Copenhagen, and then we heard the engines slow. The word went through the masses, "Copenhagen is mined. The British have mined the harbor. We must turn back."

The blow was devastating. We were headed east again. But instead of going back to Danzig, we headed for the coast, finally coming to the mouth of the Oder River which separates Germany from Poland now. It was a dark journey of three days, during which time I was given one drink of water a day. Off the coastal town of Ahlbeck on the Usedom Peninsula we dropped anchor, and I waited patiently for the little boat that shuttled us off the ship and onto German soil. A couple of kindly souls helped me onto the little tender, but as we started to bounce in the rough water I was near the end of my endurance and became violently ill in the boat, vomiting and coughing blood. I no longer cared about living or dying, my body and my spirit had exhausted their reserves.

All of us were taken to a hospital and revived enough to feel very relieved. At last, I would get the medical care. And even better, for the first time in what seemed like an eternity, we were not in danger of being mined, shelled, bombed or hung by the last of the Nazi zealots. I dared to think I just might make it after all.

The little makeshift hospital, formerly a school, was reserved for the most serious cases. But the hospital and medical staff were ill-equipped to handle so many of the serious cases they now found themselves burdened with.

I had been laying in bed there for a few days when I had the sensation of wetness around my lower torso. I felt it with my hands, and it felt warm and wet. Oh no, I thought. Now I'd lost bladder control. As I lifted my hand it was bright red. The wound was bleeding so much I was literally bathing in it.

The soldier in the next bed saw my hand at the same time, and we looked at each other and yelled out at the same time. *"Schwester! Schwester!* (Sister, Sister)!"* A nurse came running in, and when she saw me laying in a bed of blood she panicked and went running madly down the hall yelling for help. In a moment or two the room seemed to be full of men who quickly pulled me, sheet and all, onto a stretcher and rushed me into surgery. They carried me down a stair, and I remember all the blood spilling onto the floor so that I was afraid they would slip in it and drop me. When they got me to the operating room the nurses were frantically running around, and one of them jabbed a needle inside my left arm at the bend of the elbow. I wished they had taken more time because in their haste it is likely the needle they used was contaminated. It was the last thing I remember. When I came to I found myself in a big room with about 30 others, some also recovering from surgery.

About two days after the surgery I noticed pain inside my left elbow that didn't seem to be going away. It was red and swollen, and I immediately suspected blood poisoning. They applied a splint on my arm, suspending it from a hook on the headboard, and I lay there, hardly able to move. My lung wound was discharging pus continually, the boil on my arm was growing hourly and the pain was getting worse and worse. All I could do was lay there like a chicken on a rotisserie. Then the patient in the next bed totally lost it.

The beds in this overcrowded hospital were practically touching they were so close. He was a soldier with very serious wounds, and he suddenly became delirious and started singing *Ave Maria* and tried pulling at my bed sheets. I was stuck and couldn't move and in sheer misery myself. I was yelling *Hilfe, hilfe* until an orderly came rushing in and harnessed the poor fellow to his bed, still singing *Ave Maria*. The next day he was much quieter, and he went quietly out of this life as I watched him go.

My elbow infection was now huge with the red skin stretched tight. It was almost ripe, so the doctor came to my bed, sat down on a stool, brandishing a little knife. An orderly hung onto my legs as the doctor jabbed the knife into the boil. It exploded, spraying reddish pus all over his white coat. Then he took some tweezers and pushed gauze deep into the now open wound. The pain was unbelievable. I was yelling my head off as he kept pushing gauze around, cleaning out all the infection. He kept at it and kept at it, and I found out there was greater pain than what I experienced as a young boy with a broken leg set by the village doctor. It was not the most elegant or pain-free way of dealing with the infection, but it was effective, and I am certain this doctor saved my life. When he was finished he almost ran out of the room, he must have felt sorry for me.

There were many who entered that hospital in Ahlbeck in spring of 1945 only to leave in a box. For reasons I can't explain, I was not to be one of them. Still, after that my condition deteriorated. I felt myself getting weaker and weaker. Earlier I had watched as patients who were dying were rolled out of the wards and put into a special room we called the hopeless chamber. No one lasted more than a day in that room. Now I waited for them to come and roll me there. I couldn't eat anymore and never in my life had that happened before. I faced many days of battle, many times of near death in combat, but rarely did I think of dying. Now I found myself praying for almost the first time in the war. I felt in my bones that I would be in the next world in a very short time and thought it was time to get prepared. I had little fear of dying but great curiosity and wondered if I would meet up with Herman and Franz in the world beyond, and contemplated if they would look human as I remembered them. I worried about my family since they had no way of knowing where I was and perhaps would never know what happened to me. I was dreaming that my mother was offering me to make *Tyrolean Knoedel* if I only would come home again. I was too weak to write and knew that there was no more mail going out with the war going as it was. I resigned myself to the fate of the Unknown Soldier. I closed my eyes with weariness, waiting to see what it looked like behind the curtain.

Why did I live through this? I have pondered this often. Of course, it is possible to leave this all in the hands of fate or whatever other name you wish to call "IT." The upbringing I had on the steep slopes of the Alps may also have had a lot to do with it. The summers of swinging a scythe, or packing building materials up the steep meadows, the winters of non-stop skiing, mountain climbing. Who can tell?

Somehow, I began to recover, and when *Ivan* came close
to Ahlbeck it was time to be moved again, this time 70 miles
by train to Teterow, a small city northwest of Berlin. Here I
started to feel my strength coming back. Unfortunately, the
Russian push continued; by the end of April they were near
Teterow, so we had to move again. Here we heard on the
radio that Hitler had died in Berlin fighting with his soldiers.
The Nazi regime was a big lie from beginning to end. He shot
himself, 30 yards deep under the earth in a concrete bunker;
he knew when the reckoning would come, he would look like
an insane man, causing tens of millions of death and unimaginable hardships and miseries to hundreds of million people.

April 30th we were on a Red Cross train being moved further west to the coastal town of Wismar. From here we were
loaded onto trucks which had Red Crosses painted on their
roofs, and headed further west toward Lübeck. In the trucks
we were attacked several times by Allied planes on strafing
runs. I watched some of the trucks in our column destroyed
by these deadly, accurate weapons, but none of the trucks
with the red cross painted on them were hit. Were we just
lucky? Were the Allies lousy shots? We had heard how devastating these strafing attacks were to our army. I could see
their accuracy with my own eyes now, so it became clear they
were simply avoiding Red Cross vehicles.

This was a different kind of warfare I wasn't used to. I
realized again what I had said before and said after: had I
been lucky enough to be posted to the western front I would
have found the first Allied soldier, dutifully following the
Führer's orders of "Not one step back," I would have stuck my
hands straight up in the air and said, "Take me prisoner,
please." I didn't lack the courage. If I could have found a way
out of the Russian front, I would have taken it a thousand
times. But I couldn't have surrendered to the Russians.

We were now unloaded in a hospital in the city of Lübeck.
Rumor had it the mayor was going to declare Lübeck an open
city: it wouldn't be defended and accordingly not attacked by
artillery, air attack or anything else by the Allies. It was a
relief, but we still were afraid if some fanatical Nazi bigwig
would order to defend it and consequently going to be bombed.

We were now what would become West Germany, a real
relief to us. We were so aware that the end of fighting was

near and of being the last and most meaningless casualties of the war. We heard stories from the vets of the first world war that the British were gentlemen and that we would not be shot. The endless propaganda of the Nazis tried to convince the German population that Allied victory would mean that everyone would be declared guilty and be punished. Hitler ordered *Reichs Minister* Speer that all bridges, water mains, electrical installations, factories and more to be destroyed in the whole *Reich*. Thank God that many of the leading Nazis had sense enough not to follow this insane man's order.

We soldiers felt if we could surrender to the British or other western Allies that we would be safe. I was in the hospital in Lübeck when I saw the first British uniform. It was May 2, 1945. The foreign soldiers came in, looked around but didn't say anything. They didn't gloat or rage. They looked grim and decidedly unfriendly. I would guess that the full horrors of the concentration camps were just being realized by the Allied troops at this time. They were quickly forming their own opinions who these German's were.

I was quite uncomfortable when I looked into their emotionless faces. They saw a soldier in a German soldier's uniform, the enemy. They didn't see me as a young man taken from his home in the Tyrolian Alps to fight a war he didn't want and thought was wrong and unjust. They saw a face like many others who had killed their comrades and buddies and who might have taken part in the gruesome massacres they had just discovered. They didn't see a man who lived through four years of hell, fighting daily just to stay alive to see this day finally come when the fighting would be over and go back to his family and ski, climb mountains and just enjoy life. They saw a representative of a system, a party, a policy that can only be called evil. I wanted to tell them it was different. I can only say that questions of good and evil are never as simple as we might prefer to make them.

Escape from Russian P.O.W. Camp

Within a few days after the British entered Lübeck we were driven by truck north to a town near the Danish border called Schönberg. At least we were in British hands and began to feel somewhat safe. It was a very reassuring feeling after the tension and dangers of the last few months of the war.

I was still in the hospital and very weak, but my appetite had returned. Unfortunately, there was little to no food. For two days we didn't get a bite to eat. Our rations, now controlled by the British, was a small bowl of watery soup and a slice of bread a day. I began to experience true hunger, the kind that goes far beyond an empty gnawing in the stomach. I would almost go out of my mind thinking about food and the pain of starvation. When the emptiness got too bad, some of us patients would go outside and start eating handfuls of grass from the lawn just to get something in the stomach. During this time I had to think about all the hungry, starving people and refugees I had seen in the past four years. Now I knew their pain. I hope God is more merciful to the ones responsible for this than I would have been if I had been the one to judge them.

For some reason our British captors decided to move us. This time it was back to the east to another town called Schönberg, this one about ten miles east of Lübeck in the Province of Mecklenburg. At the time it was confusing to us. Later we realized that the British must have known that east of Lübeck was the occupation territory granted to the Russians in the Yalta agreement between Roosevelt, Churchill and Stalin in February 1945. Those of us in the hospital were sick or wounded; the British seemed to want this burden to fall on their Allies in victory, the Russians. We of course didn't know that this Schönberg would be in the future Russian zone of occupation. We certainly would have moved west, out of this future Russian zone. Here I became a good friend with a sixteen-year-old boy Willy Feiler who had fought with the *Volkssturm* (Hitler Youth Army). He had two dozen small shrapnel wounds all over his body from a mortar grenade. His home was in Ellbogen, a town in the Sudetenland, which was Czechoslovakia before Hitler annexed it back to Germany in the fall of 1938. We two would now share for two and a half months the fate as P.O.W.

While here in the hospital we heard the news of Himmler's capture. He was the leader of the infamous *Gestapo*. This scum was discovered in a British P.O.W. camp near the Danish border disguised as a plain soldier. He wore a regular German soldier's uniform, had shaved his mustache and hidden his eye glasses to conceal his identity. Eventually, by the end of May he was recognized by some soldiers and turned in. This scumbag of course did not fight to the death like he and Hitler had ordered all soldiers. He was the one who ordered his S.S. police to hang thousands and thousands of our own soldiers on trees or any signpost they could find, with a sign hanging around their broken necks, "I did not fight to the last," or "I was a coward," or shooting them outright. In the hospital we were discussing the capture of Himmler, remarking that he and his henchmen did not fight to the last. When recognized, Himmler swallowed a poison pill which he with foresight hid in his mouth and ended his pitiful life that way. Eichman and Kaltenbrunner, the two Austrians and highest ranking S.S. leaders after Himmler, Mengele, the butcher of Auschwitz and hundreds more stole at the end of the war millions of *Reichsmark*, disguised themselves and fled to South America or other places. Eichman and Kaltenbrunner and many more got their just reward—death by hanging.

On June 30, 1945, our worst fears were realized. Our British guards told us we were not to leave the hospital in Schönberg between 6 p.m. and noon the next day. During the evening the British army with all their vehicles left, and by the morning our new guards were wearing the brown, baggy uniforms with the red stars, the Russians. Instead of being my enemy across a field, *Ivan* was now my nurse and guard. I had that uneasy feeling like something dreadful was about to happen. The war is over, I thought, they wouldn't take us out and shoot us now, would they? If not that, then they will wait until we are all well again and send us to Siberia. Just like the vet's of World War I had said. In my now yellowish calender is written: *1. Juli, 1945, "In Russische Gefangen-*

schaft (P.O.W. of the Russians)." One cannot describe what that meant at that time for a soldier who fought for four long years on the Russian front.

While guarded by the British, Willy Feiler and I were going into the village of Schönberg during the day, to beg for food. One would go to a bakery, when successful, somehow we would let each other know, then the other would enter that store within ten minutes, but never at the same time. We would enter the store, then stand near the entrance and wait till all the customers had left. By then the bakery owner had only two choices: hand over a piece of bread or say, sorry, no bread today. I can't remember once being turned down. Once, I remember, I got a whole loaf. It is hard to describe what that meant to a starving young man at that time.

Even though the war was over and things were gradually getting back to some semblance of normalcy, I started to feel alive again. When the Russians came, those of us who had been on the Eastern Front had a special knowledge and fear of their infantry men. We knew that, as the common saying went, "the bullets sat loose in their guns."

The day after the Russians arrived at our hospital, we had a noontime visit from a party of Russians in uniform. We still had our German doctors and nurses in the hospital, and this official visit seemed to be some sort of inspection. They went from room to room, muttering quietly to themselves. It made us a bit nervous. Still, I did not fear them too much now that the fighting was over. Although we had been told throughout the war that the Russians were *Untermenschen* (subhuman). I knew better. I had seen their strength in enduring the devastation that our invasion had brought on their land. I had seen great courage, and I had seen generosity and kindness greater than from anyone else. The fanatical communists I didn't trust, but the Russian people I knew had good hearts. I really didn't know what to think about these people now checking us all over. As it happened, our stingy rations were slightly increased. The Russian appetite, it seems, is more like the healthy German one; these people couldn't see how we could survive on one bowl of thin soup and one piece of bread a day.

After we became a little more comfortable with our new captors, Willy and I started to venture out to town again during the day. Our begging for food was as successful as ever. Thank God for those generous bakers and townspeople in Schoenberg. It is interesting to note that I would receive a request for an autograph from a lady in Schönberg about 40 years later, because of the Olympic Medal. She then sent me several postcards.

By now it was mid-July, and I was feeling better and could feel some of my energy and youth returning. And when it did the first thing on my mind was skiing. The more I thought about skiing, the more I longed to get home again. In mid-July at home the haying is just getting going, the edelweiss are coming into full bloom, and the snow is clearing from the high peaks leaving the path open for glorious hikes and thrilling climbs. Yes, I was starting to feel like I could hike and climb and ski. But, would I ever get home? Would these captors give me my freedom or would they make me pay for my participation in this war by sending me to the coal mines in frigid Siberia. Inquiring around, I became less concerned about being sent to the labor camps. I was an invalid and found out that the Russians were only sending *Kriegsverbrecher* (war criminals) to Siberia. Those who once had been so proud to carry the S.S. tattoo under their arms now found it a dead-giveaway and a certain sentence to the far side of Russia's Ural Mountains. For myself, I could find nothing wrong with the treatment we received from the Russians so far, which did not mean I was in the least content to languish in the hospital while the winter was just around the corner.

Willy and I started to plan our escape to the west. The British occupation zone was only about ten miles west. By now I was working in the kitchen, which not only helped my hungry stomach, it gave me the opportunity to stuff a little food away for our journey. The plan was simple. We would leave the hospital at 6:00 in the morning and head west. When we saw a friendly looking villager, we would ask directions to the nearest forest to the west and that's what we would head for. We figured our survival skills in the forest would help us get through any Russian guards posted at the border.

We got up that morning, July 17, 1945, one of the many dates I wrote in the little calender, filled with excitement, anticipation and a little fear. We knew the risks we were taking. I was getting my things together when one of my buddies ran into our room. "Look out the window," he said with a panicked look in his face.

Willy and I went to the window. The hospital was completely surrounded by Russian troops which were all carrying the PPSH, a very familiar sub machine gun. "Somebody found out," he said. I had to agree. After a couple of nervous hours we were told to get our personal belongings together and assemble in front of the hospital. "Where are we going?" I asked. "To a camp," I was told gruffly. "Then you will be given your papers and allowed to go home." I looked at him intently and wanted to find some sign that he knew what our true fate was going to be. He was stone-faced. If he was lying, he was good. Maybe that's what they told him to keep us from panicking.

Pretty soon all of us men from the hospital were assembled at the front gate. They marched us into town, and there were hundreds of young German men. Many were in civilian clothes. My buddies and I looked at each other with great confusion. Slowly it dawned on us that the Russian soldiers coming to the hospital at the very moment we were about to escape was simply a great coincidence. This was planned a long time ago. Wherever we were going, it was to be with all the German soldiers and young men from the province of Mecklenburg.

We marched together out of town onto a main highway. We had formed into a marching column and suddenly it seemed all so familiar to us. It could have been a training drill in Salzburg during *Reichsarbeitsdienst*. It could have been down the dusty Russian highway just past the Dnieper east of Kiev. But we were German soldiers marching to an unknown fate. Then a joker, also feeling the familiarity of marching, broke out into one of the *Soldatenlieder* (campaign songs). It was the marching song of the *Panzer* men. *"Ob's stuermt oder schneit--ob - die Son--ne uns lacht-- ob heit-er der Himmel -- ob finster -die Nacht--verstaubt-- sind die -Gesi--ichter und froh - ist unser Sinn--ja unser Sinn -- dann braust un-ser Pan--zer- im Sturmee --dahin."*

These were the famous marching songs that so stirred the blood of the German soldiers and the population in general. Soon there were many of us joining in the singing. It was too much for our captors. *"Stoy!"* they yelled. We could tell they did not think it funny or even nostalgic. The music quickly stopped, and the only sound was the clumpf, clumpf, clumpf of our high German boots on the paved highway.

We were out of town a couple of miles when we were turned left toward a forest. We marched through this and came out on the other side onto a grain field. We started to become very uneasy. We had heard rumors, including one about a Russian massacre of thousands of Polish officers in the Katyn Forest of White Russia in 1939 which the German propaganda machine reminded the population frequently. Someone whispered the fear we all felt gripping our hearts. Was this to be our fate. To be marched out of town, away from staring eyes, to a lonely spot where we would dig our own graves and be shot. The wild rumor spread through our midst. We were lined up into three rows and told to lay our belongings, few as they were, out on the ground and spread them out. The English had already taken our watches. Now the Russians took the rest. Each was allowed one blanket, a spoon, a pencil and a comb. In my calender which I hid in the inside pocket, I wrote down the names and addresses of my buddies. Then we were marched back to the highway. On the way to the P.O.W. camp near the town of Rhena, some of our men were told to stop when a Russian guard noticed a good pair of German high top boots. The man would be required to sit down on the shoulder of the highway and take them off and exchange them for the Russians poor quality boots. It was a scene straight out of 1941 and 1942 in Russia. This time the shoe was on the other foot.

Somehow, taking our few belongings and our boots eased our minds. If the Russians were going to shoot us, wouldn't they wait until after we were dead to take what they wanted from us? Ironically, this process of being relieved of what value they could find made us feel wonderful. Perhaps we would live after all.

We marched for about seven and half miles and arrived at a camp with barracks, where we joined a huge crowd already there. Altogether there were about 4,000 men from the province of Mecklenburg on the Baltic Sea gathered in this camp. Again, we were told that from here we would be sent home. After being assigned a bed, some had to do farm work, others

were ordered to help build more barracks. My luck continued. Willy and I were ordered to be kitchen helpers. Giving
us kitchen duty was like making rabbits gardeners. We stuffed
ourself like there was no tomorrow. After all, we were not
sure there was. We were careful not to be seen, but after
months of near starvation, we had practically an insatiable
appetite.

All Russian soldiers had their hair cut to the skin, and we
prisoners were lining up in the evenings where our own men,
who had a hair cutting machine, kept busy until dark.

After two days in the camp we saw no sign of being released any time soon. It was July 20th, and autumn wasn't
far away; after that came snow and then skiing. I had to get
home. Willy and I began to make new escape plans. If *Ivan*
wouldn't let us go, we would have to take matters into our
own hands. We scouted out the situation. The fence surrounding the camp was not exactly high security. It was the
kind used to keep cattle in a pasture and would represent no
problems. What about the guards? At night the Russians
posted few guards, and even they seemed a little tipsy. Clearly
they felt they had nothing to fear from the *Germanskis* now.
No one was thinking about doing battle any more. Everyone
was mostly concerned about the next meal.

We waited until dark. About midnight we headed for the
fence, stealing carefully through the lines of barracks and
slipped through the fence with stealth that came from practice. We disappeared into a high grain field and found a hay
barn. Here we decided we might as well catch some sleep.
Early in the morning we were up and walking along a road
toward a small town. The road took a bend and as we turned
the corner we ran right smack into a two man Russian patrol.

"*Stoy!*" they yelled. Our hands shot high in the air at
once. By now we certainly knew what this Russian word
meant. We also knew that the bullets sat loose in their guns.

They took us to their commander. It was still early in the
morning, and the commandant took his time shaving and eating breakfast. We watched him through the window. We
were not so calm. He motioned for us to come into the house
and began to question us through an interpreter. He seemed
an elderly, well fed gentleman, kindly, almost bemused. My
friend was just 16; I was a war-weary 23, but I was small,

wiry and could have passed for 17. Besides I was not yet recovered from my serious wound. We didn't seem much of a threat to this man.

After the questioning, one of the guards took us to a building up the road. There we found ourselves in the midst of a group of other P.O.W.s gathered for work. We told the guard that we had just gotten out of the hospital and were in no condition for work. *"Nix rabodney, nix kushajty* (no work, no food), he said. It made sense. Here I heard Austrian dialect, particularly Viennese. There were two men who told me they were both from around Vienna. I at once noted their addressees in my little calender: *Karl Dolezel, Wien VI., Webgasse 15, II. Stock and Karl Reisenberger, Bruck an der Leitha, Altstadt 34, Oesterreich.*

Willy and I sat there all day without working while all the others went with the guard, where I don't know. In the evening the P.O.W.s came back from working, and the guard took some of them to a shed some distance away to store the shovels, rakes, hoes, and other tools. While he was gone a friendly Russian officer came by, sat down on the grass with us, and started to talk to our little group. I think it was the commandant who interviewed us in the morning. He spoke some German, and we had learned some Russian so we managed to talk a little. We knew he was a good natured man, and we knew where the Russian's soft spots were.

"We wanted to go home to *madka* (mother) we said plaintively. We looked as young, doe-eyed and homesick as we could muster. *"Tawai,"* he said with a smile, waving his hand away. Go home. We stared at him. Did he say we could go home? *"Tawai!"* he said again. He gestured definitely, and now we knew he was serious. This Russian officer was telling us to go home! He couldn't have known that I was 1,000 kilometers from my home.

We didn't need a third invitation. In an instant we were walking fast down the hill toward the main highway to Berlin. We did not want to run to make it look like we were running from a guard in case other Russian soldiers saw us. For the first time since I had left St. Anton, almost four years earlier for the eastern front, I felt a sense of freedom and life. Home! It was if I had been repressing my desire to get home to protect myself against the disappointment that something would happen before I got there. That fear was stripped away, and I let the reality of actually going home take hold of me. Though I was still far from safety and freedom and had frontiers to cross to the U.S. occupation zone in Bavaria and then into the French zone in Austria. The urgency of getting home so filled me that I would let nothing stand in my way. I would take whatever risks, whatever chances were necessary, but, by God, I was going home!

There were about a dozen of us in the group walking along the highway to Berlin, and some were faster than others. Suddenly we heard yelling behind us. It was the Russian guard, the one who had been putting the tools away with two men. He was on his bike pedaling furiously toward us and pointing a pistol at the sky and swearing in Russian four letter words. He couldn't have known that the *Offizer* told us to go home. Willy, the two Karls and I were near the back of the pack, so he came upon us first, but he kept on going, trying to catch the ones ahead of us. His thought was to stop those in front and then hold us all up, like you'd stop a cattle stampede. We accepted the first Russian's authority to send us home. Now we were supposed to accept this Russian's authority to stop us? That's the way it was at that time. The orders you follow are the last ones you are given. In this case, the last orders were the ones we chose to disobey.

I was walking with the two Karls and Willy when the guard passed us on his bike. Before the guard had a chance to round up the others ahead of us and come back for us, we decided to head for the high grain fields to the right and one by one we disappeared. I lay down in the grain and caught my breath. It was just getting dark. After it was completely dark I decided to try and find the others. "Willy!" I whispered. "Karl! Karl! Feiler! I crawled around and after a while I heard Feiler answer. "Here," he said with an urgent, fearful whisper. "Gabl, is that you?" We called for the others but heard no answer.

When I made it back to Austria in August I wrote to both Karls' families in Vienna. I heard from Reisenberger's family that he made it home in November. But Karl Dolezel was captured and sent to Siberia. He finally returned home to Vienna in 1952 after being moved around five different cities in Siberia. He had been in the Division Brandenburg, that was on the Russian's blacklist, which is why he was sent there. The men from Division Brandenburg were a special unit of the *Wehrmacht*; they were all volunteers and totally dedicated to Nazism. They spoke the language of the countries they operated in and wore their uniforms. They were dropped by parachutes behind the enemy lines to blow up bridges or remove signs or just plain raise havoc and cause confusion. If caught, they were executed on the spot. They were not protected by the Geneva convention because they didn't wear the regular uniform of the combating enemy. Less then 5% survived the war. Karl Dolezel was one of them; he wrote me from Vienna in 1989 that he served in this division. I didn't find out about this until 1989 when a friend from Seattle, who made frequent trips to Vienna, looked him up. Since then Karl and I have maintained frequent correspondence, and I routinely send him money and a carton of American cigarettes which he greatly enjoys. In 1993 Karl passed away at age 83.

Willy Feiler and I walked through the grain field in the dark and found a small farmhouse on the edge of a forest. We could see a light in the distance because finally the hated *Verdunkelung* (blackout) was over. It was a sheer joy to see lights on at night again. How we miss the little things. The farmer at the door was not particularly pleased to see us and told us to go sleep under the cherry tree. He could get in big trouble with the Russian occupiers if he was caught harboring P.O.W.s in his house. We hadn't eaten for a while, since we had avoided work, so in the middle of the night we climbed into the cherry tree and had a delicious dinner of black cherries.

Food was our main concern. We had found that the people in the cities generally were pretty generous towards us ex-soldiers when it came to handouts. I don't think I had a real meal ever since the British army occupied Lübeck on May 2, 1945. We decided to head for Berlin. It was to the south and east of where we were, and so in the general direction of Austria and home. Also, Feiler used to work in a plant in Berlin before joining the Hitler Youth Army, and he had friends there. Perhaps they would help with our escape. But to get to Berlin, we had to stay out of sight of the ever-present Russians. The Russians stuck to the main roads, so we avoided these as much as possible and used the paths through the fields and stayed away from villages and towns. Often we would see a Russian or a group of them from a distance. Then we would hunker down and stay quiet or move as stealthily as our four years of survival skills had taught us. We had only gone a few miles and already were tiring of the hide and seek game. Hunger was our constant companion, and we were getting anxious to make faster progress toward Berlin and then home. This slinking around like snakes was not much fun.

'Why don't we pretend we are cripples?" Feiler asked. "Great idea," I answered. Russians wouldn't send cripples to Siberia. As emaciated as we still looked it wouldn't be that difficult to convince them that we were in bad shape. And in that case, they would just as soon be rid of us than have to care for us in an overcrowded hospital or camp. So we each fastened a sling on our arms and hobbled our way onto the main highway toward Wismar. Almost immediately we ran into a detail of Russians, these soldiers looked so young, like school boys. Instead of arresting us, they offered us their ungodly smelling *machorka* cigarettes rolled in newspapers which we pretended to greatly enjoy. We played our cripple roles to the hilt until the Russians turned their back then we broke out into big smiles at each other.

Now our confidence was unbridled. We thought we had this game figured out and hobbled boldly in broad daylight to the train station in Wismar to catch a train for Berlin. We had no money, but soldiers didn't need to pay for a ticket. The trains were absolutely jammed with passengers. The aisles were crowded with people standing and there were even people jammed into the passageway between train cars. We were treated very kindly; frequently civilians gave up their seats so we could sit down for a few minutes and if a lunch was unpacked we were sure to get a few bites. We had lost the war, but it was clear that the German people didn't blame us for the defeat. We looked ragged and hungry; in fact we were hoboes. But we didn't care. The knowledge that we were on our way home kept us feeling great and full of hope. We arrived in Berlin and began looking for the plant where Feiler had worked. The city was a mess. The relentless Allied bombing, unhindered at the end by our brave fighter pilots, had caused unimaginable devastation. If Feiler thought he could get us some work in the factory he was sorely disappointed. The building itself was a total loss. Only one man was there, but he was a good friend of Feiler's. The two of them hugged like long lost buddies, and I started to feel like the homecoming was beginning.

We went door to door in Berlin looking for food. At that time there wasn't a single restaurant in all of Berlin operating. Willy and I where approached by a man asking if we wanted to come with him for a bite to eat. He led us to a bombed-out building on the first floor, his apartment had most windows covered with planks. As we entered his wife greeted us and said, "Sit down, we will have some bread and ersatz coffee." They also had two small children, and we felt bad, but we were so hungry and accepted. We thanked them profusely and left. The same day, as we walked along on another street, a woman had a tailor shop in a basement of a bombed out building and when she saw us approach, she came out and almost begged us to come and have something to eat. Again, we found people were very generous. We didn't get a lot of food, but we did get enough to keep the painful edge off our hunger. In war, I have seen the very worst of the human race; but also the best. *Heil* to the Berliners.

Everywhere throughout the city people were trying to clean up the rubble. It was less then three months since the shooting had stopped, but the citizens were trying to pick up life as best they could. One could see already lines of old men and women separating whole bricks from the broken ones and pile them up. It was going to be hard work and many years before new buildings were to be erected. Their heart and resilience was an encouragement to me. Maybe, just maybe,= life could get back to some sort of normalcy, someday.

After just two days in Berlin we decided to continue our journey south. Feiler had relatives near the Czechoslovakian border, so that's where we decided to head. He thought they would put us up until the world settled down a bit. Early in the morning of July 25th we went to the train station looking for a train bound for Dresden. Again, the station was crowded and the train heading for Dresden was so packed already at this time of the day that we had no chance of even getting on board. We went to the other side of the train, looking into the windows to see if we could find any room, some passengers on board waved at us to come. We came nearer and before we knew it they were dragging us on board through the open windows.

Hours later we arrived in Dresden. In my calender I wrote: *25. Juli, Ankunft in Dresden um 12:00 hr., 13:45 hr. nach Chemnitz.* Dresden had been one of the most beautiful of German cities. Now there was almost nothing left. Words cannot describe the total destruction. The repeated Allied bombing and the fierce fire storms that were caused by the intense heat of an entire city burning had caused havoc almost as bad as the atomic blast in Hiroshima, Japan. I remember so well, half the city was only a dust heap the other half had only very high bare walls standing. There was such a sadness among these people. The waste in lives, in property, in history and beauty was as total as it was meaningless.

We continued on the train past Dresden, to the south and west, paralleling the Czech border and stopped at Chemnitz and then went on to the town of Plauen. Near here is where Feiler's relatives lived. On the train I had decided I didn't want to wait until more order was restored in occupied Germany. I was in the Russian zone and wanted out. The Iron Curtain wasn't even thought of yet, but I was afraid of taking chances. Feiler and I said our good-byes. It was hard since we had become good comrades in the hospital and on the journey. We wished each other luck with great sincerity because we knew we needed it just to get home, and then to try to get our lives in order.

I had to get off the train at Plauen as well because a large railway bridge over a valley had been destroyed. I tramped with other passengers across the valley on the way to a little town near the Russian-American zone border and stayed here for a day, reconnoitering the situation. I knew this was tricky business, passing from the Russian zone, what would be known for nearly fifty years as East Germany into the American zone in Bavaria. There were numerous stories of people getting killed crossing the border. The bullets hung very loose in *Ivan's* sub-machine guns. The Russians just seem to have a different idea about human life. Their job was to protect the border, so if they saw someone trying to cross it, it seemed to them the right thing to do was to shoot them. It didn't seem a big deal. I went to the city hall to get food coupons, but the *Bürgermeister* had placed a notice on the fence of the house where I was directed for coupons. "No food coupons for Austrians," the cold message said. There were camps in this town for Italians, Hungarians, Croatians and Slovenians, they all were supplied with food and shelter, except the Austrians. Of course, we had only been forced to fight a German war for nearly six years for the glory of their damned Thousand Year Reich but share their food with their Austrian friends? Not a chance. And unlike Berliners, the villagers were not very generous with their food, or shelter. I slept in hay barns at night, and during the day I dug potatoes in the fields, boiling them in an open can over a fire. Still, it was late July and the weather was warm. Sleeping in a pile of hay without fear of being shelled or overrun was still a welcome luxury. I had no complaints whatsoever as long as I came closer to St. Anton with every step.

The closer I got to home the more I had to fight the urge just to make a run to cross the border and out of the Russian zone. It was so close. I knew once I crossed that line I would be all but home. But I knew that if I got crazy I was risking capture and a Russian P.O.W. camp or worse, a bullet in the back. Patience, I kept telling myself, patience.

The border was now only a few miles away. One afternoon I decided to see how close I could get and what I could find out. On the way I met another Austrian who was also heading toward the border. He lived only about twelve miles from St. Anton in the town of Pians and wanted to get home as much as I did, but as we got closer to the Russian-American border I noticed he was dragging farther and farther behind. He was hesitating. I kept going and looked back several times but finally lost sight of him altogether. I had talked to farmers along the way so I knew pretty well where the border was located. Within a few hundred yards from the border I came to a crossing in the road and saw a small group of civilians standing, talking. One of them was a woman with a baby carriage. This was a common sight at this time. The carriage did not carry a baby but it held all the woman's personal belongings. I approached the group.

"Do you know where the border is?" I asked cautiously.

*"Ja, "*they said and pointed ahead toward a forested area. "We have tried twice today, but the Russian guards have turned

us back." They were clearly dejected. I stood looking in the direction of the woods then made an impetuous decision to go for it and started walking quickly toward the trees. I heard a noise behind me and noticed that one of the young men and the woman were following me. It was amazing, having been turned away twice and now they were trying again. But they must have thought this soldier must know what he was doing.

"My God," I thought. "There's just no way that three of us can make it, and with that carriage." I figured to have a good chance with the sneaking skills I had developed in Russia how to crawl on my elbows and sneak up on a guard post. But with them, what could I do.

"Hurry!" I said impatiently and grabbed the carriage away from the woman so we could move faster. In a few minutes we had disappeared into the trees. It was not a dense forest, and we could see some distance around us. About 150 yards in we came to a clearing about 40 yards wide. This was the real border. Across the clearing we would find *Ammy*'s, the Americans. My heart was beating furiously. We stopped at the edge of the clearing, and I told my companions to wait here. Then I went out into the open first.

"*Stoy!*" The dreaded command. My instinct took over and my hands shot straight into the air. The Russian guard to my right was about 50 yards away and started walking toward me. The two behind me had not been seen yet. I slowly started backing up, in my mind I knew if I would run, the guard no doubt would use his P.P.S.H. sub-machine gun with its 72 bullets. This was the scariest moment in my whole life, with the exception of the war years in Russia. I expected any moment this guard would open fire. When I was back in the woods I told the man and woman in a subdued voice, "Run! Run to the left, over there!" "Take the carriage," she whispered back at me. With a curse I grabbed it and ran.

We moved as quickly as we could through the woods and stopped about a hundred yards farther down. We would make for the clearing again. This time as I approached the clearing I was more careful. It was only about 10 to 15 yards wide and would make it easier to cross. The woods on the other side represented freedom. I hid behind a tree right at the edge of the clearing and looked for Russians to the right and to the left. I saw two to my left, maybe 60 yards away. They were just lying down in the grass right at the edge of the forest. Good. These *Ivans* were not too wary.

"Keep low, very low!" I instructed my fellow escapees and led them on my knees pulling the carriage behind me. Again I cursed that damn carriage. The man and woman followed me, keeping a close eye on me and not looking to the right or left. Within a few seconds we were on the other side in the trees. This was *Niemandsland* (no mans land). I wanted to yodel out loud, but was thinking keep your head, keep calm and you'll get home alive.

In the last town where I stopped, people told me that if you are caught in no man's land to tell the Russians you wanted to go to the Russian zone. They would figure you were trying to escape from the American zone and send you back. They didn't care which direction you were going, they were just told to keep people from crossing the border.

We stayed down on all fours as we kept crawling closer and closer to the American zone. The trees here were very young, only about ten feet high. "Wait!" I whispered. I could hear someone moving. We held perfectly still. There were two figures, also crawling on their knees, heading in our direction. It was a man and a woman. They saw me, and we eyed each other carefully then crawled to meet each other. They were from the American zone and trying to get to their home in eastern Germany in the Russian zone. I told them the way we had come, about the guards laying in the grass and told them if they were caught to say they wanted to go to the American zone. We continued crawling until the trees started getting taller and then we stood up and almost ran to the edge of the forest and out of no man's land. When we emerged from the trees onto a field we saw Americans. A couple of soldiers were riding in a jeep along a narrow path adjacent to the forest. They saw us but didn't even give us a second look. It was weird. On one side the Russians would shoot you like they were guarding the front line in a war. The *Ammy's* could care less.

It was getting dark by now and we had to find shelter before the curfew. Curfews were taken very seriously in occupied territories at this time. Before long we came to a village and found a schoolhouse. Inside were many refugees so

we joined the crowd and made ourselves at home. It was August 2nd, and I was in the American zone. I allowed myself to
breathe a huge sigh of relief. In my calender I wrote, *"2. August über die Grenze bei Muenchreuth* (2nd of August across
the border near Muenchreuth, Bavaria)."

The next morning I was told to report to the American
authorities as soon as possible if I came from the Russian
Zone. I needed to get authorization papers from them because if I was caught without the right papers it was quite
possible to get sent to a P.O.W. camp for several months. I
hurried to Hof, the largest city in that area, to report to the
authorities. I found the compound where the occupation forces
command post was and joined a small group of other ex-soldiers waiting outside a fenced area. A guard motioned for us
to enter a small room where we were instructed to remove
our shirts. Here they lifted our arms, checking carefully for
the S.S. tattoo that would mark our membership in this military unit. I had none, and in one hour had my papers allowing me to roam freely in the American zone. I was still over
two hundred miles, as the crow flies, from home, at least three
hundred miles by road or rail. To get home I had to enter the
French occupation zone. They were not quite so gracious to
ex-enemy soldiers. It was their policy to send them to P.O.W.
camps in France for two years for reconstruction, rather than
let them simply go home. My troubles were not yet over.

In the American zone passenger trains were reserved for
the *Ammy*'s, a name which was always used by the local population. If you wanted to use the rail you had to go in freight
cars. I was eager to be on my way so that night jumped on a
train and settled into the coal tender, turned, facing backwards and pulled my army jacket over my bald head. I kept
this jacket for many years, it had all kinds of burn marks
from the coal sparks. I was an experienced beggar by now,
and in the morning whenever the train stopped I made my
way to farm houses to gather my meal for the day. I was
becoming blacker and blacker from my close acquaintance with
the black, greasy coal.

August 5th I arrived in Munich and headed for the
*Bahnhof*Restaurant. I'm not certain if I had been given some
money while begging or if I was just going to see what nourishment I could find. My head was shaven to the skin, my

clothes were tattered and filthy. I had hardly slept in a bed since leaving the hospital in Schönberg ,and my face was covered with coal dust, so I looked almost African except for the white creases around my eyes. In other words, I was no doubt a sight. But I had no awareness of this as I sat down in the big Restaurant in Munich. I didn't look into a mirror since I left the hospital in Schönberg. Before long a waiter brought a beer on a tray and set it down in front of me. He pointed at another table telling me the people there had paid for it. I looked over at them, but they quickly looked away. Then I looked around the restaurant and began to realize that many were looking at me,but no one would meet my gaze. They all turned quickly away. Perhaps I was a frightening bit of reality brought into their lives of what warfare was really like. Maybe I reminded them of what had been revealed to them about the activities of Dachau's concentration camp, literally just a few miles from where I was now sitting.

Passenger trains from Munich were now running regularly, and after my beer I boarded the train headed for Garmisch. My excitement was growing. Garmisch is a famous tourist town in the Bavarian Alps, and it would be the last major stop before coming to the Austrian border. About halfway to Garmisch I had to get off the train at Tutzing. It was getting dark, and that meant curfew. I got off the train and headed for a hotel nearby to ask them if they knew a place I could stay for the night. I wasn't asking and certainly wasn't expecting a room, maybe a shed or a cellar. Instead they invited me warmly in and told me I could have one of their rooms, a bath and a meal. A bath! I'd almost forgotten about such things. I couldn't believe my good fortune. The world was definitely turning into a more friendly place to be.

I finally soaked off all the coal dust and weeks of dirt that I had accumulated crossing all of Germany from the Baltic Sea in the North to the border of Austria in the South. I was getting close to home and wanted to be somewhat presentable. In the morning I boarded a train to Garmisch where I had to check in with the *Ammys'* MPs at the railway station and show my papers. I remember there were two guys, they looked like giants. I had to look up to them, and they somewhat stared at me. Then I got back on the train for the few minutes ride to the village of Mittenwald. The German rail ended here. It was the end of the line. The Austrian border was just a walk of about three miles.

It was near evening when I approached the border and was thinking about the French soldiers but was not really afraid of them knowing they were nothing like the Russians. Still, I didn't want to be foolish. I certainly didn't want them to pack me up and ship me off to France for a couple of years reconstruction. I was sitting on a big boulder by the side of the highway when a couple, a man and woman, came up to me walking very quickly. "Guten Tag," I said. "Are you a *Heimkehrer?*" They wanted to know if I was going home from the war to Austria. *"Ja,"* I said hopefully. Perhaps they could help. "What is your name?" they asked. "Franz Gabl from St. Anton," I answered. "Do you know Pepi Gabl?" *"Ja*, he is my brother."

They had become acquainted with my brother from skiing. Now they were employed in the business of helping German families who had been booted out of Austria by the French to recover their lost property. Many Germans had moved to Austria following the *Anschluss*. But the French occupiers decided they should go back to Germany, so they were told to leave but were not allowed to take any of their possessions with them except what they could carry. Smugglers, such as this couple, were hired by the Germans to recover their goods and carry them illegally across the border. It was a risky but very profitable business. And the best part of it was, they were accustomed to avoiding the French guards who were patrolling the frontier.

It was dusk when we were nearing the border at Scharnitz before crossing into Austria. Again, my excitement was running high. Austria! Almost home. But it was dangerous business. We were in rugged Alp country with steep cliffs. There was an old Roman wall up the hillside with an opening towards the town of Scharnitz. This was an ancient passageway through the Alps. It guarded the village in old times where travellers had to pay toll, and to get through it we had to find one of the openings that used to be places for the wooden gates. It was dark by now and I was following them as best I could along a narrow rock ledge that overlooked the valley below. They were very familiar with the territory but moving this quickly on treacherous and unknown trails was scary to say the least. I'm sure I kicked down a rock or two which made noise as it clattered down the steep cliffs into the valley. French guards below on the highway must have heard a noise and immediately started shooting. I hadn't counted on this. Perhaps they were shooting in the air. I am sure they had not seen us because it was pitch dark. One can never tell for sure with the French. My partners scattered instantly like chamois and were gone.

There I sat all alone crouched behind a narrow rock ledge. Down below me were men with guns who didn't seem to have a problem using them. Also down below was a hard valley floor that would be quite unforgiving should I make a wrong step and fall off the cliff. Ahead was an unknown trail. And it was very dark. Very slowly and cautiously I made my way forward. There was no bright moon to light my way. I crossed over several more stone ledges and gradually began working my way down to the valley floor. Finally, after midnight, I was there and stumbled across a farmhouse near the edge of the forest. I knocked on the door. An old woman came to the door and informed me very directly that she had no interest whatsoever in harboring German soldiers. I was still wearing my army jacket, so she figured that I must have escaped from a prison camp. Welcome to Austria. Not that I really blamed her. There were severe penalties for getting caught with German soldiers in your house at this time. But I kept arguing the point, pleading with her to give me some shelter for the night. After a while her husband appeared and he seemed a bit more reasonable.

"Come in," he said gruffly, and I stepped into the farm house. "What will you have to eat?" the woman said begrudgingly. Now that I was a guest in her house the Austrian habits of hospitality took over. The man knew my father. He was also a painter and the two had talked together often. I was given some bread, some *Speck* (smoked bacon) and then told to sleep in the hay barn. They didn't want trouble if the French came looking for me and searched the house.

I climbed high into the hay and went to sleep. Anyway, my journey was almost over. The next morning when I woke up my legs felt lame and I couldn't move. I was sweating, water running down my face. I knew what it was: Malaria, just like I had in Russia. I called down from the hay to the

farmer. Soon he came up to see what it was all about. He
went back in the house and brought me some pills. I dozed
off again and about noon woke up feeling better. Shakily I
got up and went to join them in the house. The man went out
and hitched his wagon to the only mode of locomotion available to him—his milk cow. He told me to get on the wagon
and we would go to the railroad station looking to the French
like we were just a farmer and his son heading to the hayfields.

An hour later I boarded the train to Innsbruck. Now this
was definitely familiar territory. St. Anton was just a couple
hours on the train. Still, I was very wary of the French. That
old feeling came back—don't let something happen to me this
close to home. I got off the *Westbahnhof*(west train station).
On the train I had been told that the French soldiers were
checking I.D.'s. on the *Hauptbahnhof*(main train station),
and I had no I.D. from the French. I then caught a train to St.
Anton and started to relax. Everything was familiar now.
My heart was near to bursting. I was going to make it after
all. On the train I saw a very familiar face; it was Maria, the
sister of our neighbor Louise. I said to her "*Grüss Gott*, Maria."
She looked at me, and looked, then asked, Who are you?" I
then said, "Don't you know me?" As soon as I opened my
mouth she knew who I was.

About six in the evening on August 7,1945, I got off the
train at the familiar little station at St. Anton. I stood and
just stared at the Galzig. It glistened in the August warmth,
reminding me of all the joy I had felt on her slippery sides
and would find there again. Yes, there was nothing like it in
all the world. I gazed around at the mountain meadows now
blossoming with the favorite alpine flowers and with the black-
berries and blueberries just ripening for the harvest.

I started down the street toward my home. The first familiar face I saw was Karl Seeberger, an old school friend. I
called across the street, "*Servus* Karl." He looked over to me
and called, "Who are you?" "Don't you know me?" I questioned. "*Na.*" Then I called over to him, "*s' Gabl's Franz.*"
"*Na*, really is that you?" I didn't want to start a conversation
on the street. I needn't have worried. No one recognized me.
Several towns people I knew passed me, but I didn't want to
stop, so I walked as fast as my legs carried me and dropped in
at my sister Kathi's apartment. The hotel bath had taken

much of the black away, but I looked every bit the tattered, beaten hobo. Then I went to house Nr. 14. I stood on the threshold of the kitchen door, not saying a word. Hilda, my youngest sister, was sitting at the table looking at this stranger. Then she said *"Oetz, wer bischt du (*who are you)?" My head was shaven because all Russian soldiers and German prisoners had the hair cut to the skin. "Franz! Franz!" she said, and immediately I was in a warm, familiar hug. She at once asked, "What would you like to eat?"

My family had not heard from me since January 1945 when the big Russian push was on and I was deep in Poland. All mail had stopped since then. They had no reason to believe I was alive, and they certainly had no inkling that I was coming home. My mother was in Bludenz visiting her sister Maria that day. Sixteen years earlier, when she arrived on the same 6:30 train, she was told that Franz has both legs off. This time no one knew that her son Franz was already home. She came home to one of the biggest and happiest surprises in her life. "Franz," she said, laughing and crying at the same time. "My Franz!' Turning to the others as if she was telling them the news, she said, "Franz is home!" and she asked me, "What will you have to eat?" I gave her a gift of silk stockings given to me by the woman whose baby carriage of personal belongings I had dragged across the Russian border.

My father came home a little later, shook my hand solemnly in the Austrian fashion, and we sat down to one of the most enjoyable suppers of my life. I asked about my brothers. Karl was in a French P.O.W. camp in Landeck not far from home. He was to come home in November. Nobody had heard from Pepi. There was no mail service from any nation except within Austria. We didn't know if he was dead or alive, but I felt confident that he would come through.

On December 20th someone told us they heard Pepi was on his way home. Our home did not have a phone at that time. We were afraid to believe it was true. On December 22nd he walked in, unannounced. He had been in an English P.O.W. camp near the Danish border, not far from where I had been before being turned over to the Russians. He told us the story. On May 8th, his unit of *Luftwaffe* fighters were on the Russian front. Their commander assembled all his men from the fighter wing and in a somber tone said, "*Kameraden,* the war is over. Germany has surrendered unconditionally to the Allies. You must not be ashamed, you have done your duty with honor, but now your oath to our *Führer* does not bind you anymore. He died fighting with his soldiers in Berlin, and now you are free to go and fly anywhere you choose. I would suggest you either fly to neutral Sweden, but there is a chance that Sweden might turn you over to the Russians, because they had requested it, or better fly to Denmark where the English have now occupied that country." With the Hitler *salut* they parted and all of them flew to Copenhagen, Denmark. Of course there was not a single man willing to surrender to the Russians. When they approached the airport in Copenhagen, they were to tip the wings back and forth so as to let the British air force know they were giving up.

Christmas 1945 was a great celebration. Though we were in poverty, we were once again together as a family. All three boys in our family who went to war had returned safe and in one piece. We celebrated our blessings and started to have hope for what life might bring.

Our villages of St. Anton and St. Jakob took a terrible toll in this war. With a population of 1,000 one has only to read the names in the cemetery chapel which were carved into a stucco wall by one of my father's employees Fritz Berger of Innsbruck, whose left eye and right arm is now fertilizing the Russian Steppe. Fifty-six were killed with 22 still missing, and one of two Jewish men, Rudolf Gomperz, the genius who put St. Anton and Hannes Schneider on the world map as a ski resort, was supposed to have died in a concentration camp in Poland or White Russia.

On the next page you can read the cost in lives and miseries brought to the Russian and the German peoples, not to mention to another 50 or more nations. This was Hitler's **legacy**, and there are still now many who say that Hitler was a great man!

War to men is what childbirth is to women!
Benito Mussolini

Table E. Wehrmacht Casualties in World War II, 1939–1945

Permanent Losses
(dead, missing, or disabled)

Sept. 1939–1 Sept. 1942	922,000 (14% of total force)*
1 Sept. 1942–20 Nov. 1943	2,077,000 (30% of total force)*
20 Nov. 1943–June 1944	1,500,000 (est.)
June–Nov. 1944	1,457,000*
Dec. 1944–30 April 1945	2,000,000**

Losses

Total to 30 April 1945	11,135,800 (including 6,035,000 wounded)**
Total armed forces losses to war's end	13,448,000, including wounded (75% of mobilized force and 46% of 1939 male population)**

Krivosheev, 391, places the Eastern Front losses of Germany's allies at 1,725,800, broken down as follows:

Nation	Dead and Missing	POWs	Total
Hungary	350,000	513,700	863,700
Italy	45,000	48,900	93,900
Rumania	480,000	201,800	681,800
Finland	84,000	2,400	86,400
Total	959,000	766,800	1,725,800

Krivosheev, 392, cites Soviet POW figures and deaths (in Soviet captivity) as follows:

Germany	2,389,600	450,600
Austria	156,000	N/A
Hungary	513,700	54,700
Rumania	201,800	40,000
Italy	48,975	N/A
Finland	2,400	N/A
Others (French, Czech, Slovak, Belgium, and Spanish in SS and auxilliary formations)	464,147	N/A
Total	3,777,290	

Sources:
*Earl F. Ziemke, *From Stalingrad to Berlin: The German Defeat in the East* (Washington D.C., U.S. Army Center of Military History, 1968), 213–214, 412.
**G. F. Krivosheev, *Grif sekretnosti sniat: Poteri vooruzhennykh sil SSSR v voinakh, boevykh deistviiakh i voennykh konfliktakh* [Losses of the armed forces of the USSR in wars, combat actions, and military conflicts] (Moscow: Voenizdat, 1993), 384–392, places German dead at 3,888,000 and POWs (including Austrians, SS, and foreign auxiliaries in the German Army) at 3,035,700.

Table A. Red Army Personnel Losses, 22 June 1941–9 May 1945

	RED ARMY PERSONNEL LOSSES			
Period	Average Strength (monthly)	Killed or Missing	Wounded and Sick	Total
1941, 3d Quarter	3,334,000	2,067,801	676,964	2,744,765
1941, 4th Quarter	2,818,500	926,002	637,327	1,563,329
Yearly Total	3,024,900	2,993,803	1,314,291	4,308,094
1942, 1st Quarter	4,186,000	619,167	1,172,274	1,791,441
1942, 2d Quarter	5,060,300	776,578	702,150	1,478,728
1942, 3d Quarter	5,664,600	1,141,991	1,276,810	2,418,801
1942, 4th Quarter	6,343,600	455,800	936,031	1,391,831
Yearly Total	5,313,600	2,993,536	4,087,265	7,080,801
1943, 1st Quarter	5,892,800	656,403	1,421,140	2,077,543
1943, 2d Quarter	6,459,800	125,172	471,724	596,896
1943, 3d Quarter	6,816,800	694,465	2,053,492	2,747,957
1943, 4th Quarter	6,387,200	501,087	1,560,164	2,061,251
Yearly Total	6,389,200	1,977,127	5,506,520	7,483,647
1944, 1st Quarter	6,268,600	470,392	1,565,431	2,035,823
1944, 2d Quarter	6,447,000	251,745	956,828	1,208,573
1944, 3d Quarter	6,714,300	430,432	1,541,965	1,972,397
1944, 4th Quarter	6,770,100	259,766	1,026,645	1,286,411
Yearly Total	6,550,000	1,412,335	5,090,869	6,503,204
1945, 1st Quarter	6,461,100	468,407	1,582,517	2,050,924
1945, 2d Quarter	6,135,300	163,226	609,231	772,457
Yearly Total	6,330,880	631,633	2,191,748	2,823,381
Wartime Totals		10,008,434	18,190,693	28,199,127

Total Armed Forces Losses by Category

	Number (%)
Irrevocable	
Killed in battle or died during evacuation	5,187,190 (17.5)
Died of wounds in hospital	1,100,327 (3.7)
Died of illness (nonbattle)	541,920 (1.8)
Missing in action or captured	4,455,620 (15.1)
Total	11,285,057 (38.1)
Sanitary	
Wounded	15,205,592 (51.3)
Sick	3,047,675 (10.3)
Frostbitten	90,881 (0.3)
Total	18,344,148 (61.9)
Total armed forces losses	29,629,205

Note: Red Army personnel losses include those of the air force.

Back from the War for Good

At the end of 1945, I started my second life. It was a life I didn't really expect to have. Too many times in the past four years I had clearly understood that it was not reasonable to expect to live through this war, let alone have a healthy, happy life beyond it. After all the comrades I had left behind in the Russian steppe, some buried, the birch cross decorating their graves, many just being left on open ground and many blown to bits. Now it was up to me to enjoy it. I felt I owed that much to Herman, Franz, Konrad, Herbst, Wensky, Wagner, Jenewein and on and on.

Still, life was hardly like the pre-1938 days in St. Anton. At first I feared the French occupation forces would catch up with me and still send me off to France for two years of reconstruction to make me pay for what our army destroyed in their country. Fortunately, Willy Schaeffler, who was actually from Germany, and was also a well known ski racer came to my assistance. We both had competed in some of the same races years ago and knew each other. He was a leader of the anti-Nazi resistance in St. Anton during the last few months of the war and because of this was well known and trusted by the French occupation forces. Willy offered to accompany me to the French commander to plead my case. I gladly accepted his generous help. The French questioned me thoroughly, asking for a complete explanation of the units I served in and my activities during the war and checked if I had the S.S. tattoo under my left arm, which would have given me away as having belonged to that organization. I had none. Willy helped point out my numerous war wounds, twelve of them. That was enough for them, so they decided I had suffered enough and gave me my unconditional release. The last burden was lifted; now I knew I was home for good.

The second problem was hunger. It is hard to imagine and even harder to describe the conditions in the war ravaged countries at that time. A meal in a restaurant, if you could get one, cost almost a week's ration card. In spite of strict laws, every one participated in the black market in one form or another. This included policemen, farmers and regular townspeople. Survival was the name of this game, and survival meant working hard or being a smart trader to make sure you had some food in your belly, daily.

We were quite lucky in our family. We had three cows, several goats, pigs and chickens. We delivered our fair share and then some to the local distribution center for the authorities to dole out to those with ration cards, but we still had enough for our extended family. By now, in addition to my brothers and sisters, my parents also had several grandchildren. My mother was exceptionally generous. Knowing, a mother's love for a child or grandchild knows no bounds. Often my father's employees would board with us when no one else would take them. Because with the ration cards, the homes who took in our boarders, would hardly have enough food for them to get the necessary calories, so there would be even more mouths to feed.

Trading was the normal business of every day. Money was worthless except for items one could buy with coupons. If you wanted something, you had to find something that someone else wanted and trade for it. At times you had to go through several complicated trades to get the item you wanted. To get real coffee, not roasted barley, you might have to trade butter for sugar, sugar for bacon and finally bacon for coffee. The currency of the day was butter and cigarettes. One French cigarette was worth one hour of labor; one American cigarette was worth two hours. A kilogram of butter could be purchased with one month's wages, that is, on the black market, though with a coupon it was only about two hours of wages.

Once I traded a pair of *Lederhosen* (short, leather, Austrian pants) to a French soldier. I was astonished when he gave me 700 *Uman* (French) cigarettes. My mind flashed back to the incident in Poland in 1941 when German soldiers were trading with Polish Jews and taking their blankets and other goods from them after the exchange. I half expected him to demand the cigarettes back. But he didn't. What a deal, I earned the equivalent of 700 hours of labor for one pair of leather pants! Perhaps the man was new to Austria.

Because I was a *Heimkehrer* (war returnee) I was entitled to receive enough material for one suit. Of course I had to buy it. After I managed to locate the material which took me several months, I then had to wait several more months for the tailor to make it, who made it clear he was only doing this out of the goodness of his heart. To get a toothbrush required a prescription from a doctor, then take that to city hall for a coupon, then try and find a store that still had a toothbrush for sale.

Life in the cities was particularly hard. Many families sold furniture, art objects and personal belongings of high sentimental value just to get enough money to buy food on the black market that was sold at 100 times the coupon value. The rations were ridiculously small. The allowance for one person for one month was eight pounds of bread, one pound of meat and one pound of fat. Potatoes, vegetables were only available sporadically. To get anything not on coupons, housewives would have to stand in line for hours and hours, and even then would find the door closing in their faces as the merchant ran out of his small allotment. Needless to say, there were not many obese people walking the streets of Vienna, or St. Anton for that matter, in those days.

Another thing that changed was, when it came to attending church on Sundays. Before the war, almost all the local people would go to Sunday mass, and nobody would stay outside the church. But now, it was common that many younger men, many ex-soldiers, would stay outside while mass was held inside and discuss the problems at hand. It seemed as if these men lost some of the belief in a higher being. Then, every once in a while someone, who was still a strict catholic, would quickly open the large back door of the church from the inside, all these men would now scramble to enter the church through the two small side doors. It didn't deter any, and the same would happen the next Sunday.

In small towns in Austria there were some customs observed for centuries. One of them was *Katzen Musik* (cat music). It meant, if a young couple was seen together frequently arm in arm going to church on Sundays, going to the dances Sunday night, as if they were engaged, and then suddenly broke up, the man was then subject to cat music. The young men in town would then organize a hilarious procession to this man's home. It was all very secretly organized. On that particular evening, one was sent to be the spy and

made sure that this man was home. At the place of assembly
in town, each was to bring a noise maker, there were pans
and ladles, musical instruments, which of course used all the
wrong notes, also a thrashing machine pulled by horses and
many more. About seven in the evening this column started
to march through town to this man's home. Everyone was
crying and calling the girl's name. You might say, it was a
riot. When this procession arrived at this man's home, he
would come out and show himself. He was required then to
take now the whole group to the nearest beer parlor and pay
for a round.

My spirit was far from complaining, however. I sucked
life in like someone who had been buried alive and survived.
Everything was precious to me. The beautiful autumn
weather, the haying in our own meadows and harvesting the
potatoes and barley, hiking in the alpine meadows and above
all berry picking on steep mountain sides in the fall when all
the leaves turned to beautiful colors and some of the high
mountain tops sported white snow caps. I could feel the pain
of the war experience begin to be washed from me. I was
being revived, slowly, gently as the flakes quietly fell to begin
covering my favorite ski runs, especially the Galzig.

Snow meant one thing above all—skiing. Early in December, at the very start of the ski season I had in mind to
head for the cable car and get to the top of the Galzig for the
first skiable snow. I found just one pair of skis in the attic at
home, however, an old hickory pair. They were warped beyond use. I remember very well that when I was home from
my sick leave in September 1944 after I was discharged from
the hospital in Goslar, Germany, and had my papers to report in Buedingen for transport to the Russian front, I sold
my 210 cm Hofbauer skis with which I had won many races
and also my accordion which I bought in 1939, knowing full
well that the war could not be won, and I would never return.
Fortunately, Walter Schuler, the owner of the Hotel Post,
kindly let me borrow a pair from the hotel's stock. They were
205 cm Sertorelli hickory skis, made in Italy, but never mind,
they worked.

I really wasn't certain my body was up to the challenge of
skiing. I feared especially for my knee since it had locked on
me so painfully on the desperate march to escape an encircle-

ment in Russia in October 1943. Then there was the fact that without the nourishment I needed, I still hadn't fully recovered from the infection that nearly killed me in the spring. But, I wasn't going to waste any time finding out. If there was a way I could ski, I was going to do it or I'd die trying.

The ski racers now were the young boys who were too young for the war. They had spent the war years practicing while we had been spilling our blood in Russia. Frequently I trained with them and often came home discouraged. Had they gotten that good, or had I lost everything I had worked so hard for before the war?

My brother Pepi came home at Christmas and almost immediately we hit the slopes together. I told him that I was afraid I had lost my skill and wouldn't be able to race again. "I've been watching you, Franz," Pepi said seriously. "You're afraid. You're not pushing yourself."

The lights went on just like when the movie director told me to just let myself go and not be afraid of the landing when I was ski jumping over the castle wall at Ladis. Yes, I would let myself go, and more than that, I would push myself harder than ever. This was the best advice I could have.

Our first halfway-serious races were with our French occupiers. They had taken over all the hotels for their headquarters. The men stationed in the Tyrol were mountain troops and many were ski racers. Some of them were even on the French National Ski Team. They did not seem to be particularly unhappy to be stationed in our little village. They would challenge some of us to race. They usually won which we credited to their vastly superior equipment and to some degree on their food.

That first winter at home, December 1945 to April 1946, I worked once again for the St. Anton Ski School. A ski team was formed to enter into the races around Tyrol, but we went to few of them. To go would mean using up precious food coupons to eat in restaurants, and that would mean going without them for the rest of the time. It was just too expensive.

Spring 1946 saw me standing on top of the famous *Hahnenkamm* (Rooster Comb) downhill course in Kitzbühel. Life is strange. It was the Tyrolean Championships and it would be my first real test, my first opportunity to see how I would stand up to the competition. I was disappointed to find that I was put in class II with my two ski club buddies Robert Falch and Edi Mall. The racers were divided into two classes, the first being for the elite racers and the second for those not expected to place.

While disappointed I also understood it. In 1940 I would have been in class I. But that was over five years ago. A lot of young new talent was on the scene. Downhill racing was considerably different in those days. There were few gates to slow you down. The risks you took were controlled by yourself much more than by the course. The downhill was two miles long with a vertical drop of 2,400 feet. The slalom, on Ganslern Hill just above Kitzbühel, was also challenging, nearly 60 gates with a vertical drop of over 700 feet.

My heart was pounding as I entered the starting gate for the famous *Hahnenkamm* race. But now it was with as much joy as excitement. There were thousands of spectators below on the hill. I was an unknown, a vague name from the past for this crowd. "Five, four, three, two, one, go!" My second skiing career was underway. I won the class II downhill and slalom races with ease. And my times were good enough to place me third among all racers. I would never ski in class II again.

On Sunday was the slalom on Ganslern hill. In both my two runs I was near the top finishers. After the race several people came up to me to talk about my revolutionary new technique. "What technique?" I asked innocently. I didn't know what they were talking about. "The shoulders, how you turn your shoulders when going into a turn."

After a bit I figured out what they were talking about. A month before I joined the bicycle battalion in Volders in May 1941, I broke my shoulder in a race in Zuers. I crashed into a giant slalom pole which was very solid. They were rigid poles in those days. The pain it caused me created a long memory and a strong desire to avoid cutting the corners too close and hitting my shoulder again. But if I didn't cut the corners close, my times would be off, so I developed a habit of turning my upper torso 90 degrees away from the turn of my skis, putting my back parallel to the direction I was going, and slipping the shoulder past the slalom pole. I wasn't even aware of what I was doing, but when I saw photos of my slalom runs in the newspapers it became obvious that my technique was different from all the other racers. This became then known as the "extreme reverse shoulder technique," and I was amused to find my name connected to this technique in several ski manuals since the year 1946. This, then, is how the great innovations in sports are created, by the instinct of someone who doesn't want to make the same painful mistake twice. When slalom poles became flexible this technique was obviously no longer needed.

Once again I was a celebrity of sorts in my hometown. But the ski season was soon over and it was back to painting, haying, hiking and berry picking in the fall. The routines of normal life were once again becoming comfortable, maybe even humdrum.

I'm not sure if I had become accustomed to living life a little closer to the edge or if during the summer I just longed for the excitement I found in racing, but in the summer of 1946 I began to take a strong interest in mountain climbing and steel my muscles still more. I first was introduced to the thrills that can be found challenging sheer rock walls when my father assigned me to fulfill a painting contract for a mountain hut called *Konstanzer Huette* in the summer of 1937. It was a two -hour hike just to get to the hut. I became friendly with the hut operator Ludwig Tschol. He said that he and a friend of his from a nearby mountain Alp called Seppl, were going to climb the Patteriol. This was a Matterhorn-like peak that towered another 4,000 feet above this already high mountain hut. Of course I said I would go.

We left at 4 a.m. and approached the mountain through a steep chimney. It was nothing but steep rock. One scrambled for toe holds and places to insert your finger tips so you could take one more torturous step upward. Pitons were laughed at as something only flatland sissies would use. Our equipment was limited to special boots for the rock climbing portions and our guts. I was a bit scared, though I trusted Ludwig, and at the same time I was completely hooked.

So that summer after the war I ventured out to find the vertical drops and cracked rocks that would give me the thrills I was seeking. I made several climbs and although each was filled with its own dangers, I kept looking for the greater challenge. In my earlier days I put all my confidence in the skills and good sense of Ludwig Tschol. He was the leader and I trusted him. Now others were putting their trust in me, and I was leading some of the more difficult climbs.

Karl Frei was my regular climbing partner now, and we were climbing that summer with Karl Fahrner and Toni Spiss, both ski racers from St. Anton. The challenge was the Rockspitze. We climbed the difficult, almost perpendicular front face and decided to go back down the easier backside. We had to cross a steep ice field to shorten our route on the way down. We didn't have ice axes or crampons, so I picked up a sharp rock for each hand to use as simple ice axe if I should slide. The ice field was less then the length of a football field, at the bottom was a narrow strip of gravel and below that, nothing. A sheer drop off for about 600 feet. Carefully I led our group onto the steep, slick ice. My feet slipped and I started to slide. Desperately I dug my stones into the ice, yelling, "Karl! Karl!" There was time to think as I picked up more and more speed, slipping and sliding toward the abyss.

"Pity," I thought. "Live through four years of Russian hell and die on this mountain." I dug my stones in as hard as I could. My hands were numb, raw and bleeding from the scraping the imbedded stones in the ice. My one chance, I knew, was to land feet first on the gravel and hope there was enough space to stop me. I kept my nerve and kept thinking. Feet first. Dig the feet in. Suddenly the ice ended and I landed feet first on the gravel strip. I stopped a bare two feet from the edge of the cliff. I lay there for a time, letting the trembling out of my knees. Not only in Russia does one need luck.

Of course, that didn't keep me off the mountains. Karl Frei and I now became steady climbing partners. His previous partner was Herman Buhl, but Herman was always pushing a little farther, a little faster than Karl was comfortable with. Herman was soon to earn fame as one of the greatest climbers of his day, well known for incredible and dangerous climbs. Karl and I were more in the same league and while not as spectacular as Herman, we weren't afraid to take our chances.

In November of 1946, I was invited to join the Austrian national ski team squad. This was a direct result of the success I enjoyed on the *Hahnenkamm* course earlier that year.

Training was to take place on the Stubai Glacier just south of Innsbruck. The snow was deep which excited us; the more snow the better we thought. But there were no lifts, so to get to our runs we had to hike. The first day we climbed the steep slalom run eight times through the soft, fresh snow. The second day we had the strength only for three climbs. By the third day we could hardly make it twice. It wasn't so much that we were in bad shape; after all, I had conditioned my body during the summer with high meadow haying and those rugged rock climbs. It was more the food, or lack of it, that weakened us. It just wasn't enough nourishment to give us the strength for all those climbs even though it was all our ski association could afford at the time. After three days we were sent home to build up our strength and mom's cooking.

I was also hampered by the lack of good skis. My practice skis were warped, and I had to borrow skis whenever I raced. The borrowed skis were barely adequate. Hickory racing skis, used by the victorious nations after the war, were not available in Austria. Hickory came from the U.S., and Austria had no credit with the U.S.

By springtime I was getting discouraged. I thought maybe the war had taken too much out of me. Maybe I was getting too old and tired for this; after all I was 25 years old. But the words of Pepi formed a question mark in my mind: maybe I just wasn't trying hard enough. I worked harder, practiced longer and pushed myself further than anyone else. The desire was definitely there.

During the 1946–47 season I also had the opportunity to coach the Belgian and Czechoslovakian national ski teams. The Belgians, of course, had no ski resorts in their own country, so they came to St. Anton for training. It was the rich, young people who were the skiers and frankly, they were a little less than serious about gaining fame on the course and they lacked experience. Enjoying the apre's ski life was a primary concern. At five p.m. the Hotel Post bar would be filled with skiers and racers for the famous five o'clock tea and dance.

There was a large group of skiers from Czechoslovakia, and I remember them as some of the most congenial racers I ever had the privilege to coach. Since they were victors in war they seemed to have plenty of food which they brought

with them from their home country. They offered to pay me
with food rather than money and I gladly accepted. They
were still a free and democratic country at that time, not falling to the Communist regime until 1948. Racers like Antonin
Sponar, Lubo Brchl, and Sasha Neckvapilova were already
well known ski racers internationally at that time.

In 1948 they competed for their now Communist nation
in the Olympics, but some did not return home. Sponar and
Neckvapilova emigrated to Australia to build ski chalets in
ski resorts down under.

The Hungarian team also came to storm the Galzig. Unlike us Austrians, skiing was relatively new to them and they
weren't born with skis on their feet, so they couldn't match us
in skill. On their highest mountain one could hardly set a
slalom course. But they improved rapidly and we enjoyed
getting to know them.

During the winter we had been very delighted to find a
special gift waiting for us at the ski school. Hannes Schneider,
still living in North Conway, New Hampshire, had kindly sent
several pairs of seven-foot hickory skis, made by the Northland
Manufacturing Company, to us racers of the Ski Club Arlberg.
It was good to know his heart was still with us St. Anton
boys, and it was very good to have some equipment that put
us on better footing with many of the other skiers.

The eyes of all of us on the national squad were being
focused more and more on the Winter Olympics in St. Moritz
in 1948. The beautiful Swiss ski resort would be the site of
the V Olympic Winter Games, and we were all hoping for a
chance to compete before the world for Austria. In spite of all
the disadvantages of being ravaged by the war, we felt we
had a chance of competing well against the top skiers of the
world, and we were all dreaming continually of being the ones
to bring fame and renown to our suffering country.

We were thrilled when we found out our team was invited
to compete in the Arlberg Kandahar race in Muerren, Switzerland. This famous race was originated on the Galzig above
St. Anton in 1928, but because the founder, Sir Arnold Lunn
of Great Britain, had a home in Muerren and lived there part
of the year, the race location alternated every other year between St. Anton and Muerren. We were going to Switzerland. It's hard to explain our excitement because after all,

the neighboring country was only 24 miles from my home. But I had never been there. After the war Switzerland was viewed as the land of milk and honey since it didn't have any of the shortages that were starving our people. We heard many stories about the full shops and especially all the chocolate. Chocolate! The closest I had gotten to the delightful stuff in five years was when we were quartered in a wrecked chocolate factory in 1941 in Kiev. But then the chocolate was all gone.

Switzerland was a fantasy land, and now we were going there. Before we boarded the train I scrounged as many Swiss Francs as I could beg or borrow from family and friends. When we crossed the border we jumped off the train at the first stop in Buchs and literally stormed the Bahnhof Delicatessen like it was a full fledged infantry attack. We bought enough chocolate to last us for days. Unfortunately, it was gone by the time we arrived in Muerren.

The people in Switzerland at that time always called us *die arma Österricher* (those poor Austrians). Our poverty and deprivation was well known, and the Swiss were very generous to us. They seemed to understand very well that just across the border from them, people were going to bed hun-

Josef and Kreszenz Gabl with their children Karl, Maria, Hedwig, Kathi, Pepi, Franz and Hilda, 1947.

gry every night and they seemed determined to use us as representatives of their generous natures. We appreciated and accepted it.

For several years after the war the good Swiss people offered to take many thousands of children from Vienna to their private homes in Switzerland knowing full well that many would not survive in Vienna. They not only fed them, they clothed and they spoiled them with chocolate, I am sure.

The food and chocolate were my best memories from the Kandahar race in Muerren. The snow was deep and unpacked. In the downhill run we were racing in two or more feet of powder. Near the bottom of my run my skis got stuck in a snow drift, and I had to get help from a spectator to pull me out. Not exactly a glorious finish. I ended up 41st which was bad news since the first 40 racers go on to race in the slalom for the alpine combined. It was the first time in my life that I failed to qualify for the slalom. I didn't mind it one bit. Chocolate, chocolate was the reason.

After the ski season in the late spring of 1947 I returned once more to my father's painting business. The painting aggravated a pain in my shoulder, and I finally went to the doctor. An X-ray revealed a piece of shrapnel from the tank blast in March 1945 outside Danzig was still stuck in the shoulder. I cursed that damned officer once again who ordered me to shoot the machine gun even though it was pointless and would just give away our position. But also, he might have saved me from a P.O.W. camp in Siberia! An operation was required to remove it. The doctor suggested I apply for invalid status with the government. I thought it was a joke since I had heard you practically had to come to them carrying your head under your arm if you wanted to be considered an invalid. Since I was spending a good deal of time on the downhill race course I didn't think I'd have much of a chance. Apparently the government felt otherwise after reviewing my records. In a few months I was declared a war invalid and given a government stipend of 22.50 Austrian *Schillings* per month. The *Schillings* were hardly a big deal. I had 3,000 German *Marks* in my savings account from my military salary which in prewar value I could have bought three brand new Volkswagens which were selling for 998.00 marks each, in 1938. Now my 3,000 marks would buy me one ski boot. Not a pair, just one.

Invalid status papers issued to Franz Gabl in January 1948.

The 22.50 *Schillings* were hardly worth putting in my pocket. I could buy one American cigarette and would have 2.50 *Schillings* left. However, as an invalid I could receive medical care for my wounds and illnesses related to the war so that was worth something.

Years later, when I stayed in the U.S. after the F.I.S. in Aspen in 1950, I was still getting my invalid stipend of 22.50 *Schillings* per month which my mother kept for me. The Austrian government decided then that I didn't deserve this, because I was now residing in USA, and they threatened to jail my mother for it. So much for the Austrian generosity! Didn't Austria vote overwhelmingly—97%—for *Anschluss* and therefore take responsibility for the harm to Austrian citizens? *"Soldaten, der Dank des Vaterlandes ist Euch gewiss*(Soldiers, the fatherland's thanks is assured you)." These words I had heard hundreds of times from veterans of the first world war and seen the blind cripples sitting on a pillow on the side of the street, hat in hand, a dog barking each time some samaritan threw a nickel or other money into it.

When I thought skiing was over for the year and I was getting settled into the painting business for the summer, I got a call from the Tyrolean Ski Association. Would I race in the annual Gross Glockner Glacier Ski Race? This was a summer race on the glacier on the side of the Gross Glockner, the highest mountain in Austria, a 12,500 foot peak in the Province of Carinthia. It was considered a very tough race and very steep, but with the Olympics coming up soon I wanted to get all the practice I could get and also improve my chances at getting a berth on the team. I had consistently come in the top five in races around Austria, but I knew it wasn't enough to assure me a place on the team, because eight men and six women would represent Austria in the 1948 Olympics. I gladly accepted.

When I boarded the train in the first week of June it was beautiful weather in St. Anton, and I packed summer clothes, but not enough winter skiing clothes, a mistake I would very much regret. The night after we arrived at the Kaiser Franz Josef Haus, the hotel across from the glacier we would race on, a storm blew in from the Mediterranean and brought blizzard conditions to the high mountain. All day Saturday it stormed so I couldn't get out to ski and have a look at the course. Sunday morning, race day, dawned crystal clear to a most beautiful sight. Across the valley the Gross Glockner towered above us, covered with a fresh coating of soft snow.

The *Adlersruhe* (eagle's nest) was a mountain hut not far from the summit and the starting point for the downhill race. Some of the racers had climbed up the day before and stayed overnight to be rested for the race. Those of us who got stuck in the hotel put our skis on our shoulders and started the three- to four-hour hike up in the soft snow in the morning. But there were many thousands of hardy souls who were ahead of us, and we had a well packed trail to follow.

By the time I got to the *Adlersruhe*, over 10,000 feet above sea level, I was tired and very cold. I quickly rubbed some wax onto the bottom of the hickory Northland skis, the gift from Hannes, and got ready for my turn to race. Not that I thought waxing would do much good on this very steep and normally icy run. Unlike most of the others, I had never raced this course before. The favorites were Hans Nogler, Christian Pravda, Hans Senger, Eberhard Kneissl, Herbert Zitterer, the winner in 1946, and others. There were no women as this race was considered too tough and dangerous. Nogler, like some of the others, had raced all during the war since his task had been to stay in Austria and train the Hitler Youth.

I watched Nogler and the others take off. One every minute. Racer after racer. Meanwhile, I was freezing and feeling more and more like I was back in the winter of 1941 in Russia. Then my name was called. Some friends, who were guests in St. Anton for years, handed me a cup of coffee to try to warm me up a bit. I moved stiffly to the gate.

"Three, two, one, go!" I pushed my skis into the deep, soft snow to try to get a fast start. The start of the race was very steep, and soon I just bent into a low crouch to cut down wind resistance and pick up as much speed as possible. The course was long and steep with only a few long direction changes. A speed demon's course definitely. The snow was soft, and I noticed how my seven-foot Northlands were keeping me riding high on the soft, creamy snow. But there were deep tracks from the other racers which made the course dangerous and caused me to nearly fall several times. Still, I kept in my tuck and felt good schussing down that beautiful mountain.

As I came to the lower portion, thousands of spectators along the course were yelling at me. Cheering? No, they seemed to be trying to tell me something? Well, I couldn't stop to ask them what they wanted. Just stay down low, cut wind resistance. The last schuss was especially steep, and now my speed was blinding me. I was really moving and accelerating all the time it seemed. By the time I hit the transition to the finish line I couldn't stay on my feet and slid across the finish line on my behind, biting my tongue in the process.

I stood for a moment, catching my breath. I could hear the crowd was cheering, wildly I thought. People were coming toward me running and gesticulating. I saw Nogler and Pravda who had been first and second. They were just looking at me shaking their heads. I knew my time was good, but when someone told me that I beat Nogler by twelve seconds? In a short downhill that kind of margin is unheard of. My time was 2.12.2 minutes, Nogler's was 2.24.00 and Pravda's 2.24.2 It was like running a three minute mile. Now I found out what the crowd was yelling at me. "Slow down!" they were screaming. They were sure I was going to kill myself.

I was surprised and could hardly believe my time and I felt I had secured a place on the team for the Olympics in St. Moritz. Who is this guy they seemed to wonder. A war invalid. An old has-been. My success, I was sure, was due to two things: first, the skis; they were wider and more flexible than the skis used by some of the other racers, they were designed for the deep snows of the American West. The snow conditions were perfect for them allowing me to ride higher on the soft snow than the ones with stiff skis which were ideal for icy courses. The other reason was my ignorance combined with guts. I had never seen the course before. If I had known in advance how steep and fast it was, no doubt I wouldn't have done all the schussing I did. On the other hand, I just might have. Konrad told me, cowards died just as fast as heroes. That being the case, why not be a hero?

At the awards ceremony, Major Goshen, an officer of the British occupation army in the province of Carinthia, handed me the 16-pound heavy trophy, a shell casing from a 88 mm anti aircraft gun, made into a flower vase. Major Goshen raced himself; it was just fun for him. His time was nearly ten minutes.

When I arrived back in St. Anton the buzz in town was not just my exploits on the Gross Glockner. Hannes was back in town. For the first time since he was arrested by the Nazis nine years earlier, the skiing god had returned to his home. Before the war it was his custom to sit in the lobby of the hotel post with the hotel owner Walter Schuler and almost literally hold court. The tourists from around the world including many of the rich and famous, would come by his table where he was sipping tea or a glass of wine and give a little bow. He would acknowledge them with a nod and perhaps a few words. He was, after all, the most famous ski pioneer and teacher in the whole world. Imagine my surprise and excitement then when I received a note after I returned that Hannes wanted me to visit him at the hotel post.

With excitement and a little awe I walked to the hotel post and entered the lobby. There, he and Walter Schuler sat like the past ten years had not happened. I approached the table, and Hannes saw me and extended his hand to shake mine. To win this man's approval was a goal almost as great as Olympic gold. At least I felt that way that summer day in

1947. My dreams were finally coming true. A few days later Hannes invited me and several other of the young hopeful racers from St. Anton to join him on a hike on the mountain we all dearly loved, the Galzig. In the coming years, Hannes made it a custom to return to St. Anton every fall to engage in his second passion: hunting chamois, elk, deer and marmots.

The ski season of 1947–48 was now upon us. This was the Olympic season. The games were just months away. All the Austrian hopefuls were invited to a two -week training camp at the Zugspitzplatt. The Zugspitze is the highest mountain in Germany and straddles the German-Austrian border near Garmisch on the German side and Ehrwald on the Austrian. We were quartered in the town of Ehrwald and every morning took a cable car up the Austrian side, then walked through a tunnel more then a quarter of a mile long to the German side, emerging at the front of the Zugspitz Hotel. Since we were in Germany, the *Ammy's* (American occupation forces) were in control there. They were running the hotel which was used as a recreation resort for the American soldiers stationed in Bavaria. The man in command was a colonel Ed Link, an avid mountaineer from the 10th Mountain Division. He seemed to have forgiven us for being his enemy a couple of years earlier and was very generous. He and captain Floto who ran the hotel made sure that we received a bowl of hot soup from the hotel every noon. I well remember captain Floto's engaging smile and his enthusiasm for our racing skills. Col. Link made the hotel's rope tow available to us on the ski runs near the hotel. Rope tows were a new innovation to us.

In spite of the hot soup, we again had to cut our training short because of lack of food. We had no lunch from our hotel, and even though our government gave us more than standard rations, it was not enough to keep up with the energy we were burning on the ski course. We became tired and weak and decided to go home and get some more of mom's cooking. It was the last time we would train together as a team until we arrived in St. Moritz.

It was now December and the Olympic team would be selected in January. The Olympics were in February. I wanted more practice so we racers from the Ski Club Arlberg, my brother Pepi, Otto Linher, Othmar Schneider, Herbert Jochum, Sepp Staffler, Edi Mall, Toni Spiss, Karl Fahrner and I organized our own training camp, packing as much food as we could, and headed for a mountain hut above Zuers, just across the Arlberg Pass. There we skied as much and as hard as we could until the food ran out.

Whenever I wasn't racing or training, I continued to teach skiing. One experience reminded me that the world had still not been healed of its diseases of killing. My student was a Swedish diplomat who was stationed in Vienna and came to ski on the Arlberg. I was to be his private instructor. Since there were no helicopters or snowmobiles, the instructor had to carry all the safety and first aid equipment in a packsack on his back. We hiked with sealskins on skis to the *Ulmer Huette,* a hut high above St. Anton, and I was carrying a large packsack filled with equipment. On our way down I stumbled over a hump in the flat light and fell face first into the snow with the packsack on top of me. I was stuck and couldn't get up. It was very embarrassing to be a ski instructor, and well known racer at that, to be lying face down in the snow and needing help from his student. Ever the diplomat, he tried to keep me from seeing that he was laughing inside, he helped me up from the snow and I brushed it off and tried to restore my dignity, and we continued our trip down to St. Anton.

A few weeks later I was very saddened to hear that my gracious student had been shot dead by a Russian patrol on a street in Vienna. I wished I had told him that "the bullets sit loose in the Russian guns." Apparently he drove through a checkpoint without noticing and didn't stop quickly enough when he was told.

On December 29, 1947, I turned 26. The Olympics were a month away. I had two chances to make the team. The men's coach Rudi Matt; he was also our ski school director for the St. Anton ski school and Pepi's and my boss. Theus Schwabl of Kitzbühel was the coach for the women. Two races in early January would determine who would earn the opportunity to race with the world's best and maybe, just maybe, bring honor and fame to St. Anton and Austria. I wanted to be on that team as much as I wanted to breathe. I knew I wouldn't get another chance.

The first race was the Tyrolean championships held in Sölden in the Oetz Valley. All Austrian hopefuls from the mountain provinces were there. We were all issued brand new ski boots with double laces at Christmas time, and I would have to pay a price within a few weeks by not being able to race the slalom in the Olympics because of it. The lining of the boots was very rigid and it rubbed against the ankles, mainly on the outside ones. At one time I just cut the stitching and ripped out some of the foam on one boot, but not on the other one. What a mistake!.

I stood once more in the gate, feeling my heart pound. This one really counted, I knew. In the downhill I came in under the first five. My chances were good, but the slalom was coming up, and I always did better in the slalom, because in the slalom a fast ski is less important then in a downhill. One has to understand that in ski racing it is not always the wax that makes a ski run fast, there are other factors to consider: for instance camber of the ski, stiffness, width, all this in relation to the weight of the racer and snow condition. My first run was one of the fastest, but in the second run I hooked a gate and it turned me around, the time was still good enough to be in the first group.

My brother Pepi won the Alpine Combined and seemed a sure bet for the Olympic team because there was only one more race which would decide who would go to St. Moritz. I would have to wait another week for the second race to know whether I made the team.

This next race was the Westen Cup in Lech, on the other side of the Arlberg Pass and not far from home, where I had raced often. This was last call. I tried as best I could and made good runs. Good enough for the top six in downhill, slalom and combined. After the races were over, all waited nervously to find out who would be chosen to go to St. Moritz.

Rudi Matt, our men's coach, Theus Schwabl, the women's coach and members of the selection committee would decide who was going to represent the Austrian colors, red-white-red, at the V Winter Olympics.

We gathered at the hotel in Lech where the names were to be announced. Finally I heard them call, "Franz Gabl." I felt a burden fall from me. I had worked very hard for this day; perhaps harder than anyone and now it paid off. I was on the Olympic team. Pepi, having won the Tyrolean championships in Soelden two weeks earlier, was surprisingly left off the team. Some people shaking their heads.

For six years the darkness that had come over the world had conspired to take my joy away. It had failed. I couldn't help feeling that I had conquered an enemy greater than anything I had faced in battle. But the victory was incomplete. Herman and Franz were left behind on the Russian battlefield. Pepi Jenewein, perhaps the greatest skier of our little group, had flown his plane into the bloodied Russian dirt. I made this unspoken commitment to them: I would do my very best in St. Moritz. My very best.

The V. Winter Olympics, St. Moritz 1948

And now it was time to leave for St. Moritz; the V. Winter Olympic Games were about to start. For twelve years no Olympic champion had been crowned. The world, preoccupied with its dreadful struggle, quite understandably had no appetite for the enjoyment of watching young athletes give their best. One thing that had changed was the press. The press had grown up during the long war years and now used its new skills and tools to keep readers and listeners informed of every detail of the preparations for the competitions.

Reporters were with our Austrian team constantly, reporting our moves to the Austrian sports fans and beyond. The world was watching and listening. The interest in the ski-minded nations was intense. Who would come out on top? The Swiss were the hosts, and of all the European nations had suffered the least both in the loss of young men and in devastation to its countryside, villages and cities. It was an island with all its bordering countries in a life and death struggle. France and Italy were both making rapid recoveries. But Austria had suffered immensely. Many of its best skiers were now buried in the Russian steppe. For Austria, downhill skiing is king of sports, and that meant the attention of all Austria was on our little ski team. I laughed to think we were now the Austrian elite. We were underfed, underequipped and overeager. Would our desire be enough? I hoped, so but inside I doubted.

Still, no team could have been prouder. We had worked exceptionally hard to get to this point and knew that many others had also worked hard but had failed to make the team. Some of these joined us at the train station two weeks before the Games were to begin as we prepared to board the train for St. Moritz. We proudly carried the red-white-red Austrian flag as we headed for our train car. We tried to focus on the noble thoughts of Baron De Coubertin, the French nobleman and founder of the modern Olympics in 1896, who said that winning is not the most important thing, only taking part; the fight was unimportant, but sportsmanship was everything. I was more than happy to be taking part. But I also wanted to win a medal.

My brother Karl left for the *Bahnhof* with my large suitcase and the two pairs of Northland skis, compliments of Hannes Schneider. It was time to say good-bye to my mother. With her much practiced worried look she begged me to be careful. "I don't want you to be brought home on a toboggan again," she said, reminding me of the accident I had on new year's day 1932, with my new hickory Christmas skis. "Yes, *Mammi*," I replied soberly. "I promise to snowplow all the way down the hill." This brought a laugh from her and a knowing smile. She understood that her son was going to give it everything he had and that he would take some chances. She also understood that if I hadn't taken chances, and hadn't had the blessings of good fortune, I would be under the Russian soil like Pepi Jenewein, Herman Ladner, Franz Klimmer and so many other brave Austrian skiers.

"I'll hold both my thumbs for you, Franz," she said as I shook her hand and left. Like crossing fingers, holding thumbs is an unspoken and somewhat desperate wish for good luck in Austria.

Edi Mall was already at the railroad station when I arrived. There was a crowd of well wishers, mostly in family groups, to bid us farewell. Young girls were there to watch their heroes leave, and I well remember one cute girl with blonde pigtails who called out to me, "Break your neck, break your leg." It was the most common expression of good luck in Austrian sports, and I whiled away some of the time playing flirtatiously with her around a metal post until she disappeared into the crowd. I watched my father push through the crowd toward me. The concrete station platform was a swirl of people, many clomping around in ski boots as they had come straight from the ski slopes to join the farewell party. "Good luck, Franz," he said as he finally reached me. "We'll all hold our thumbs for you."

"*Danke, Tatti,*" I said simply. Here was the jolly Santa Clause who had arranged that the *Christkindl* would leave a pair of hickory skis under the Christmas tree in 1931. He always believed I was a natural and maybe would someday be a champion. No one, through all the years, had supported my desire to be a ski champion more. When I looked at him, especially now as I saw tension in his face and his constant smile subdued, I wanted to tell him how much his support meant to me.

"*Achtung! Achtung!* The Arlberg Express will arrive shortly. *Bahn Frei!*"the loudspeaker announced. My sisters grabbed and hugged me. Karl, Pepi and my father shook my hand as did many of the other well wishers. Slowly the train came into view, looking first like a small toy train winding its way around the last turn, then closer until I could see the faces of my Austrian teammates who were already on the train. As the train came to a stop, some of them jumped out to help Edi and me with our luggage. We jumped aboard, clambering for a window seat so we could wave to everyone on the platform. No sooner were we aboard than the train began moving and we waved our final good-byes. Within a quarter of a mile the train entered the seven-mile-long Arlberg Tunnel on the way to St. Moritz.

As we entered the dark hole a lump grew in my throat: apprehension, excitement and pride. St. Anton was left behind. We were off to the Olympics. My teammates on the men's team were Christian Pravda, Hans Hinterholzer, Eberhard Kneissl, Egon Schoepf, Hans Nogler, Engele Haider and Edi Mall. Rudi Matt, the ski school director in St. Anton was our coach. On the women's team were Trude Beiser from Lech, also Ski Club Arlberg, Erika Mahringer, Sophie Nogler, Anneliese Proxauf, Annelore Zueckert and Resi Hammerer; their coach was Theus Schwabl of Kitzbuehel.

In less than an hour the train was in Switzerland. At each stop the crowds shouted from the *Bahnhof*, *"Hals und Beinbruch! Hals und Beinbruch!"* At Buchs, on the Swiss border, we stopped for awhile, and I took the opportunity to exchange the five American dollars into Swiss *Francs*. Chocolate simply wasn't found in war-ravaged Austria let alone on the eastern front, so I looked at the mounds of chocolate candy in the stores with childish amazement. My Swiss *Francs* were quickly gone, and Christian Pradva said I was going to eat myself to death with chocolate. "Better than starving to death," I said. He said no more. He knew, too, that I had

gotten those five precious dollars from a Swedish diplomat who later was shot dead in Vienna by the occupying Russians.

We arrived in St. Moritz and were lodged in the Grand
Hotel on the lake in St. Moritz Bad, a half mile from the town
center. We felt like kings. St. Moritz—the dream destination of the wealthy and the sick. The majestic hotels drew
the world's privileged. The clean mountain air at 6,000 feet
ministered to the sufferers of tuberculosis and other lung diseases. The carpets in the hotel felt like six inches of pure
powder snow to us. "Almost as good as the Russian bunkers,"
I joked to Edi. The Swiss called us *die arma Oestrricher* (those
poor Austrians). Perhaps it was our somewhat drab, gray
team uniforms, but I think, the Swiss knew that we Austrians had known only hunger the last nine years. Still no one
could make us feel less than royalty.

The next morning it was time to inspect the course.
Though the race was two weeks away, our first look at the
course made the tension rise. This was for real. It was also
our opportunity to have a look at our competitors. We knew
it would be difficult. The Swiss, always strong skiers, had
been hurt little by the war. The French and Italians had
been pretty well restored, and there was plenty of talent on
their team. But it was not so for the Austrians. Many of our
greatest skiers were dead, many others maimed. We knew
that our bravery would be more important than our skill or
our inferior equipment. I knew that it should have been
enough to be satisfied with being on the team, to participate
in this great worldwide and historic pageant, but I also wanted
to win a medal.

My Austrian teammates and I were quiet as we rode the
cog railway up towards Piz Nair on our first day for inspecting the downhill. From the top of the cog railway we were
pulled to the top of the downhill start by a wire rope tow. Our
hope above all was, that it wouldn't be a "wax race." If the
downhill here at St. Moritz was the same course as the pre-
Olympics run the year before on another hill, we knew we
didn't stand a chance. No Austrian had placed better than
fifteenth in the downhill. A flat course placed emphasis on
fast skis and the waxes used. That was not our advantage.
We didn't have the experience about waxing and our skis

weren't up to the standard of the day. All on our team had laminated ash skis except for Mall and I who had hickory Northlands from the United States, thanks to Hannes Schneider. Hannes, my idol and my employer before he was ousted in March, 1938, sent these from his ski school in North Conway, New Hampshire. Most of the competitors from other countries had five or more pairs of skis, some as many as eight, and all tuned to different snow conditions and events. Some of their skis had phenolic bases, a kind of plastic covering the running surface. Ours were plain wood.

The night before at dinner in the hotel we had been told the course was a monster. My teammates and I looked at each other with a faint smile of satisfaction. We hoped it was a monster.

Finally, we were ready to inspect the downhill course. It was everything we wanted. Courage and nerve would be the determining factors, though wax would also play a role at the top where for the first 41 seconds, each racer just schussed without any turns.

Mentally I divided the course into three sections. The top was rolling terrain, not too steep and lasted about 41 seconds. Here, the racer would ski straight and crouch to minimize the wind and let his skis and wax do the work. This was the wax section, where we were at a disadvantage, where the wrong skis or wax could cost you seconds. The next section were the *Steilhangs*, three steep hills. There were no control gates, so it was totally up to the skier to use his judgement in controlling his speed. Schussing would mean a trip to the hospital at minimum, a trip to the morgue if your luck was bad. The last section was the timberline with its *Kiesgrube* (gravel pit) because that's what it was in the summer time when the snow was gone. After this section came the rollercoasters of wicked, man-made bumps and then a washboard-like flat portion towards the finish line. This sure would give tired knees a thorough workout. It was a devilish course and would yield only to a daredevil. We all were thrilled. We might have a chance.

On the following days we got to know the course intimately and duelled down the mountain like we had done so often before on the hills of St. Anton and on so many other courses around Austria. First we carefully checked out the different sections. But after a couple of days we went all out. I watched Pravda take a straight line down from the *Stangenpass,* the sheer drop that started the series of steep hills. I thought, "He's crazy." But, if Pravda could do it, I knew I had to try, for prides sake! After awhile we began to get more comfortable with the course. We noticed other teams watching us and began to hear rumors around the village of "some Austrians that were going like hell."

At first I used my 210 cm Northlands thinking they would handle better on the bumps where racers spent most of the time in the air rather than touching the snow. But after two days I had switched to the 218 cm Northlands and then felt solid contact with the snow. The bumps became my friends; my confidence was growing. I thought of Dr. Wieser, the director of the movie, who said, "Let it happen." I tried to relax, not think about the landings. After the first week of practice, we were running the course in our sleep.

And so we practiced, and practiced some more. The course was exhilarating to me. Every morning after breakfast our men's team went by bus to the cog railway station in the middle of St. Moritz *Dorf,* the business district. On top of the cog railway, there was a wire rope tow which pulled us to the top of the downhill course on Piz Nair mountain. After the starting gate, it was straight down on rolling hills. No turns. Here you need to build speed so you crouch as low as you can, killing the wind. We called it the *Waxstrecke* (wax section) and we feared it, not because of the danger and skill required, but because we knew our equipment and wax abilities weren't up to Olympic standards. Austria at that time could not import ski waxes nor hickory, as it had no credit rating in the world.

At the end of the *Waxstrecke* we practiced the sharp turn to the right at the *Stangenpass,* then the course dropped away from under us. Down, down, down. There was a huge bump which the course builders had built up. Then there was a long, steep Schuss alongside the mountain where you could side slip and cut some speed. At the bottom of this hillside there were a series of man-made ridges that provided opportunities for the daredevils. In practice I would jump from one ridge to another, flying over the little valley in the middle and landing on the fall away side of the next ridge. Next, the *Steilhangs*, just plain, steep slopes. These reminded me of the Black Forest course where I had first raced in 1939, eight years earlier. To slow down here you had to turn several times. To go straight without slowing meant a great buildup of speed and a likely trip to the hospital, or perhaps a view of the Olympics from under the snow.

After the *Steilhangs* the course flattened a bit, but to make sure this didn't turn into a *Waxstrecke* the Swiss course designers built a number of bumps to keep a skier in the air long enough and give the legs a good workout. Finally, the course disappeared into a narrow trail through the woods to the gravel pit, called the *Rominger Schneisse*. Too fast and you'd land on the flats and drive your bouncing knees into your chin. This was a truly Olympian course from beginning to end.

I loved *Gelaendesprungs*—flying through the air on the giant man-made bumps with downhill skis and poles was my forte. From my earliest days on skis, nothing thrilled me like ski jumping; after all I earned my first silver ski pin for jumping in the 1929 ski club championships.

After the Olympics I wrote to the Austrian Olympic Committee about my Olympic experience: I was actually amazed

Gabl executing a Gelaendesprung *at Mount Baker Ski Area in 1968.*

that I did not spill once in the two weeks training on the Olympic downhill course. But there were plenty of spills. We avoided watching other racers; it was unnerving—bodies flying, somersaulting, spread-eagled. There were broken bones, thumped heads and plenty of muscle strains. Each time the sled would take the injured skier down the mountain, another Olympic hope would be broken. We didn't like to watch.

We did, however, enjoy watching the practice for other events when we weren't practicing downhill or slalom. Next to the finish line of the downhill was the Skeleton run—the course for the one man sled. The course was like a bobsled run, but the drivers would lie flat on their stomachs and steer with their toes which each had a saw like piece of metal attached. We watched them every day and decided the *Steilhangs* weren't so frightening after all. The spills we saw made the downhill spills almost look tame.

The slalom course was on the hills just above St. Moritz *Dorf,* and we watched as the fire department sprayed the hill with water to ice-harden the snow and support the late starters. In the afternoons our Austrian team practiced the slalom. In slalom it is less important to have a fast ski then in downhill because the ski's edges are touching the snow more then the running surface.

Everyone on our team skied on Austrian equipment except Mall and me, and although our Austrian manufacturers did the best they could, without hickory wood they couldn't make the skis needed for this level of competition.

One of the joys of Olympic competition is becoming friends with other athletes from around the world. Cafe Hanselman was in the middle of St. Moritz *Dorf* and a favorite of myself as well as most other skiers. Each day, after training we would gather for cake and coffee. We could hardly believe what we saw, all the sweets, especially the chocolate cakes in this store. One day we were offered free cake by a cute, blonde waitress. "Compliments of the management," she said a little shyly. Did she find us Austrians irresistible? Or was it our gray uniforms with the double eagles that gave us away as *die arma Oestrricher*—those poor Austrians? Nine years of nothing but ration cards and a steady diet of hunger. We enjoyed the cake, and the company and thanked them profusely for their generosity.

Two members of the Czech team, Antonin Sponar and Lubo Brchl, were sitting at a next table next to some of my team members one day when we had our coffee and cake. "You guys looked good in practice," one of them said. "Who told you to take such a direct line in the *Steilhangs*? Are your coaches pushing you?" Some of my teammates and I had been pushing the edge in the middle section knowing this is where our opportunity was. We explained that we were really coaching each other, training in groups of three or four rather than as a whole team.

We wanted to ask them questions about waxes, skis, snow conditions and anything else they might know that would help our training. But we wanted to give nothing away ourselves and were afraid of showing any of our weakness. So I changed the subject. "Who are the favorites?" I asked Antonin and Lubo, the two Czech skiers. "You guys," laughed Sponar. "And Molitor, and Couttet, Oreiller and Colo, maybe another Swiss, Frenchmen or Italian." "Ha!" I laughed, "not me!" It was true, but my confidence was growing.

We also met some old friends who were at the games as spectators. Mrs. Alice Chiar had been a regular visitor to St. Anton before the war. She had her heart left in St. Anton, you might say, and was a great friend of Hannes. She gave Edi Mall and I each a pair of United States Air Force goggles. They were completely airtight and kept the wind out of our eyes at high speed, preventing our eyes from watering and blurring our vision. They were a great help.

The modified 218 Northlands continued to feel great, and I was skiing with greater abandon every day. Still, I had been erratic on past downhills, and felt I had to take more chances than the racers who were able to race during the war years.

Our philosophy was that it all comes down to how you feel on race day and the wax, the wax. If you feel good and the downhill suits your style and have the right wax you just might win a medal. But, if you don't feel so good, well, "We'll know after the race."

Race day was drawing closer. On January 30th, 1948—three days before our big race—28 nations gathered to march together into the Olympic Stadium and swear the Olympic oath. For twelve years the Olympic flame had been but a

glowing spark, patiently waiting for the world to end its sei-
zure of hatred, terror and killing. Now it was about to burst
into full fire again, but with friendship, not hate, and we
would be a part of it.

  We were, of course, nervous about our reception. After
all, only three years ago we Austrians who had been in the
uniforms of the German *Wehrmacht* and were occupying many
of the countries now represented here. Norway insisted ada-
mantly that Austria should not participate in the Olympics.
They didn't forget. Eventually they were overruled, and Austria was admitted.

  The glorious peaks of St. Moritz provided the backdrop
for the Olympic Stadium. The teams in the uniforms of the
many nations were arrayed in alphabetical order, ready to
march before the crowd. The Greeks first; the privilege was
theirs since the founding of the games some 2,000 years earlier. The host Swiss would enter the stadium last. Paul
Haslwanter was the proud bearer of our sign *Autriche* (Austria) since French was the official language of the Olympics.
All our fears about how we would be received were washed
away in a flood of cheers as our Paul entered the Olympic
Stadium. That was glory to march in front of that crowd. It
was as if the relief the world felt in being freed from tyranny,
hate and bloodshed, and our relief and joy in having been
spared certain death. And that feeling continued on through
the Games as losers would congratulate the winners. It was
a competition with friendship instead of animosity, a battle
that ended with backslaps and handshakes rather than spilled
blood and lonely graves.

  I thought of Herman Ladner and Franz Klimmer, my un-
shakable comrades from the early army days in Russia. How
they would have loved this. And how much more it would
have been for me had they been there to share it. I wondered
if the birch cross that marked Klimmer's grave near Kursk
was still standing and how the patch of grass was looking
above Herman's last resting place. How I would like to go
back there some day and look at the spot where Herman was
missing, 400 meters to the right of the Kunatsch River.

  It was three days from the opening ceremonies to our race
day, February 2, 1948. We could feel the tension in us building. Frantically we tried different waxes. Our coach was

hardly ever seen on the downhill course. There never was a discussion between our team regarding wax or tactic. So everything we needed to know we had to learn ourselves. We tried to learn as much as we could, knowing full well that the most experienced on our team would keep their best secrets to themselves.

The day before the downhill the narrow streets of St. Moritz began to fill with *Schlachtenbummler* (groupies), those who followed their teams faithfully. Austrians came to see how their countrymen and women would fare against the world's best. Throughout the two weeks we had stayed away from the news media, not wanting all the speculation and the thought of the expectations of the people at home to distract us. We knew it was there, we just didn't want to think about it. Now we couldn't avoid it. The talk was all around us. James Couttet, Henry Oreiller, Karl Molitor, Ralph Olinger, Zeno Colo and one of the Alvera brothers of Italy and maybe a Swede were the favorites since they had won many international races. Couttet had even been a world champion at the age of 17 in 1938, the year before Pepi Jenewein won in Poland. Now he was 27 and hungry for the gold. Austria had never won an Olympic medal in skiing. Never. Would this be the year? And who would carry home the glory to the whole nation?

On the day before the race each country had to name its downhill team. There were six men and six women chosen, and four of the six on a team were also chosen to run a special slalom race, which combined with the downhill, would determine the winner in the Alpine Combined. This was to give the alpine nations who had so many world-class downhillers more of a chance to ski in competition. Egon Schoepf from Innsbruck and I were chosen to be the two to race only the downhill. The reason was simple. The coaches considered us the gutsiest. They wanted us to just go for it and not have to worry about running the slalom for the alpine combined. As if they needed to tell us to go for it. I knew if anyone wanted to have any chance in this race they would have to go for it like never before. No slalom possibilities could have stopped me from giving it everything I had.

After a final piece of cake provided by the good owner of the Cafe Hanselmann, without doubt the finest delicatessen

in world, it was time to head to our hotel. Race day was tomorrow. And now we had to settle once and for all the questions about wax. Schoepf, Kneissl, Nogler, Haider, Mall and
I were clearly nervous and uncertain. Mall and I headed for
the wax room in the attic, we were ski club buddies and used
the same wax on many occasions. Our coach Rudi Matt never
discussed with us strategy or questions about wax. As a matter of fact, we hardly ever saw him, except at dinner time.
The other team members went their own way. I fell back on
a wax that had felt good to me in training. On top of the
lacquered base I rubbed Toko 1, a black Swiss wax. After
that went a thin layer of Tento, a Swedish lacquer. Then, in
the morning, I would crisscross this surface with a thin layer
of paraffin and hope for the best.

The 2nd of February, 1948, dawned with a beautiful, blue,
cloudless sky. By the time the sun lit the Swiss mountain
tops, we had already eaten breakfast and loaded our two pairs
of skis onto the bus for the ride to the cog railway. Later we
were told that all of Austria was listening on their radios,
waiting anxiously to hear news from St. Moritz. Our thoughts
were on the race, our equipment, the wax. The Bulgarian
racer David Madjar decided to ease the tension on the bus
with lusty renditions of some popular songs. Though it didn't
help; all our minds, I am sure, were on how to take the three
Steilhangs and the *Kiesgrube* (gravel pit). When we got off
the cog railway I put on my 210s, saving the 218s, with their
fresh wax for the race. We had even put paper between the
bases to prevent them from scratching each other. We wanted
every advantage we could get. At the top, Hans Hinterholzer,
who was already at the start, but didn't get to race, made a
comment that got us all nervous again. "I sure went faster
when I crisscrossed my skis with silver paraffin," he said.

We debated and discussed and decided to try a little test
run. Hans, Edi Mall and I linked arms, then let go and skied
together for about 80 yards to see who would arrive at our
imaginary finish line first. We all arrived at the same time.
Now what? We decided to stick with what we had. The
indecision was getting to us.

We had a moment to look around and try to soak in this
incredible time in our lives. Slowly teams from countries
around the world were arriving at the mountain top. The

village of St. Moritz, deep in the alpine valley, was spectacular in the cold mountain sunshine. I was looking around, watching a small plane sail through the clear blue sky, leaving a wispy cloud of vapor trail, when the first racer was announced. It was James Couttet, the world champion in 1938 from France. At 10:01 a.m. he pushed through the starting gate, and the Olympic downhill race of 1948 was underway.

From then on, every 60 seconds, another racer would give that burst of energy he hoped would propel him to glory. Edi Mall, my teammate, was number 2. He stepped quickly into the gate, leaning towards the little thread stretched across the gate attached to the electric timer. Five, four, three, two, one and Edi was gone. "Hals und Beinbruch, my friend," I breathed to myself. In a few minutes the racers' times would be telephoned back up to the starting gate. James Couttet, France: 3:07:3. Edi Mall, Austria: 3:09:3, down by two seconds. No gold for Edi. For awhile their times stood. Then a message was phoned up that sent a shock wave through the starting area. 2:55 flat! Who? Who did it? Nobody had broken three minutes. Two fifty five? Unbelievable. The word came back up. Henry Oreiller, a Frenchman.

My God! He beat Edi's time by 14.3 seconds! Was it the wax? The best 112 downhillers in the world were on this course today. Over fourteen seconds behind? My mind was racing faster than the downhillers now on the course? What could I do? I couldn't make up more than a few seconds, even by taking great risks in the *Steilhangs*.

"Number 24! Are you ready?" That was my number. The last of the second seed. Now I was calm. "*Jawohl,*" I answered, my voice steady. The race nerves had taken over, like so many times before. My mind would push me, and my body would respond. I would let it happen, like the castle wall jump in Ladis. Like the *Schlosskopf* dare with Pepi Jenewein. Edi was down by over fourteen seconds. If the Austrians were to win a medal, it had to be me. "Hold nothing back, Franz, go for it," I said to myself.

"Five, four, three, two, one—GO!" The little thread snapped as I pushed with all my strength against the poles to get out of the gate. Skate hard. One—two—three—four. Forty-one seconds of *Waxstrecke*. Crouch low, lower. The wind whipped over my American air force goggles, my eyes clear. My ski pants whipping in the wind, even though I had the ski pants on the lower part of the legs tightened with shoelaces. There's the *Stangenpass*. Jump and fly. The slope falls away below me, and I land many yards down the steep slope then immediately stand up and open my arms as wide as I can to slow myself down because I am determined to make no turns. All or nothing. Later, observers told me I was the only one to make no turns.

At the bottom of the *Steilhang* was a big dip. Two choices: stay on the ground or jump over it completely. Fourteen seconds—to win one must jump. I jumped. Landing far down the next *Steilhang*, I snowplow quickly, pre-jump a ridge, airborne again, and land on still another steep hill. Thank you, Eugen and Theoni, the two ski mechanics in Hannes Schneider's Ski Schop who altered my downhill skis. The hickories flex and propel. Thank you, Hannes.

I can hear yelling alongside the course. "Must be *Schlachtenbummler*," I thought. Austrians, cheering me on. But they were not just Austrians. Ski enthusiasts from many nations were encouraging me on when they heard my interim time, which was identical to Oreiller's time, announced by the public address announcer.

The tree line comes into sight. The *Kiesgrube*, the gravel pit. A sharp ridge followed by a vertical wall and a flat landing spot. Too fast and you land hard with a difficult time standing up. Too slow, and, well, no medals. Now the ski jumping practice paid off. One hundred feet—thirty—ten—pre-jump and fly. Let it happen. I land solid, a little farther down than I wanted. Now the course flattens out, but the man-made bumps keep any thought of relaxation far out of my mind. Here the course disappears into the woods. The branches of the trees from each side touching each other above my head. It's just a narrow trail. A giant washboard with wicked, cruel bumps. In practice we called it the *Danauwellen* (the Danube waves). My legs are tired, rubbery; they're working like auto shocks. The light flashing through the snowy branches like a giant strobe throws my senses off. The finish line is coming up, but the waves get smaller like a real washboard. Just a little farther now. Stay in a tuck. It's there.

I coast for another fifty yards, breathing like an asthmatic, my legs feeling tired like never before in a downhill. Slowly the sounds and sights of the cheering crowd comes on me like someone gradually turning up the volume. I am exhausted. I droop over from the waist. Then, straightening up, I look into the stands. They are shouting. I see Mrs. Chiar, our American friend who gave me the air force goggles. Then I see people running toward me, laughing and smiling. At first I thought they did this for everyone, but I soon realized that my time must be good. I looked up to the big blackboard and saw them move the names of the two Swiss skiers, Molitor and Olinger. I watched as they started putting up new letters. "G-A-B-L." There was only one name above of mine. My time was posted: 2:59:1.

How can one describe that feeling? I had no right to be alive, let alone stand on the top of this mountain. The race wasn't over yet, but everyone seemed to think that no one else had a chance to break the three-minute mark. The Swiss who had just been celebrating the sharing of the silver medals by Molitor and Olinger with times of 3:00:3 had to settle for the bronze. No one was going to beat Henry Oreiller that day with his spectacular run. He was truly the Olympic champion that day. But a little known Austrian skier had taken the silver, and in so doing, won Austria's first ever Olympic skiing medal.

Henry and I met at the finish line. We congratulated each other with gestures. Microphones were thrust into our faces; a BBC journalist from London, wanted both of us to describe our tactics. Henry spoke French and I spoke German so the interviews were babel-like pantomimes, Henry stone-faced when the microphone was pointed at me and I doing the same when he talked.

That afternoon, after the men's downhill, we went to watch our women teammates compete in their downhill. Our women were considered to have a better chance than the men, so we had high hopes, especially for Trude Beiser. But, in a great race, Switzerland's Hedy Schlunegger beat Trude and teammate Resi Hammerer, who took the silver and the bronze, respectively. One day, three medals. Not bad for our Austrian ski team who had never before won a medal.

In the evening after the downhill race, Dr. Geroe, the head of the Austrian Olympic Committee, came to our hotel where the Austrian team was celebrating the two silver medals of

Gabl and Beiser and the bronze medal of Hammerer. Dr. Geroe congratulated us heartily. We knew without him telling us that Austria had arrived as an alpine ski nation.

In the late afternoon, the awards ceremony was held in the Olympic Stadium. With a sense of gratitude I walked toward the platform and took my place just below the Frenchman, Henry Oreiller. How could it be that I stood here now, representing Austria and receiving the applause of all these nations represented here? I thought of all young men I raced with who were now dead, sacrificed to an ignoble cause and buried with the shame of the world. Pepi Jene-

FRANZ   HENRY   KARL   RALPH
GABL   ORЗILLER MOLINOR OLINGER

wein, top fighter pilot and world ski champion, killed in 1943 after downing 86 Russian planes. Albert Pfeifer, fighter pilot, killed over Holland in 1943 after downing 18 Allied planes. Herman Ladner, big lighthearted Herman. Franz Klimmer and many more. Less then three years earlier I was a Russian prisoner of war, weighing hardly 100 pounds, not knowing if my next stop would be Siberia and the coal mines. Now I stood on the Olympic platform, on top of the world.

Trude Beiser went later on in the games to win a gold in the alpine combined, and Erika Mahringer won a bronze medal in the alpine combined and the special slalom. The gold medal in the slalom and the silver in the combined was won by the pigtailed U.S. girl Gretchen Frazer.

As a top seed for slalom, I was given the Number 8. But I had been having trouble with my new ski boots which we had received at Christmas. My ankle was rubbing uncomfortably against the outside of one boot ever since. Normally after downhill practice I would join my teammates for slalom practice but skipped it lately as the ankle became infected and

Descente Messieurs	Abfahrt Herren		
DOWNHILL	MEN 1948		
Rang Nom		Nation	Temps
1. Oreiller Henri		France	2.55,0
2. Gabl Franz		Autriche	2.59,1
3.a Molitor Karl		Suisse	3.00,3
3.b Olinger Rolf		Suisse	3.00,3
5. Schoepf Egon		Autriche	3.01,2
6.a Alvera Silvio		Italie	3.02,4
6.b Gartner Carlo		Italie	3.02,4
8. Grosjean Fernand		Suisse	3.03,1
9. Nogler Hans		Autriche	3.03,2
10. Hanssen Hans		Suède	3.05,0
11.a Lassen Urdahl Sverre		Norvège	3.06,4
11.b Odermatt Adolf		Suisse	3.06,4
13. Couttet James		France	3.07,3
14. Haider Engelbert		Autriche	3.08,2
15. Kneisl Eberhard		Autriche	3.08,3
16. Arentz Bjarne		Norvège	3.09,0
17. Sponar Antonin		Tchécoslovaquie	3.09,1
18. Spada Romedi		Suisse	3.09,2
19. Mall Edi		Autriche	3.09,3
20. Eriksen Marius		Norvège	3.09,4
21. Chierroni Vittorio		Italie	3.10,0
22. Reinalter Edi		Suisse	3.11,0
23.a De Huertas Guy		France	3.12,0
23.b Panisset Georges		France	3.12,0
25. Johannessen Sverre		Norvège	3.12,1
26. Reddish Jack		U. S. A.	3.12,3
27. Brchel Lubos		Tchécoslovaquie	3.12,4
28.a Clifford Harvey		Canada	3.14,1
28.b Sutherland Hector		Canada	3.14,1
30. Isberg Sixten		Suède	3.15,0
31. Eriksen Stein		Norvège	3.15,1
32. Bonicca Eugenio		Italie	3.15,4
33. Pazzi Jean		France	3.16,1
34. Penz Claude		France	3.19,2
35. Marusarz Josef		Pologne	3.20,2
36. Mulej Tine		Yougoslavie	3.21,1
37. Gasienica Ciaptak Jan		Pologne	3.21,3
38. Nilsson Aake		Suède	3.22,2
39. Alonen Pentti		Finlande	3.22,3
40. Sollander Stig		Suède	3.23,1
41. Dalman Olle		Suède	3.23,2
42. Movitz Richard		U. S. A.	3.25,2
43. Knowlton Steve		U. S. A.	3.26,2
44. Blatt Robert		U. S. A.	3.27,4
45. Jennings Devereaux		U. S. A.	3.28,2
46. S'lachta Daniel		Tchécoslovaquie	3.29,4
47. Mc. Lean Barney		U. S. A.	3.30,1

extremely painful. With foresight, our team chef, got permission from the race organizers, that if I wouldn't be able to race the slalom, he could substitute someone else. How generous. The evening before the slalom race, our team Physician Dr. Prokop put alcohol compresses on my ankle during the night, thinking it might go away, but in the morning I could hardly walk on it and lacing up my boot was out of the question. My hopes were raised when Dr. Prokop went off early in the morning to a pharmacy in St. Moritz to get a pain killing injection. I went to the starting gate with my boot unlaced and a spare racer, Hans Hinterholzer, ready to take my place if Dr. Prokop didn't make it in time. The time to start was coming and now I cursed my starting position requiring me to start early in the race. I was waiting near the starting gate my boot unlaced to be able to quickly lace up and race. Then I saw Dr. Prokop huffing and puffing up the mountain. It was too late. Hans skied in my place. He fell and missed a gate. I was disappointed but took comfort in my silver medal.

Home Coming
from the Olympics

And now as the V Olympic Winter Games ended it was time to leave for my home , St. Anton am Arlberg. We arrived after midnight; there were few people at the railroad station when Mall, our coach Matt and I arrived. My father, brothers and two sisters were all beaming with pride when we exited the train. Immediately I heard "let me carry your luggage and skis." My oldest brother Karl took my suitcase another two youngsters the two pairs of skis. It was always an honor when someone asked a champion skier, "let me carry your skis." When I arrived in my home, *Mammi* was brimming with pride; she was smiling and was so glad to see me without crutches. I said to her, "*Mammi*, I snowplowed all the way down in the downhill." She knew that when I left for the trip to St. Moritz I told her I was going to snowplow all the way down. "*Mammi,* you know what? I didn't spill once in all my two weeks training and racing in St. Moritz. In the report I will have to write to the Olympic committee I will tell them that I didn't spill once in the two weeks in St. Moritz." The local music band was supposed to have been there to play a march or two, but as we arrived so late they went home. One could feel a sense of envy. Wasn't he the son of a strong Nazi family? I took it all in stride and tried to get along with my fellow instructors and ski school directors.

In the fall all members of the teams and officials were invited by the president of the Austrian Republic Dr. Renner to Vienna for a celebration. The women who won medals received a gold brooch, the men a gold ring with five stones, depicting the five Olympic colors. A letter from the Austrian Olympic committee states: "Dear Mr. Gabl: the Austrian Olympic Committee congratulates you for winning the silver medal in downhill and thanks you for representing the Austrian colors. We are happy to let you know that you will receive from the Covoy-Mejor-Kollonen, a United Nations sponsored food distribution organization, 1 package of rice (5 kilo) and 1 package of sugar (5 kilo), which you will receive by show-ing this certificate in Vienna, IX. Lichtenstein Strasse, 43. I had to travel to Vienna, an 800-mile round trip to receive the rice and sugar, but it was worth it at that time.

The first race after the Olympics was the Hannes Schneider Cup right in St. Anton. I was looking forward to it very much. The American team and others came to partici-pate and honor Hannes through their presence. It was sup-posed to be held on the regular Kandahar downhill course from the Galzig, but it snowed every day. Eventually it wasn't possible to hold it there because of high avalanche danger. It was diverted to the *Osthang*, the narrow steep strip right un-der the Galzig cable car. On the day of the downhill, it was still snowing, with over three feet of unpacked, powder snow, and getting warmer. Packing a downhill course in the morn-ing after a snowfall just wasn't done. You raced in the snow under your feet. There were a few gates at the top and a few near the bottom of the course, but in the *Osthang* the very steep strip, one could go straight. I wore my American Air Force goggles as in St. Moritz, but as I came down toward the steep part right under the cable car, the airtight goggles fogged up; all I could do now was go straight down in the deep pow-der, seeing only darkness to the left and right where the trees stood. Before long my skis dug in at the tips, and I somer-saulted several times before stopping. At once I knew it was my knee and also to some extent one ankle which hurt badly. What a disappointment it was for me. The racing season was over for me until the late spring races. The big surprise was that Jack Reddish of the US won the downhill, in the lion's den you might say, though Jack would have to be recognized in the future as a potential threat any time he stepped into a starting gate. After some weeks I could walk again without a cast, my legs felt good and I knew that the injuries were not permanent.

Late in march, my father in his good natured way then said, "Franz, now you have to go back to swinging the paint brush, climbing ladders and no more flirting with the *Fraeuleins*." I knew there was no arguing with father, so I settled into a daily grind after my legs felt better.

In the summer months of 1948 I was determined to train very hard for the coming racing season. Toni Spiss and Karl

Fahrner became regular climbing partners of Karl Frei and myself. Frei was the chief of the railway engineers in St. Anton and a competent, enthusiastic mountaineer. He was, at one time, partner to the famous Herman Buhl. They both grew up in Hall near Innsbruck.

Usually we would leave town around 5:30 on Saturday evenings and hike one and a half hours to the *Ulmer Huette,* the mountain hut administered by the German Alpine Club, carrying our skis and a packsack. After a night's rest we waited for our ski club buddies Othmar Schneider and Otto Linherr who came from Lech on the other side of the Arlberg Pass, to join us for some on snow slalom training on a piece of summer hard snow below the Valluga peak. I was still using my 218 cm Northland from the Olympics, but now 4 cm shorter because I found out that the binding mounted on them were 4 cm too far forward, and as I had no giant slalom skis they had to do for the time being as giant slalom and downhill skis.

After our training we would ski from Kapall all the way down to the bottom of the Galzig Bahn on grass. It was not the best way to treat skis, but in the fall I just scraped the bottom flat with a piece of glass, painted a few more layers of lacquer on it and replaced the steel edges. These skis I then used all through the Winter of 1948-49. In the Tirolean championships held on a mountain near Innsbruck, at Wattens, in February 1949, I would beat Christian Pravda and Egon Schoepf by over ten seconds in downhill. These skis I also used in the slalom and the combined DH-SL time gave me the alpine combined. I knew then that the skis were all right.

Late March of 1949 was the scene of the Arlberg Kandahar race in St. Anton where Hannes and Sir Arnold Lunn originated it in 1928; it was the 21st anniversary. I was looking forward to race before my home town crowd. On Saturday was the downhill. In early morning Rudi Moser, Edi Mall, my brother Pepi and I boarded the Galzig *Bahn* cable car and hiked up to the very top where the World War I memorial stood and next to it the starting place for the Kandahar race. It was a clear, cool day and the corn snow was frozen. Most of the racers painted wax on the running surface the night before, thinking by the time of the race the snow would be softening up. My starting was No.2; the snow still frozen at the top, and now I had to make a decision: scrape the wax off to keep the skis from scraping on the frozen corn snow, or take a chance and leave it on and hope on the lower half of the mountain the snow to be soft where the painted wax would have been by far faster. Finally I decided and scraped the wax off—big mistake. I ended up almost 20 seconds behind the winner Zeno Colo of Italy. In the slalom I redeemed myself and came in on the podium, but in the combined was an also-ran, a disappointment for me and many St. Antoners.

The last big race was to be the *Zuerser See* Giant Slalom in late April 1949. Most of the great names from Austria were competing, and it was always one of the most fun races. Our Hannes Schneider happened to be there as honored guest, and we St. Antoners tried to show off. My first run was not so hot, but in the second I beat the field handily. On my way up to the start after the race to bring my spare skis down, my right knee got blocked. The meniscus jammed it, and now I had to walk with a bent knee. It was the same what happened on a march in Russia in 1943 to escape an encirclement by *Ivan*. In the Hotel Post was the ceremony to give out the trophies. Toni Spiss had to collect the trophy for me; it was embarrassing because of the knee. For two weeks after the accident I got treatment from Dr. Schalle's office, our local specialist for ski related injuries, though to no avail. I phoned then a friend in Vienna Elfriede Steurer who was on the 1948 team and in the 1952 Summer Olympic team as an 80-meter hurdler. She, at once contacted Professor Felix Mandl of the main *Wiener Krankenhaus* (Vienna hospital). He sent a wire advising me to come at once to his hospital. The train ride to Vienna was hell; I couldn't straighten my leg. In Vienna I was admitted at once to the hospital and within a day my knee was operated on. Though it was painful; there was only a local anesthetic. Professor Mandl used a pair of pliers to pull the meniscus out. I took it home as a souvenir. Within two days I was bouncing a small sandbag into the air with this leg. I asked Prof. Mandl if I would be able to ski or race again. I was worried that now my racing days would be over. He then said, "Franz, do not worry, you will be racing before long, and you shouldn't have problems with this knee for a long time." He proved right. It put my mind to rest.

I want to mention that Professor Felix Mandl was from

Vienna, he was of Jewish descent, and left for America before
Hitler *Anschluss-ed* Austria. He came back right after the
war, and he was the one to whom all soccer players in Austria
went for ailments concerning limbs and joints. Ever since,
my knee has been all right, except for an occasional swelling.

By training very hard I conditioned myself like never before to make sure to make the F.I.S. team and represent Austria at the upcoming World Alpine Ski Championships in
Aspen, Colorado. I flirted with the idea as a young boy to go
to America, and now I saw my chance to fulfill my dream. I
remembered too well that when Toni Matt left Austria in the
fall of 1938, he had to leave on the sly across the border to
Switzerland, because the new regime required every German
citizen to get a visa to leave the country. This faraway land
intrigued me to no end. I had visions of gold- digging in the
far north, seeing Indians in their wild environment, bears
and buffalo. How much wilder it all seemed to me then. In
reality it was quite different, much tamer.

In early winter the hopefuls who would represent Austria
at the F.I.S. World Championships in Aspen, Colorado, were
called for a training camp at the German side of the Zugspitze,
the highest Mountain in Germany, the same place we had
trained for the 1948 Olympics. We were quartered in the
Hotel on top of the cable car station on the Austrian side and
had to walk every morning through a tunnel, less than half a
mile long to the German side. Every afternoon, when we were
walking back through the tunnel to our hotel, the electricity
was shut off for conservation, and we walked in the dark. We
pointed our ski poles ahead of us, and each time there was a
corner we would hit the wall and then change direction.

The American Occupation Forces were still in charge of
the Zugspitz Hotel and let us Austrians use their rope tow
which to us was already familiar from the 1947 training for
the Olympics. This time, unlike in 1947, we had enough food
and didn't have to go home to mother's cooking anymore. The
U.S. forces again served us at noon a bowl of soup like they
did two years earlier. The end of food rationing cards came to
Austria in 1952.

Two races were to decide who would go to Aspen for the
F.I.S. The Hannes Schneider Cup in St. Anton, and in January the Westen Cup in Lech. My training and physical condi-

tioning left nothing to be desired. The weekend hiking and climbing put me in great shape. I won the Hannes Schneider cup combined in my home town, it was a thrill when Herta Schneider, Hannes's daughter, handed me over the beautiful trophy. Two weeks later in Lech, I won the Westen Cup downhill, slalom and the combined. There was now no question of me going to the land of my dreams. I sold my motorcycle and with the money bought two new Leica cameras, which I intended to sell for $200 each and use the money for a start in America. At home I had a long talk with my father, saying: "*Tatti*, I want to stay in America and not come back and see how I get along." Rudi Matt and Sepp Fahrner seemed not pleased with me anyhow; I wanted to get away from them. I recalled flunking the ski instructor exam in 1947 at St. Christoph when Rudi Moser (also a ski racer) and myself flunked the test and the other instructor from St. Anton, who was not a ski racer passed it easily. The examiners, including Rudi Matt, the co-director of the ski school in St. Anton and coach of the men's team in St. Moritz said, "We don't want the ski racers heads' swell too much." In spring of 1948, Rudi Moser and I passed it hardly answering any questions; all I had to repeat was the demonstration phase of the test. I knew then that as a ski racer and being an instructor in St. Anton I would have to kiss asses, and I am not the type to do that.

My father said, "Franz, I'll bet you will get homesick and then gladly come back home." "We will see, but if I endured four years on the Russian front, how could I get homesick being in the land of plenty?" I asked. His belly jiggled, and he had kind of a smile on his face. He knew many St. Antoners had emigrated before the war—Otto Lang, Toni Matt (famous after he shussed Tuckerman's Ravine on Mt. Washington, New Hampshire, in 1939), Luggi Foeger, Friedl Pfeifer, Otto Tschol, Benno Rybitzka and Franz Koessler. Others who left before the war were Sigi Engl, Hannes Schroll, Sepp Ruschp and Bill and his brother Fred Klein, to name a few.

Off to the Land of My Dreams

In the middle of January 1950, our Austrian team flew to New York where Hannes Schneider and a large delegation of Austrians awaited us at the airport. The following were on our team; Ernst Scarderassy, the Hotel owner from Zuers was our manager, he spoke English very well because he emigrated before the war to Australia and taught skiing there. The men's coach was Toni Seelos with his charges: Hans Nogler, Hans Senger, Engele Haider, Edi Mall, Christian Pravda, Egon Schoepf, Toni Spiss, Walter Schuster and myself. On the women's team were: my brother Pepi, coach; Erika Mahringer, Trude Beiser, Dagmar Rom, Resi Hammerer, Anneliese Proxauf, Lidia Gstrein and Rosemary Gebler-Proxauf, the racers.

We were all taken to a hotel in the middle of New York City, in the big Apple. We couldn't believe that we were now in America, the Land of our dreams. This was another world. The tall buildings—we called them *Wolkenkratzer* which means "cloud scratchers" in German. This was all new to us, but we had heard so much about New York and, of course, America.

The next evening we were introduced in Radio City Music Hall to a full house of invited guests. Hannes Schneider was there, and he was an icon in the eyes of the skiing world in America. Hannes was also the uncle of Edi Mall. He and I roomed together, and we watched for hours—half the night—from our hotel room on the twenty-something floor down below to the street. I thought, "My God, if I only had a car." I said to Edi, "I'll bet you, before long I will own a car." This was the dream of my life. It was less than six months, and my dream came true.

One evening we were all invited to a bar to watch television. We didn't know that in America they had TV. It was a boxing match. The reception wasn't too good, but it was TV.

From New York we traveled by train to Chicago where another group of Austrian-American friends drove us around the city. I remember Erika Mahringer driving the car at 80 miles an hour, never having driven a car. I was scared silly and am sure others were too. In Chicago we boarded a train again and traversed the wide open, flat and rich farmland until we saw the Rocky Mountains in the distance. We didn't stop until we arrived at Glenwood Springs, deep in the Colorado Rockies, forty miles from Aspen, our destination. It was wonderful to see the countryside from the upper level of the observation cars.

I remember seeing photos when in this area millions of buffalo roamed in this open range land, a hundred years ago, and I remember seeing paintings of how the white men drove them over cliffs to kill them, mostly for the hide's sake. When I was a teenager we would read late into the night stories of *Karl May and Rolf Torrings Abenteuer* (adventures). Some evenings our father would check on us in bed and give us hell for burning electricity.

Finally we arrived somewhat tired from the sleepless travel in Glenwood Springs where an array of autos waited to drive our team to Aspen. Edi Mall and I were driven by the famous Dick Durrance who participated in the 1936 Olympics at Garmisch, Germany, for the U.S. My English wasn't too good yet, but good enough to hold a conversation and besides Durrance spoke some German. He had lived in Garmish for a winter season or two.

It was late evening when we arrived in Aspen. Our team was quartered in the Roaring Fork, an old, decrepit, red brick building left over from the silver mining days 60 years earlier. It had bunk beds, a far cry from the castle-like Hotel in St. Moritz Bad. But we didn't mind one bit, the reason was the food, the food. The cafeteria-style food service was unknown in Europe. Austria still had food ration cards, and there were not many days since September 1939 when war broke out until now, that we could eat all we wanted. Here we indulged to satisfy our constant hunger to our heart's content. For breakfast we loaded our trays with ham and eggs, toast, cereal, pancakes, syrup, milk, coffee and more. It was no wonder when, weeks later, we arrived in Sun Valley for the Harriman Cup, the manager from the Roaring Fork in Aspen phoned Mr. McCrea, the manager in Sun Valley and said, "Next time you take the Europeans first, they eat to make you poor." For us it was like *Schlaraffenland* (Utopia).

It was not only we Austrians who ate ourselves silly; all other ski teams from Europe did the same, except maybe the Swiss and the Swedes who were the only nations in Europe who hadn't joined in the massacre from 1939 to 1945.

Germany was still banned from International Competition. Finally in 1952, at the Olympics in Oslo, the hatred and animosity of the six years of war was forgotten, and they were again welcomed by the International Olympic Community. These young athletes certainly couldn't be blamed for what the ruthless Nazi leaders did to the world.

In Aspen, Edi Mall and I each awaited a pair of 218 cm Northland skis, compliments of our Hannes Schneider. My pair was warped, and I knew they were unusable, so I fixed my 1948 Olympic Northland 218s, now 4 cm shorter and hoped for the best. Our primitive accommodations didn't bother us in the least; the reason was the food, the food.

In the morning after our arrival and a hearty breakfast, it was now time to inspect the downhill course. We were quite happy with what we found on this mountain. The top part was very steep, then came some *Gelaendesprungs* (bumps), after that a (too) long valley where the wax played a vital role, which for us Austrians was bad news. Then came the famous jump and a steep headwall. After that it flattened out towards the finish line. It reminded me of the Olympic downhill in St. Moritz, except the *Waxstrecke* here was in the middle of the run; in St. Moritz it had been at the beginning of the downhill.

We Austrians were happy with what we saw, and our hopes were high, though the long, flat valley in the middle gave us concern when we saw the bundles of skis the Swiss, French and Italians had. Zeno Colo's downhill skis were 225 cm long with inlaid edges and a plastic base. We had never seen skis with only a fraction of the steel edges showing. He even had the giant slalom skis 215 cm in length with inlaid edges and the bases were of some kind plastic.

Afternoons we practiced GS or Slalom. To make more runs, we Austrians would take the chairlift part way up, but jump off at the start of the GS hill. We threw the poles down and quickly got off the seat, turned the body downhill, held on with our hands on the chair and let go with skis pointing downward. It was quite high, but we were young and always daredevils. It didn't take management long before word got around that those crazy Austrians should stop this foolish practice or they are going to walk up to the top of the down-hill. It stopped quickly.

There was not much to do in Aspen after skiing, and we would go to the movies in the evening or have a beer at Steve Knowlton's bar which was the in place at that time. Steve Knowlton was also a well known racer and later became a famous speaker for Colorado skiing, telling anecdotes from his service as a soldier with the U.S. 10th Mountain Division in Italy. His favorite was: he was given an assignment to contact a German outfit across from them and yell over to them *nix schiessen* (do not shoot), but Steve was not versed in German and he yelled *nix scheissen* which in German means no shitting!

One evening Klaus Obermeyer, who came from Garmish a few years earlier, took Edi Mall and me to the movies. Edi hardly spoke any English and mine was adequate for basic conversation, though not yet good enough to understand what was said on the movie screen. Klaus explained to us what was going on. He was the inventor of the quilted ski jackets. Klaus was a ski instructor in Aspen after he emigrated from Garmisch in 1947. It was so cold in that high altitude in Aspen that he tried to find a way of licking the immense cold by stitching together jackets made of sleeping bags. Remember the mountains around Aspen have an altitude of over 10,000 feet, and at that altitude it can get cold as hell. Within years he not only had quilted jackets made for him and his friends; he also deserves credit for having started the quilted clothing industry. Tens of millions of skiers should thank him for it

Finally the F.I.S. races got underway with the GS first. It was a total disaster for our men. I went in as one of the favor-ites to do well in Aspen, having won both big races in Austria. I placed 36th, after somersaulting over a road. Christian Pravda was the best Austrian coming in 12th.

But it was different with our girls. Blond Dagmar Rom, the darling of the American news media, won both GS and Slalom, and in all the women's races our girls came in first, second and fourth. In the GS the six girls took first, second, fourth, fifth, sixth and seventh places. Trude Beiser won the downhill gold.

The men's downhill I really liked and like in St. Moritz didn't spill once in training. It sounds like an excuse, but my skis didn't run the way I expected them to. Skiing on grass down from Kapall in the summer could have been used as an excuse, but why did I win the Hannes Schneider and Westen Cup just a few weeks before with the same skis? I came in 11th, seven seconds behind the winner Italy's Zeno Colo. Our Egon Schoepf won the only medal for the men, a bronze, in the downhill. In the Slalom again no medal, coming in ninth, less then three seconds behind Georges Schneider of Switzerland, the World Champion.

After our races in Aspen, we were all invited to the North American Championships in Banff, Canada, through the efforts of Georg Eisenschimmel. Georg had a beautiful villa built in St. Anton in the early thirties, and he skied there every winter until the *Anschluss*. I skied frequently with him and got to know him well; also my father had the contract to paint his home in St. Anton. Georg was from Czechoslovakia and Jewish. His family owned a glove-making factory there. He emigrated to Canada after the Nazis took over Czechoslovakia in the fall of 1938 and with foresight got involved in the ski resort business. He had one of the earliest chairlifts installed in Canada, on Banff's Mount Norquay, four miles outside town, though the first chairlift was built in eastern Canada.

George said to me at one of those evening parties which we had to attend, "Franzl, if you would like to stay on this continent I would be happy to get you a visa, and you could run the ski school here at Mt. Norquay." "For years I had planned to go to America and I might take you up on your offer," I said to him. In Banff I was sick and couldn't race, but the knowledge that I might be able to get a job and stay here made me happy. The scenery here was spectacular; the Canadian Rockies are a sight to behold.

From Banff all European and North American teams went off to the Harriman Cup in Sun Valley, Idaho. We had heard so much about Sun Valley; after all there were ski school directors there at one time or another who came from my hometown—Otto Lang, Friedl Pfeifer and Toni Matt. Sun Valley was completely different from what we had expected. The timberline in America is generally much higher than in Europe where it ends at about 1,800 meters. Here it can go as high as 3,000 meters, about 10,000 feet.

We started inspecting the downhill course from Baldy Mountain. The top part had several turns in it, then came the compression near the "Roundhouse." After that came the "Exhibition" run—a long, steep, open meadow and it ended up near the bottom on the nearly flat, river run. It might have been the fastest downhill I had ever experienced. It was scary. Two days before the downhill, one of the Swiss Perren brothers, either Gottlieb or Bernhard, gave me a pair of their racing skis, how generous. They were 225 cm Attenhofers made in Switzerland, and they were fast. I wished I had them in Aspen, instead of my old 214 cm Northlands and wished to have used my 214 cm Northlands here on this downhill.

In Sun Valley, our team was invited almost every evening by one of our old friends for a typical American party. Mrs. Alice Kiaer, who was a guest in St. Anton every year since the early 1930s, but suspended her vacationing during the *Anschluss*, had us Arlberger's for a party. Even Ernest Hemingway, who had a little house on a river nearby, had us for whisky and snacks, and our yodelers Hans Nogler and Lidia Gstrein yodeled their throats hoarse. We didn't know then who this Mr. Hemingway was. Later on, we realized that he was a world famous writer, whose books *For Whom the Bell Tolls* and the *Old Man and the Sea* won many awards.

On Friday, our last day of training for the downhill in late afternoon, Hans Senger, Christian Pravda and I started out for the final practice run. I said to Hans and Christian, "Let's *tuschen* on our last practice run." *Tuschen*, in our Tyrolean dialect means no holds barred, all out. I was leading, Pravda right behind me and Senger last. The corn snow had a frozen crust on top and was really fast as we three daredevils shussed the exhibition run from top to bottom. We must have travelled at least 85 to 90 miles an hour. At the bottom of the exhibition run it flattened out some what, and there was a slight turn to the right. That's where I caught the inner edge of the right ski. It turned me around, and then I somersaulted at least a dozen times. It was by far the greatest spill of my life. I couldn't move and thought every bone in my body was broken as if Joe Louis had pummeled me around a ring for fifteen rounds. My face was bleeding with scratches all over; my legs felt as if every bone was broken. The new pair of Attenhofers, compliment of one of the Swiss Perren brothers, lay in pieces around me, only the wood under the binding was still on my feet, the other wood only good for the fireplace. There were no release bindings then. Zeno Colo, the world champion, saw the spill and was supposed to have waved his arms and hands and winced as if to say, "What a hell of a spill." He didn't win the downhill the next day; Hans Nogler did.

At once the ski patrol took me to the hospital. I knew then that my racing career might be over. I approached 29 years of age and was now looking for other worlds to conquer. Still I travelled with my team to Sugar Bowl in the Sierra Nevada, California, where Hannes Schroll, the yodeling Tyrolean arranged for our team to compete. He was the one who was responsible for developing Sugar Bowl as a Ski Resort in the 1930s. Now he came to Aspen to cheer his countrymen and women on and had several cars and station wagons arranged to take our whole team to his resort for the Silver Belt Ski Race.

On the way to Sugar Bowl one of our cars broke down, and we waited in Reno, Nevada, for them to catch up and in the meantime started gambling. This was new to us. What we saw there was something out of this world. We could only gape at all the slot machines, the conestogas hanging from the ceilings, and the noise when a slot machine released the jackpot. It sounded like a coin avalanche, and this noise went on without intermission. Now, is this what the wild west is all about?

Some of the gamblers saw that we were gambling neophytes and asked us where we were from, in English of course. Our manager Ernst Scarderassy then told them that we just came from the world ski championships in Aspen and the Harriman cup in Sun Valley Idaho, and now we were going to San Francisco sight-seeing; we are invited for two days and we heard that this is the most beautiful city on earth. Some of the gamblers gave us some coins to insert into the slots and when we won a few dollars, they said just keep the money! Again we experienced the generosity of the Americans.

When the broken car arrived after midnight, we continued on to San Francisco. I always excelled in geography lessons in school and to this day it is a dear subject. As our cars neared the Bay area everyone watched carefully. Finally we were over the last hill and could see an ocean of lights in San Francisco and the Golden Gate Bridge, the magic Golden Gate Bridge. It was without question one of the greatest moments and sights of my life. I had always dreamed of seeing San Francisco, the gateway to the Orient.

For two days we were guests of *Herr* Weber, manager and part owner of the Whitcomb Hotel on Market Street in San Francisco. He had come from Vienna before the war and had worked himself up to this high position. We visited many famous sights: Fisherman's Wharf, Mark Hopkins Hotel, Museums and Lombard Street, which winds down a steep flower bedecked hill with a dozen sharp turns, and rode the cable cars. From here our team went to Sugar Bowl for the Silver Belt race. I was still hurting from the Sun Valley spill and couldn't race. I had no regrets. Hannes Schroll and I had talked at length, and I told him that I would really like to stay in America. He then said, "Franz, why don't you come down to my ranch in Palo Alto for the summer and work there. You won't get rich, but you will be learning the language and get the feel of America." I agreed at once but didn't tell my team of the plan. After the race in Sugar Bowl was over the Austrian team headed to the eastern U.S. for more races in Hannes Schneider's home area of North Conway, New Hampshire, and Vermont.

When the team assembled at the Reno railroad station after the races to head east, I stood on the platform waving good-bye to my teammates, maybe forever. My ski gear was already in Hannes's station wagon. They thought I would grab my things at the last moment and enter the moving train. Hannes and I drove then to Sugar Bowl. When my legs felt better I taught for Bill Klein, the ski school director. His wife Helen ran their sport shop there. Bill and his brother Fred, both came from Austria to America before the war. They came from Lilienfeld, the hometown of Zdarsky who, you might say, invented the alpine skiing method with one pole. Both Bill and Fred were taught that technique by Zdarsky himself in the late 1920s and early 1930s.

Sugar Bowl Ski Area was started by Hannes Schroll, who came from Alpbach, in the eastern part of Tyrol. He was one of the earliest ski racers to come to America and before long married the very rich Maude Hill, the grand daughter of James Hill, the builder of the Great Northern Railroad. He was supposed to have left $200 million when he died in 1926. Even Walt Disney invested in the ski area, and one mountain there is named Mt. Disney, the other one Mt. Lincoln.

Sugar Bowl had so much snow, like St. Christoph on the Arlberg Pass. Here, I met the future Mrs. Clark Gable, ne' Kay Spreckels, who was an occasional guest at the Lodge.

When the ski season ended in early May, Hannes picked me up to drive with him to his ranch in Palo Alto, forty miles south of San Francisco.

While in Aspen I had a chance to drive Friedl Pfeifer's and Toni Matt's cars around town. Pfeifer was one of the pioneers who made Aspen a ski resort.

Hannes Schroll let me drive the car for a while on the way to Palo Alto, and I went 80 m.p.h. For me it was an unbelievable experience, but I was thinking back to Chicago when Erika Mahringer drove the car at 80 m.p.h., and I hoped I didn't scare Hannes like Mahringer did scare us.

At Hannes Schroll's ranch there was a swimming pool and Mrs. Schroll had a cook, a waiter and a gardener which were kept busy with their two children. My English was getting better, and Mrs. Schroll said to me, "Franz, the best way to learn English is by learning ten new words every day. Buy a newspaper and a dictionary and write the words down to impregnate them in your mind." The dictionary I brought with me from my home; now I only needed newspapers.

Hannes ran his dairy farm of about 200 cows on 400 acres, located only two miles from Stanford University. His employees were from Oklahoma; they were supposed to be best suited for this job. One day Hannes said to me, "Franz, how would you like to run this dairy farm of mine?" Hannes had had problems lately with contaminated milk; it seems the men didn't wash the udders enough, and it showed when the wholesalers tested the milk. Me, running a dairy farm! My God, no. Getting up at 4:00 every morning, every day of the year. A ski instructor was a heavenly job. I didn't tell this to Hannes, but he realized that I was not suited for running a dairy farm.

Eventually Hannes had to close down the dairy, and before long the land would be divided up for real estate. I occupied a small cottage near the gardeners house and did all kinds of work, such as fixing fences, hauling hay from other farmers and painting in the house. Once or twice a week, Hannes invited me to go with him to the horse races at Golden Gate or Tanforan tracks. This was a new experience for me. I had never been to a horse race before. The first time we went, Hannes said, "Franz, you select the horses, it is supposed to be beginner's luck." We both looked at the beautiful thoroughbreds as they marched them past the spectators and bettors. Not being shy about selecting, I said to Hannes, "This horse or that horse looks good." That first day Hannes won about $200, myself about $20. I only bet $2.00 a race, Hannes $20.00.

On our way home, Hannes always stopped at Uncle Tom's Restaurant in Red Wood City. He was well known in the whole Bay area, and after we entered, the first thing he did, was go to the bar and order drinks. Soon he was yodeling and once in a while stood up on a table and imitated a milking cowboy with the "cow tits yodel." He always drew a good laugh. In Palo Alto I met Fritz, a young Swiss, who was a salesman at a car dealership which sold English cars, Hillman and Humber. Fritz and I became well acquainted, and here I bought my first car for $300. It was a 1937 Pontiac. One of my life's dream came true. Fritz and his wife took me frequently on trips to San Francisco sight-seeing and to Reno for gambling. It was an exciting time in my life. Heaven could not have been better. Living in California, the most exciting part of the world. This was the reward for four years of Russian terror, I thought.

In June Mrs. Schroll's relatives from Holland visited; they were two boys but old enough to drive. They wanted to see Seattle and Vancouver, B.C., so Hannes said, "Franz, why don't you go with them and take in the Golden Rose Festival in Portland, Oregon, and the Ski Race at Mt. Hood?" I agreed at once, and the two boys, both over 18 years of age, and I started off with their rented Chevrolet.

Mt. Hood was a new experience; I had never seen such a beautiful lodge, a W.P.A. project built in the 1930s to create jobs during the depression under Roosevelt's presidency.

June 8, 1950, was a foggy day, and over 150 racers from
Washington, California, Oregon and British Columbia,
Canada, hiked from the lodge to the start high up to a snowfield at the foot of Mt. Hood. There were several gates near
the start, but then it was schuss straight down in breakable
crusty snow. I was scared like the devil and couldn't slow
down and didn't want to fall either. After the finish line it
took me several hundred yards to come to a stop. Was I ever
glad to finish this race. I won it, but it scared the devil out of
me.

At Mt. Hood, Jeanette Burr, a Seattle ski racer, invited us
three to try some water-skiing on Seattle's Lake Washington.
It was the first time in my life to see this sport done, and I
mastered it at once without falling. Twenty-six years later I
bought a home only a few hundred yards from where I first
learned to water ski. By late summer in 1950, I got a letter
from the U.S. Immigration department telling me that my
visitor's visa had expired. What now? Then I remembered
that on our trip to Banff in February, George Eisenschimmel,
the owner of the chairlift on Mt. Norquay, mentioned that if I
ever wanted to stay on this continent, he would be glad to
give me a job running the ski school at his ski area on Mt.
Norquay. George had his name changed by then to Georg
Encil by deleting eight letters. *Eisenschimmel* means in German iron white horse.

George had a beautiful villa built in St. Anton, and I knew
him well and skied with him on the Galzig and gave him ski
lessons. On March 11th, 1938, the day before Hitler's armies
entered Austria, George went over the mountains to Switzerland, only a few miles away. No doubt he would have ended
up like millions of other Jews in a concentration camp, had
he stayed.

Hannes Schroll then said, "Franz, I am going to phone
George Encil and see if he can give you a job up there." While
they were talking on the phone I got excited, hoping to be
able to stay in America, that is Canada or the U.S. George at
once said that he would arrange for me to enter Canada. He
had interests in oil drilling sites in Alberta near the Montana
border where I was supposed to cross, so he knew some of the
Canadian border patrol people there, and had talked to some
immigration officials regarding me coming, but how could I

have known? I had no Canadian visa and didn't know that in Canada they were much more liberal when it came to visas. It seemed they needed immigrants to build this immense large country and welcomed people who had trades.

Off to Canada
Coach of Canada's Olympic Ski
Teams: Ladies 1952, Men 1956

In late October, 1950, I packed my few belongings into the 1937 Pontiac, thanked Hannes and Mrs. Schroll for their kindness and headed north with apprehension, not sure of my future. George Encil told me on the phone that I had to enter Canada at Cut Bank on the Alberta-Montana border, because he knew border guards there.

On my way north my good old Pontiac lost water through a crack in the motor block. I had no idea that this could happen. I stopped once in a while and refilled at a gas station, or once or twice in the wide open Nevada dessert I just peed into it. Those cars made before the war were real rugged; you could drive them a long time without water.

In Whitefish, Montana, I stopped to see my old friend Toni Matt, who also taught for Hannes Schneider and trained with our ski Club Arlberg racers until 1938 when his foster parents, who were very religious and not happy with the *Anschluss*, advised him to emigrate to the USA.

Toni was at this time in charge of the Whitefish golf course in the summer and in winter the ski school and ski shop at the Big Mountain. Toni was already one of the greatest racers at that time in Austria before emigrating. In some races he beat the big boys Heli Lantschner, Willi Walch, Rudi Matt, no relation, Friedl Pfeifer and Pepi Jenewein. Toni was also quite heavy for his size. It was an advantage then, in downhill racing. Toni and I reminisced when we trained at home and rode the Galzig *Bahn* cable car every morning to have a quick run or two before ski school started. Toni or Pepi Jenewein were generally the leaders, then Albert Pfeifer, myself, Rudi Moser and my brother Pepi.

When I left Whitefish I became apprehensive of entering Canada. I had no visa when I approached the border at Cut Bank. I stopped at the American border station and told the man there I had no visa. The man there then said, "Why don't you leave the car here and walk over and see what they will say?" Reluctantly I trudged over to the little border station in Canada, only 25 yards away and told them my name. At once a smile came over the man's face. I will never forget. He said, "We were waiting for you for two days." I practically danced back to the U.S. station to get my car. The guard saw my elation, smiled broadly, and shook my hand. With a big smile I went on my way to Calgary to meet Bob and Phyllis Svare in the Palliser Hotel; they were friends of George and were to guide me to Banff that evening. As I drove north my Pontiac ran out of water again. I saw a big farm to my left and drove into the yard to ask for water for the radiator. What a surprise to hear Tyrolean dialect. This was a Hutterite community, a religious sect which emigrated some hundred years ago from Austria to Russia to Mexico and then to the U.S. before settling for good in Canada. It was unbelievable hearing this dialect so far from home. They all wore black clothing; the women had scarves on their heads, the men hats with wide brims. They filled the radiator up and then invited me to a meal in their community dining room. When I told them I was going to work for Georg Encil, the owner of the ski lifts at Mt. Norquay, they asked me if I was the famous skier Georg told them would run the ski school. Yes, that's me.

When I arrived at the Palliser Hotel in Calgary, one of the famous Canadian Pacific Railroad hotels, Bob and Phyllis Svare were waiting for me. They seemed to recognize me at once and made me feel very comfortable, typically American, with a smile. At once we took off for Banff 75 miles away. The next morning we met George Encil who arranged for me to live at the School of Fine Arts, an affiliate of the University of Alberta. This was now my home for a few years. Miss Stewart, an elderly, short, roundish, Scottish lady was in charge, and I was treated royally. George arranged a job for me with the National Park Service cutting trees and dragging them out of the woods with horses. It was getting very cold, and I had not much winter gear. It reminded me of the Russian winter of 1941-42, but I thought, "Franz, don't complain, within a few weeks you will be skiing."

Finally snow came, and I rode every day on the Mt. Norquay employee bus four miles to the ski area. Mid-week

Chapter 16

there were few people at the ski area and the classes were small. It was a far cry from St. Anton, but I was not complaining. I was my own boss, and weekends were very busy. By the hundreds they came from Calgary and other towns, some even from Edmonton 280 miles away. The runs from the Mt. Norquay chairlift were very, very steep and really not ideal for giving lessons, except on the lower part where there was a very gentle beginner's area with a rope tow, called the Lone Pine which stood right in the middle of the run.

George and I discussed the operation of the ski school I was to operate on a concession basis. "Franz, what you should do, is, try to make it like the Hannes Schneider ski school in St. Anton," Georg said. How easy to say this. Hannes and the Arlberg had a tradition for over 40 years, and the terrain to go with it. This was pioneer ski country, where alpine skiing was in its embryonic state, and less tradition yet, except mountaineering with seal skins and climbing.

When it got very cold, and it did in the Canadian Rockies, business was really slow. We often experienced 30 below zero, not a day or two, but for weeks. I still adhered to the class times of 10:00-12:00 A.M. and 2:00-4:00 P.M. like we did in St. Anton. It was way too long a time in that cold and often windy weather. What I should have done is, give lessons by the hour. Traditions die hard! I wore fairly tight ski boots, the ones I raced with, but they caused me to lose toe nails for years to come when it was very cold. It was a recurring problem from the winter of 1941-42 in Russia when I was hospitalized with frostbitten toes. It didn't hurt; a new toe nail would slowly emerge and push the old one out until it could be cut off with a scissor—ouch.

During the ski season I also coached some of the local racers in gate racing, GS and SL. I was surprised how advanced some of them were. They had no international experience. Gordy Morrison was the best, and he was selected for the Olympic team in 1952. Others like Ross Maxwell, Rod Adams, Edi Hunter, Bob Dawson and Don Hayes had not the ambition or time for big time racing.

After the first season, I was glad when spring came and was looking for another job. By this time my English was more than adequate, and I applied to drive for the Brewster Gray Line Sight-Seeing Co. in Banff. This company got its start in 1896 as a horse trail riding outfit. In the 1920s they replaced buggies with sight-seeing cars and later with busses and limousines. Rod Adams, the dispatcher at Brewsters Banff office, was one of the racers I coached, and he hired me at once. He probably felt that with a famous ski racer as driver, you can't go wrong, even if his English is not yet perfect to explain all the sights in the National Park. This was the greatest job in my life. There was so much to see: the incomparable Banff Springs Hotel, Upper Hot Springs, Mt. Norquay, buffalo paddocks, beaver ponds, Lake Minnewanka, and an occasional drive to Lake Louise, Moraine Lake in the Valley of the Ten Peaks, Emerald Lake and into the Yoho Valley where the high Takakkaw waterfall descends straight down over a cliff for 1,200 feet. Lake Louise, below Mt. Victoria with its Chateau, is considered by the international tourist industry as the most scenic site on earth. It is a must see for whoever comes to Banff's National Park. The Canadian Rockies are not the highest mountains in the world, but they are the most spectacular. An Australian diplomat visiting, said in a interview, "Anyone coming to Canada and not seeing the National Parks in the Canadian Rockies is crazy."

Evenings, after our twilight tours, I took some of my fellow drivers often for short climbs on the nearby rocky crags, teaching them the rudiments of holds with feet and hands. Though I didn't want to make them too difficult because mountain climbing is one of the most dangerous sports. One day I took my buddy Doug Anakin up on a ridge on Rundle mountain above the golf course. I explained to him, "Now, Duk, when you climb always try to have contact with zee mountain on three points, that is two feet, one hand or zee other way around." All went well until Doug came sliding down on a smooth rock towards me. Quickly I grabbed him and held on. He kind of was shook up a bit. It didn't deter him to continue with this climbing and eventually became a decent climber. Not only that, but years later in 1964, he won a gold medal for Canada in four-man bob sledding during the Winter Olympics in Innsbruck, Austria, with his team mates Vic Emery the captain and driver, Dr. John Emery brakeman and Doug and Peter Kirby the third and forth men.

As my English improved I drove parties up to Jasper, 125 miles to the north. This route was by far the most scenic and exciting mountain range I had ever seen. From Lake Louise you drive north to Bow Lake with its Num-T-I-A-Lodge. It was built by Jimmy Simpson who came over from Scotland at the turn of the century. Jimmy was a real character. He was a short man with a mustache which reached back to his ears. He was never seen without his cowboy hat. He took parties on packing trips and entertained them with stories, some of them were hard to believe. When good old Jimmy passed on, it was never the same at Bow Lake. He was truly missed by the people who knew him. His son is running the lodge now.

A few miles past Bow Lake at Bow Pass, you turn left up the hill for a quarter of a mile and walk 40 yards to the view point of Peyto Lake. This lake, about 600 feet below, is over a mile long and 300 yards wide, and is fed by a glacier from a nearby mountain. The color of the lake is a cross between turquoise green and aqua blue; it looks like paint. There is no lake on earth so colorful. As you drive north, the mountains get higher, and most of them have glaciers decorating their tops and sides. The countryside is teaming with wildlife, and you see bears, elk, deer, moose, mountain goat and sheep and an occasional wolf, coyote or wolverine.

Buffaloes are fenced in near Banff. Many of the little animals like chipmunks, prairie dogs and marmots, are tame and can be touched, though it is forbidden.

As you approach the Columbia ice fields the temperature gets lower, the mountains higher. The highest mountain on the Banff-Jasper highway is Mt. Columbia at 12,293 feet above sea level. From this region the waters feed into three different oceans. The Columbia River heads west, then south, then west again and drains in to the Pacific past Portland, Oregon. The Athabasca River flows north and joins the Peace River which empties into the Mackenzie River and then into the Arctic Sea. The Saskatshewan River flows southeast through Edmonton, the Capitol of Alberta, and from there empties into the Hudson Bay and eventually into the Atlantic.

The Canadian Rockies were first discovered in 1807 by an English pioneer named David Thompson. He was supposed to find a route to travel from the east coast to the Pacific on land. By the late 1850s the famous Palliser expedition under Mr. Douglas looked for a route to build a railroad. In Europe were many railroads built already, and anyone with foresight could imagine that this immense country of Canada might have a great future. The rest is history. The railroad in Canada from east to west, Montreal to Vancouver, was completed in the year 1885. For thousands of miles farms would be set up, European farmers or non-farmers were now looking for a new life in the New world, having their own farms, at that time a wish for anyone who wanted to take the gamble and work hard. Years later I would help plow my father-in-law's farm in northern Alberta, plowing 24 hours nonstop with time out only for meals and rest. It was an experience. He told me that one of his ancestors was a tailor for the German Kaiser!.

On the Columbia Ice Field Parkway towards Jasper Park an impressive chalet serves the tourists with restaurant and souvenirs. There are very few tourists who miss this stop. Across the highway tour busses which have giant wheels drive sightseers right onto the Athabasca Glacier. You hear a constant thunderous rumbling of glacier avalanches as they advance in snail's tempo over huge rock outcroppings and fall off.

From here on towards Jasper, 66 miles away, the mountains become a bit tamer, not as high and photogenic. At the Athabasca Falls you hear the tremendous rumble of the river of the same name a long time before you see it. The river drops into a narrow waterfall, then a gorge and disappears into a tunnel only to emerge way down into a very quietly moving river. You are now nearing Jasper, the sister town of Banff. Here, the valley is totally different, almost two miles wide, where as Banff, seems to be squeezed in to the valley. Jasper National Park is larger then the Banff Park, but it cannot compare in scenery. Though it has many points of interest, like the incredible Maligne Canyon, Maligne Lake with its high peaks all around and Mt. Edith Cavell, over 11,000 feet high and named after a nurse who was shot by the Germans as a spy in France in World War I. The last time I climbed it was in July 1959 with my client Dr. Archibald MacIntosh, president of Haverford College in Philadelphia.

Jasper Park Lodge, located near a lake, looks different from the castle-like Banff Springs Hotel. It has many cabins, all made from beautiful hewn logs, all spread out in be-

tween trees. Dozens of elk and deer graze right in town or on
the grounds of Jasper Park Lodge. The employees use bicycles for commuting between the numerous log cabins. An
18-hole golf course serves the lodge guests, and it is very busy
from morning to night during the summer months. Very popular are the fishing outings, especially on Maligne Lake. Guides
take you into the mountains to little known lakes and streams.
They carry a little bell on their body, because bears are always a danger and these bells give warning.

In the spring of 1951 Georg Encil had hired a new manager for Mt. Norquay, who operated the chairlift during the
summer month for sightseers, to lift them up to the top of the
chairlift on Mt. Norquay. Jim McConkey was one of the most
gung-ho men I ever had the pleasure to meet. He was a ski
instructor in the Laurentian Mountains before heading west,
and he never left it. To this day we are great friends and
have skied, hunted, golfed and partied together. He started
skiing when he was a young lad. Right after the war he became a ski instructor for Luggy Foeger at Gray Rocks Inn in
the Laurentian Mountains, north of Montreal. Later on he
taught at Sugar Bowl in California, Alta in Utah, and Tod
Mountain in British Columbia, eventually ending up in Whistler Mountain and retiring from there with lots of dough. He
lives now near Vancouver Island in a beautiful log house on
the ocean front. When we two get together one hears only
laughs when we are rehashing old times.

During my summer racing camps at Mt. Baker in the
1960s, he also coached for me with the likes of Stein Eriksen,
Willy Schaeffler, Christian Pravda, Franz Hammer and others. We are still rehashing stories of how Georg Encil, the
owner of Mt. Norquay chairlift, made his employees "pick up

zee nails" and straighten "zem" out. In Europe even before the war, but much more after it, it was the custom to straighten used nails out and use them again. Habits die hard!

In the spring of 1951, the Canadian Ski Association held tryouts on Banff's Mt. Norquay for the VI Winter Olympics to be held in Oslo, Norway, in 1952. Many hopefuls came from eastern Canada; that's where the majority of established racers came from. The officials for the tryouts asked me to set the DH, GS and Slalom courses for the try outs of those who would represent Canada.

The race courses on Mt. Norquay were very steep, some of the steepest any where, and Banff had only the second chairlift installed in all of Canada by 1948 (the first in Canada was built at Mt. Tremblant about 1938 by Joe Ryan). In Europe they operated lifts already by the hundreds, and the racers got a head start. After the races were over, they asked me if I was interested to be the women's coach. I at once agreed and was looking forward to be involved in another Olympics, this time as a coach. Alpine ski racing in Canada and specifically Alberta could not compare with the competitions held in Europe where ski racing at that time was big business for over thirty years. It was like Canada dominating ice hockey in international competitions.

Our local racers from Banff to be considered for the Olympics were Gordy Morrison, Bob Dawson and Edi Hunter for the men, the Henderson brothers, Wayne and Scott, were still to young, though they were a mainstay on the Canadian National team years later. Lois Woodward was the lone woman to be considered for the team. Gordy Morrison then was chosen as a member for the 1952 Olympic team. The eastern Canada racers dominated the team. A sponsor was found in Mr. John Southam of the well known newspaper family, Southam Press, in Canada, who published the *Calgary Herald*. He paid my way as a coach and also gave me $1,000 for personal use.

Chapter 16

COACH OF CANADIAN OLYMPIC
LADIES SKI TEAM, 1952, OSLO

Canada's Olympic Ski Team assembled in Montreal in
early January 1952, then flew to London and on to Oslo, Norway. Oslo you might say is the Mecca of Nordic skiing, that
is, ski jumping and cross country. On our men's alpine ski
team were Harvey Clifford, coach and his charges Porky Grif-
fin, Gordy Morrison, Georg Merry and Bob Richardson. On
our women's alpine ski team were Franz Gabl, coach, and his
charges Joanne Hewson, Rosemary Schutz, Lucille Wheeler
and Rhoda Wurtele.

ROSEMARY SCHUTZ— RHODA WURTELE FRANZ GABL JOANNE HEWSON LUCILLE WHEELER

CANADIAN OLYMPIC LADIES ALPINE SKI TEAM, OSLO 1952

We were received with enthusiasm in Norway. Mr.
Gresvig, who was a manufacturer of alpine and other ski
equipment, invited our Canadian team to his palatial home.
He knew that Canadian ski shops were selling his merchandise, and we in turn used his skis, which he donated to our

Canadian Olympic Ski Team, 1952 Olympics in Oslo, Norway.

ski team, though we felt the skis didn't measure up to the Italian, French or Austrian makes. But you don't look a gift horse in the mouth. Money then was not being spent like these days. Also the Canadian Amateur Ski Association had very strict guidelines regarding amateurs. Their Olympic uniforms and clothing was donated; they even had to remove the labels of the companies who donated them! In Europe the ski teams more or less trained all winter. The French, who occupied St. Anton, had several men in the army but were on their National Ski Team. Their hardest job was getting to the Galzigbahn Valley Station. The true Olympic ideals were long gone, where one was not allowed to earn even a dollar. In my autobiography you will read that in the youth races in Innsbruck in 1936, boys from 12 to 18 years of age were receiving four Leica cameras then. The one rule which could not be broken was—no cash money could be received by any competitor, not even one dollar.

Our first races in Norway were held in Voss, a town on the west coast of Norway where our team competed only against the Norwegian team. The next stop was at Gejlo, not far from Oslo, a giant slalom, and from there we went to Oslo. But soon, we went about our business to get acquainted with the terrain where our Olympic competitions were to be held—the DH and GS in Norefjell, 60 miles north of Oslo, the slalom on Roedklava, on the backside of the famous Holmenkollen *Hoppe* (ski jump).

Our Canadian team stayed in a hotel near the top of the mountain, not far from the start of the downhill. We were quartered in the same hotel with the Polish ski team, and we got to know them quite well. I thought back to June 1944 when I was in a hospital in Sokolov, Poland. I told them the story of how my buddy Raeder and I got drunk in a Polish family's home. They really enjoyed hearing of this episode. The Polish men and one woman came frequently in the evening to our wax room after skiing practice and asked me how to prepare, wax skis and sharpen edges, etc. They were still behind the times having not been in international competition as they were still a Communist Nation and were hardly able to leave their country for ski races. I was still kind of a hero to them, having won the silver medal in the 1948 downhill at St. Moritz four years earlier.

At the opening ceremony in Oslo's Bislett stadium, we marched proudly behind our Canadian flag, which still was the Union Jack of the British Empire. The Maple Leaf would become the Flag of Canada a few years later. Now, for the first time since the war ended, Germany was admitted to the Olympics. The hatred of war forgotten. Thank God.

The first race held was the GS for men. It was in a little town by the name of Norefjell in a forest 60 miles north of Oslo. There was little open alpine, treeless country terrain like we had in Europe. The local hero was Stein Eriksen, the son of Marius, who manufactured then some of the best alpine racing skis in the world. Stein won gold, the Austrian,s Christian Pravda silver and my teammate from St. Anton, called *Gummi* Spiss (Rubber Spiss), the bronze.

The ladies races commenced with the giant slalom which Andrea Mead Lawrence from the U.S. won by over three seconds against Austria's Dagmar Rom, the double world champion from Aspen in 1950.

Our Rhoda Wurtele Eaves was our best Canadian coming in ninth, beating out Trude Jochum Beiser, the world champion of Aspen 1950, who came in 11th.

Two days later commenced the downhill for ladies which

Trude Beiser won. Joanne Hewson, our best Canadian coming in eighth, Lucile Wheeler ninth, Rosemary Schutz 14th and Rhoda Eaves Wurtele 16th. Canada and I were very proud of their showing. It was the first time they raced against the powerful European ski teams, and no other team had all four ladies under the first sixteen finishers!

In the men's downhill Zeno Colo of Italy won gold, Othmar Schneider silver and Christian Pravda bronze.

The men's and women's slaloms both were held on the Roedclava Hill behind the Holmenkollen Ski Jump. Othmar Schneider beat Stein Eriksen for the gold medal and another Norwegian, Guttorm Berge took bronze.

The ladies slalom was very steep and icy. I asked if I could be a forerunner which the officials agreed. Stein Eriksen was the other. I had in mind after my run to quickly go up on the ski lift and tell my ladies team the conditions. It didn't do much good. Andrea Mead took gold again despite having to go back on a gate which she passed on the outside. Joanne Hewson was our best in 16th place.

The big story then in Oslo was the love relationship of blond, wavy haired Stein Eriksen and Kathy Rudolph of the U.S. ski team. Kathy had the looks of a movie star, beautiful, white gleaming teeth, and a steady smile on her face; seeing them together was a dreamlike couple. Publicity abounded. But Kathy was a married woman, and the headlines in the American and the European Press had a field day.

On Saturday, after all our races were over, we went to the Shrine, the ski jump on Holmenkollen, the greatest name in the history of ski jumping. As I watched them training I couldn't help but get the itch to try one or maybe two jumps myself. Ski jumping was in my blood ever since I won my first ski jumping competition in 1929. I went to Lucienne Laferte, one of our Canadian Nordic competitors and said to him, "Lucienne, you know I just love to jump. Would you mind to lend me your boots and jumping skis so I could at least make one *hop* (Norwegian for jump) on this famous hill?" "Go ahead, I give you my boots and then go up and see how you like it," he said. At once we exchanged the boots, I grabbed the skis, one under each arm and up I went to near the top of the inrun. I looked down and admit was a bit scared. Finally the starter, he didn't know who I was, but thinking

someone from some team, training, waved the starter flag. I
turned my skis downhill and without trouble landed a little
above the 60 meter mark. Once more up I went and jumped
about the same distance. This time there was no Rudi Matt
hauling me back down, and hearing behind my back "chicken"
when I had to walk back down from the inrun with skis on
my shoulder in St. Moritz in 1948. Reidar Andersen, a famous Norwegian jumper, who was an old timer and wanted a
last "hurrah" jumped after me, but he was unlucky and broke
his collar bone. These two jumps at the famous Holmenkollen
I shall remember as long as I live.

Saturday evening was the last day of the Olympics for ice
hockey competition for the gold medal—Canada versus Sweden. There was excitement in the air, and all Canadians went
to the game, expecting the gold medal. Five thousand Swedes
came over the border to cheer their countrymen on to win
gold. I was with my girls amidst a group of Swedes. We were
not worried about being insulted or harassed; we knew the
Swedes were great sportsmen. As the game went on, the
Swedes scored first. Towards the end of the third period it
was Sweden 2, Canada 1. The Swedes around us would say,
"Wouldn't you like to be a Swede now?" We, in turn told them,
"Just wait and see!" The last minutes of this ice hockey game
was by far the most exciting as any hockey game I had ever
seen. It was 2-2 with a minute and a half to go. The Canadians were attacking constantly and finally they scored. It was
3-2 for Canada. The odd thing was, the Canadian hockey
team was made up of a bunch of amateurs from Edmonton,
Alberta, called "Edmonton Mercuries" and were sponsored by
a car dealership. When we left our seats, the good Swedes
conceded that the Canadians were a better hockey team. We
were proud.

The last day of the Olympics on Sunday, before the flame
was to be extinguished, was the big event which everyone
who had Norwegian blood in his veins watched or listened to
on radios. Early in the morning columns of spectators were
wending their way to Holmenkollen, one hundred thousand
of them who didn't mind walking the three to four miles to
the ski jump. Our Canadian team had reserved seats not far
from King Haakon and Crown Prince Olav. As expected, the
Norwegians won medals. It was gold for Arnfinn Bergman

and silver for Thorboern Falkanger. The Norwegians were happy as can be. Their honor was saved. Though the fame was not only reserved for Bergman and Falkanger or the triple gold medal winner Hjalmar Andersen, a speed skater. A young blond Viking named Stein Eriksen was the darling of the 1952 Olympics. His father made the famous racing skis, the "Marius Eriksen." Stein won the GS and came in second in Slalom behind my ski club buddy Othmar Schneider.

Host Norway should have been proud of their Olympics. After the closing ceremony in Bislett Stadium, it was sad to say good by to this totally dedicated winter sports nation.

After the races we left for Switzerland, France and Austria. Our next stop was Davos, Switzerland, to race in the Parsenn Derby, the longest ski race on the regular race circuit, eight miles long. It started on Weissfluh Joch, high above Davos and ended up in Kueblis, a little town on the other side of the Weissfluh. It took a half hour train ride to come back to Davos. The vertical drop was a phenomenal 6,000 feet.

Some of our Canadian team members still stayed together, others went their own way. I had started to race for the second time in the Parsenn Derby, having placed third in 1949. My good friend Martin Strolz from Lech skied on French "Dynamic" skis which at that time were the hot ones. When he saw my skis he said, "Franz, look, I have two pairs of Dynamic skis made in France, and you can have one pair of mine, but I keep the 215s cm and you take the 220s, they are yours now." How generous of my old friend Martin. With his 215s he won the Parsenn Derby overall. When Martin gave me the 220s I figured he had tried out both pairs and came to the conclusion that the 215s were the faster pair. Generally the more running surface a ski has the faster they are supposed to be. In theory the less weight per square inch on a ski the faster it is. But this theory is faulty. There are other factors involved. Flexibility overall, camber, width and flexibility at the tips. Wax of course is also very important and is related to the weight factor. At that time in the 1950s there were no representatives from ski and wax manufacturers traveling with teams to test the equipment. You were lucky to have two pairs of skis—one pair for downhill and the other for giant slalom and slalom. When one looks at ski racing today it is a totally different game.

I started to take the long, steep schuss from the Weissfluh Joch down to the frozen lake below, turned to the left and hoped to cross the lake without having to use cross country technique before the steeps began. All went well until half way down to the finish line where one had to run under a balcony which connected two hotels. Some of the racers, who figured that their skis were either slow or fell, stopped and were already knee-deep in beer steins up on the balcony when I approached. They yelled to me, "Franz, come on up, have a beer." No stopping for me. Afterward I wished I had. One had to ski through three towns. The main roads were just wide enough for a farmer's sled. A mile before the finish line the course went along a narrow road. I tried to pass two racers but failed and flew over a high stonewall onto a frozen road. "My God, I had time to reflect." This time you are done for. I saw myself crippled. After I landed there was only one thing on my mind, lie there and yell for help, or try to get up and go on. Up I got and went lamely on to the finish line. It reminded me of the tank shrapnel in my lung and shoulder on March 17, 1945, in Danzig, when I just jumped out of the foxhole and ran 20 yards to an embankment. At the finish line some of my Canadian team mates were waiting. The British Fieldmarshall Alexander of Tunis and his wife Lady Alexander were with them when I collapsed. They laid me on the back seat of the Fieldmarshall's convertible Buick and drove me to a hospital in Davos. At the moment I didn't know who this man and woman were. On the way, at a railroad crossing, our car and a local car had a minor collision. The Swiss man was very agitated and talked in a loud voice. Fieldmarshall Alexander didn't understand a word, so they asked me to explain. When I finally explained, the Swiss guy got mad and said, "Why didn't you translate before, you speak German." I was in misery myself.

In the hospital they took X-rays, but I never found out what the real injury was. For years I had problems with my back on and off. I stayed for three days in the hospital. Most amazing was that Lady Alexander, the Fieldmarshall's wife, brought me flowers every day to the hospital. It is hard to believe—me, a simple skier, getting flowers from the wife of a Fieldmarshall, whose husband only two and a half years earlier had fought a war where I was on the other side. It reminded me of the British army when they took me prisoner on May 2, 1945. We heard that the British were gentlemen. I agree.

Now it was off to my hometown St. Anton, where they waited for my return since January 1950 when I went to America. With crutches under my arms I was greeted at the *Bahnhof* by my family and many friends. It was embarrassing coming home as a cripple. While I was convalescing at home from my back injury, the ladies team went to Chamonix, France, for the prestigious Arlberg Kanadahar race. Joanne Hewson won a bronze medal, the first ever for a Canadian.

After some weeks, I again joined Joanne Hewson and Lucile Wheeler, who wanted to travel Europe more, so I took them to some races on the Schneeberg, less then 50 miles from Vienna. After the races we visited Vienna. They are still reminding me how the Russians soldiers looked at them! Joanne and Lucille were then invited by Dick Durrance, the famous movie maker, to ski for him in Zuers, on the Arlberg.

By the end of April many of our team headed back to Canada, but no longer as a team. George Merry of Rossland, B.C., a member of the men's team and I travelled together. I went back to Banff to drive for the Brewster Gray Line again and did some mountain climbing and hiking.

In the spring of 1953 I had an offer to head the ski school at Mt. Gabriel in the Laurentian Mountains, forty miles north of Montreal. It was owned by the prominent O'Connell family of Montreal. Mt. Gabriel had a vertical drop of less then 300 feet. The language was mainly French in the Province of Quebec but in the resorts English was prevalent, because many tourists came from the U.S. and a few from Europe and overseas, from the Dominions, Australia and New Zealand.

I got to know the French people quite well and took a liking to them; they seemed so honest and polite, not that I found people impolite in the English speaking part of Canada or the U.S. for that matter. The winters there were very cold, and the ski runs were really not to my liking, but most of all I missed the Rocky Mountains; the long, steep runs, the hikes, the climbs, the wildlife, the lakes, you name it, it was paradise for me. So I headed west to my beloved Banff. Here again I went back to my trade as a painter for a short time. My friend Ken Neish, who later changed his name to Leigh

Kendall, was a contractor and had some painting work on new buildings in Banff and Calgary; he knew that my family at home was in this trade. While working for Leigh I realized that this trade was not for me, and I went back to driving for Brewster Gray Line Sight Seeing Co.

In the summer of 1955 I was lucky, though someone else was unlucky. It was the great mountaineer Hans Gmoser, who emigrated from Linz, Austria, to Canada in 1954. He was already an accomplished mountain guide, but unfortunately he broke his leg that summer and that prevented him from guiding Dr. and Mrs. Archibald MacIntosh from Philadelphia on climbs. I was then hired as a replacement, and we had wonderful hikes and medium difficult climbs in the Rockies for several summers. Mrs. MacIntosh was an avid bird watcher, and it was exciting to listen to her observation of the species she saw every day in the area.

Hans was also a pioneer who gave the world helicopter skiing. He, Mike Wiegele (another Austrian), Rudi Gertsch (a Swiss) and many others are now flying many thousands of adventurous daredevil skiers into mountains of every continent each winter and spring for helicopter skiing.

In the fall of 1955, I was approached again by the Canadian Ski Association if I would coach the Canadian Men's Olympic Ski Team for the VII Winter Olympics to be held in Cortina D'Ampezzo, Italy. How could I not accept this very honorable position? The Alpine ski team assembled in Montreal in December 1955, and we flew to Zurich, Switzerland.

OFF TO CORTINA d'AMPEZZO, ITALY, FOR THE VII WINTER OLYMPIC GAMES, 1956

On the way to my home in St. Anton for our last training before entering the *Hahnenkamm* race in Kitzbuehel, we stopped over at the Kaestle ski factory in Hohenems, Vorarlberg, to pick up racing skis for some of our team members.

It was a great coincidence that at the *Bahnhof* in Feldkirch, I saw a man who looked to be very familiar. I approached him and asked, "Are you Ganath?" He recognized me at once as his comrade when the tank shot into our *panje* hut January 1,1942, in Russia which killed four of our squad and tore several fingers off Ganath's hands. I didn't have a scratch on my body. Ganath was now employed by the National Railroad. We didn't have much time for a lengthy conversation, the train was getting ready to leave for St. Anton and I hopped in.

It was late night when we arrived in St. Anton for our final training. On my team were Andre Bertrand of Quebec, and the Tommy brothers, Andy and Art ,from the Province of Ontario. The next day, we started downhill training on the Galzig, my favorite mountain. On our first day, Art Tommy broke his left leg in downhill practice; the next day Andy Tommy broke his right leg, almost on the same spot. The third day their coach hurt his ankle and had a concussion to boot—it was Franz Gabl. What a pity! Now the team was made up of only Andre' Bertrand, ready to head to Kitzbuehel for the *Hahnenkamm* race, the last stop before the Olympics in Cortina. I was supposed to stay in bed for two weeks because of the concussion and ankle. Off to Kitzbühel I went with the team. In Kitzbühel I went with Andre' every day to the start of the downhill. I had a cast on my ankle and couldn't ski. I tried to explain and encourage him, though there was not much I could do. I had raced this course before and won in 1946; it was class II, then. Once I went down with him on one ski. I pointed out the critical turns, especially one near the top where it feels like turning on a huge basketball. Andre' hardly ever skied a mountain with more then 200 meter vertical drop; here it was 800 meters. Andre' was not trying to beat Toni Sailer that day, only stay alive.

Several evenings, Hannes Marker, the inventor of the first well functional toe release binding, the Marker Simplex, came to our hotel in the evenings and installed his Simplex toe iron on some of our Canadian team's skis. He stayed some evenings until two in the morning; he was such an idealistic man. Years later he was involved in a car accident, but he survived and continued to improve his already excellent binding. Just recently I read in a ski magazine that Hannes Marker passed away in Germany. He will be remembered for a long time.

On late Friday afternoon, the day before the downhill, I went with Andre' Bertrand for some slalom training on the local Ganslern slalom hill. We were just ready to go home when Toni Sailer walked up the Ganslern all alone. It was quite late, and the ski slopes were deserted. Toni started to set up a short slalom course. I was curious. What was he up to? I then saw something which could explain the three gold medals he won in Cortina. He ran those gates so fast and in such classy style, I had never seen anything like it in my life. I knew then that Toni could easily win three Olympic gold medals, or at least three medals.

The *Hahnenkamm* (rooster comb) downhill was the next day, Saturday. As expected Toni Sailer won, though Buddy Werner from Steamboat Springs, Colorado, already an up and coming star, was second. Austrian men were then the dominant alpine ski racers.

From there we traveled to Cortina d'Ampezzo in the Italian Dolomites. It was beautiful there; the whole town sparkled in its splendor. The sharp, steep mountains looked like giant castles.

The concussion which I had suffered at home gave me some problems, and I had to go to the hospital in Cortina, so I could only follow the races on the radio.

Toni Sailer from Kitzbühel was the unquestioned hero of the 1956 Olympics, winning all three gold medals in the alpine competitions. In GS, by an astounding 6.2 seconds. The slalom he won by 4 seconds and the downhill by 3.5 seconds. Toni was admired like I had never seen anyone before admired. His movie star looks propelled him to stardom, and eventually he became a movie star.

Our Canadian ladies team of Lucile Wheeler, Carolyn Kruger, Ann Heggteveit and Ginette Seguin was now coached by Pepi Salvenmoser of Kitzbuehel. For the first time ever, Canada won an Olympic medal in skiing, a bronze, by Lucile Wheeler. Lucile, still coached by Salvenmoser, would win another two gold medals two years later in 1958 at the world championships in Bad Gastein, Austria, and Heggteveit would win the gold medal in the Squaw Valley 1960 Olympic slalom. The first Olympic Gold Medal for Canada in skiing.

On the last day of the Olympics, the hockey game was played for the gold medal. It was Canada versus Russia. Russia, for the first time, sent an Olympic Team to the Winter Games. It was interesting. The end result was Russia 3, Canada 2. The Russians had only nine shots on the opposing goal, whereas the Canadians had 37 shots on goal. The Russsians style of play was so different from the Canadian's who shot from any angle and all the time, hoping through a lucky break to have the puck go in. The Russian style of play was, don't shoot, unless your chances are very good to score. The Russians did also very well in speed skating and cross country skiing.

After the Olympics were over, I went to my home in St. Anton and enjoyed skiing like seldom before. There was no more pressure to train, and many friends joined me on the long runs down from the Galzig and the Valluga, which by now had another cable car installed. I was thinking maybe I should stay here and build a *Pension* (bed & breakfast inn) like my brother Pepi just started to do. But without owning property it would be a struggle to build, and besides I always wanted to stay in North America anyway.

From here I went back to Banff and settled into the routine of driving for the Brewster Gray Line and occasionally guiding Dr. MacIntosh in the mountains like I did a few years earlier. Mrs. MacIntosh was an ardent bird watcher, and she stayed down in the valley while we men climbed the peaks and enjoyed the glorious views from there.

There in Banff, I met a young lady, Audrey Moorman, who was a student at the University of Edmonton and worked during summer vacation at the School of Fine Arts, an affiliate of that University, where I lived. Audrey's family was up in Northern Alberta, farming a half section of land, which is almost a square kilometer. It seems an unbelievable large farm for any European, though, for Canada it is hardly a big deal. We got to know each other quite well, and before long there was a baby on the way. By then I was 34 years old and was thinking of a family for some time, because when you get older you might be better off if you have a family of your own. Charles was our first born; he cried a lot and I thought, "My God, doesn't he ever stop?" Before he was a year old, he was the best baby you could want. He also might be the only one who ever skied before he walked. I was running the regular ski school at Grouse Mountain ski area in 1958. The Grouse Mountain Ski Resort was partially owned by the Vancouver Sun Newspaper. I had made a tiny pair of skis and ski poles for Charles and put him on skis. He was less then a year old and was just learning to walk. As it happened, the photographer of the *Vancouver Sun,* Bill Denny was visiting Grouse Mountain that day and saw this 11-month old baby on skis. He had his camera with him, and within days the front page of this paper carried the picture of Charles on skis. The headline read, "11-Month-Old Carles Gabl is Still Learning to Walk." Later on he became a good racer and had his name in *Sports Illustrated.* Rosemary was our second child; she was a most gentle baby, hardly ever cried. She also learned to ski, though she was not the competitive type.

In the spring of 1959, while I was skiing at Sunshine, a Ski Resort 14 miles west of Banff, I met Jack Snider and his lovely wife Loretta. They came for a ski vacation all the way from Cadillac, Michigan. We skied together, and then one evening, while we had dinner, Jack said, "Franz, would you like to come to Caberfae in Michigan as Ski School Director? I am on the board of directors of the ski area, and on weekends we have up to 3,000 skiers coming from all over Michigan, Indiana, Illinois and even from Ohio." Before long, Fred Bocks, the General Manager, sent me a contract which paid me much more then any other area before, and that's where I taught for the next four winter seasons.

Caberfae is a giant ski area on a mole hill. The vertical drop is an astonishing 175 feet! There were only rope tows, fifteen of them. Later on, a T-Bar was installed and then one chairlift. For four winter seasons I taught there and to this day, I treasure the acquaintances I made in Caberfae. During mid-week the area looked almost deserted, except on holidays. Fred Bocks taught me how to get publicity. He was the most competent man I had ever the privilege to work under in the ski business.

This was also the time when short skis were popular. I always felt that shorter skis for beginners was the answer. We had in Caberfae a representative for Cliff Taylor, Bill Fellows. One day he came to me and said, "Franz, I am the new representative for Cliff Taylor's short skis, and I wondered if you would be kind enough to promote them in your ski school and see if the beginners can learn skiing faster?" My instructors were all for it, and some of us tried them out. There was a very gentle slope near the day lodge. As we tried to ski down, we had to push with our ski poles to get going. We knew then that these skis were not the answer. These wooden skis were about four feet long and were much too stiff; even with good wax they didn't run well. If they had been made out of metal, like Head skis, they would have been a boon to learn to ski.

Our daughter Rosemary learned to ski there, too, but, lo and behold, she was hardly four years old when she broke a leg. The ski patrol took care of her immediately and drove her to the hospital in Cadillac, fifteen miles away. My wife Audrey stayed with her while the physician attended to her needs. The resident priest of the hospital came by and inquired about the accident. I noticed that he talked with an accent. As we conversed he told me that he was from Poland and came to America after the war. He brought out a bottle of whiskey, and when I told him of my experience in 1944 in Sokolov, Poland, when my buddy Raeder and I got so drunk in a Polish family's home, that we ended up under the table, he enjoyed that story so much that we emptied the whole bottle.

Alaskan Adventures
& Retirement in Bellingham

During the summer of 1958, Lowell Thomas, at that time the world's best known broadcaster, invited my brother Pepi and me to be part of the movie series *High Adventures* filmed in the Juneau ice fields in Alaska. When I had a chance to talk to Lowell about my war experiences, he immediately became interested and encouraged me to write them down as well as I could. That's when I began earnestly to write my autobiography *Franzl*. Every so often I sent him my writings which he then looked at and wrote comments. In dozens of letters from Lowell, he always mentioned, "Franz, you have a tremendous story to tell, you must write it down." The same time Lowell Thomas shot the scenes for his film in the Juneau ice fields, John Jay, the famous ski movie maker, also shot many scenes and showed them in cinemas all over the US and Canada. John Jay is a descendant from John Jay, the first Chief Justice of the United States.

I became enamored with the Juneau ice fields, and one day Dr. Maynard Malcolm Miller, known to us as M3, who started a scientific program to study glaciers and environments in Alaska in 1946, said to me, "Franz, would you be interested in coming up each summer to teach skiing to my students and mountaineering safety, especially, crevasse rescue?" I immediately said to M3, "Yes, I really would like to come up for a few weeks maybe, but not every summer, but whenever my job allows it." It happened infrequently that someone fell into a crevasse, but luckily, no one was ever killed. I was thinking back to the war in Russia when Konrad told me one needs luck, one needs luck.

There were 1,000 square miles of ice with about twenty camps distributed over this area. The camps were built with two by fours and sheathing and on the outside had corrugated metal nailed on the wood. We travelled by snowmobile, dog sled, on foot or on skis between the camp sites to where the scientists measured each year's thickness of snow and other pertinent facts about glaciers. Another important scientific study was to measure each of the over one hundred glaciers to determine how many of them advanced and how many receded or were in equilibrium. Students came from all over the world, many of the lecturers were famous in their own country.

The National Guard Air Force flew in tons of supplies from Anchorage every summer. The huge C-130s landed on skis not far from the main camp, Camp 10 on Taku Glacier. These planes had to use rocket assistance when taking off on the often wet, heavy new snow. When they arrived back in Anchorage on land, they retracted their skis and landed on wheels.

SETTLING DOWN IN WASHINGTON STATE

My brother Pepi became ski school director at Timberline Lodge on Mt. Hood in Oregon in 1956 under concessionaire Richard Kohnstamm. After the first winter season, November to April, he said to my brother, "You know Pepi, isn't it a shame to have this beautiful lodge almost empty during the summer months; let's try and get some business by starting a Summer Racing Camp." They put their heads together and immediately advertised it. It was the first one in the western hemisphere and was not really a hit, but became slowly popular in the next four years.

In 1960 I came down from Canada in early spring to ski weekends at Mt. Baker. One day Ivor Allsop, the manager, said to me, "Franz, why don't you start a summer racing school here at Mt. Baker like your brother did on Mt. Hood?" I was at once enthusiastic about this idea. Ivor then asked, "How should we go about this?" We planned on one ten-day session during June of 1960. Ivor had three sons—Jon, Mike and Jim, all racers—and he wanted them to become champions. There was an old lodge at Mt Baker with somewhat primitive accommodations, but the view of Mt. Shuksan on a clear day was something to behold. The lodge, which had been the headquarters for the movie *The Call of the Wild* in 1939, starring Clark Gable (no relation), burned down in 1940. The first summer we had six students, three of them were Ivor's sons, the other three paying customers. After getting publicity, for the second year 24 students came, many from Michigan where I directed the ski school at Caberfae and where I recruited many students for our summer racing camp. By then, Ivor and I knew that this was a trend for the future. Within a few years we had well over a hundred attending our racing camps every summer. Mr. Kohnstamm of Timberline Lodge when one day I just happened to visit there, asked me, "Franz, how do you do it, to have that many attending your camps?" My secret was I had ads in the Ski Racing Magazine and did recruiting in Cadillac and other Midwest ski areas. Most of the participants for the summer racing school were teenagers who came from all over the U.S. and Canada. Occasionally, older skiers over thirty would attend.

In early morning we all did exercises and running with a view of the most scenic Mt. Shucksan.   After morning toiletry, they made their own beds; I was glad their parents didn't see them. Then after breakfast we were off to the Pan Dome chair lift for gate training, slalom, giant slalom and free skiing. In the afternoon we played games or once in a while, we went to Bellingham in the afternoon for water-skiing at Ivor Allsop's home on Lake Whatcom. In the evenings I showed 16-mm movies which I took of all the racers on their first day. We sent them to Seattle for developing and had them back within two days so they could see themselves running gates, and we coaches would criticize. There were no videos then.

Mt. Baker summer racing camp participants, 1ü.

Many famous racers were guest coaches, such as Christian Pravda, Stein Eriksen, Willy Schaeffler, Jim McConkey, Franz Hammer and many more. The coaches were not only involved with on the hill training, they also gave inspirational talks. One could see on the faces of young girls and boys how they held their coaches in awe. Once in a while we took the whole group for evening skiing on Shuksan Arm. The snow then was corny and fast; it was an enlightening experience for these youngsters. When they left after a session, some had tears in their eyes, and many of them coming back year after year and attending two or even three sessions. One summer session Mrs. McKinney brought her whole brood of half a dozen children up from California. It was nice to hear later on that Steve would set a new world speed record and sister Tamara become world alpine champion and one of the great champions of the U.S.

Every July 4th, thousands of skiers and nonskiers traveled to Mt. Baker to see the Slush Cup, an event where skiers ski down a hill to a small lake and try to ski across. It's cold. Many, of course, never made it across and should one do so, he or she was roundly booed. Nobody would freeze as most of them had alcohol instead of blood in their veins by then. This celebration stopped in the early 1970s after many homeward bound cars had accidents which marred this event.

After the 1962-63 season I had a talk with Mr. Verdun Place, president of the Mt. Baker Recreation Company, and asked if they would be interested having me run the concession for ski shop and school. Mr. Place consulted with his board of directors, they agreed and we signed a contract. For the next seven years, I and all the employees at Mt. Baker braved the immense mountains of snow. This area was open only weekends and holidays. It probably gets more snow then any other resort in the world. To keep the road open the Washington State Highway department allotted several snowplow trucks for the last seven miles to the lodge and lifts.

In 1969, a new wind was blowing at the Mt. Baker Ski area. New management came in, and they felt that the summer racing school was a nuisance and thought that a new concessionaire for shop and school would be better. Eventually, they cancelled my contract as ski shop and ski school concessionaire in 1969. I packed all my equipment and con-

tinued with a sport shop in Bellingham, 56 miles away, to
keep me busy and to feed my family.

By now Audrey and I had an addition to our family Sarah
Louise. As the youngest she got lots of attention, and you
might say was a little spoiled. She of course started to ski
before she was four years old.

The northwest's climate was ideal for me. Sure there is
a lot of rain and wetness, but the higher elevations at Mt.
Baker lodge at the 4,200 foot level there could be fifteen or
even twenty five feet of snow. In the 1998-99 winter season
Mt. Baker had a world record 1,000 inches of snow fallen!

MT. BAKER SKI TO SEA RACE

In Bellingham I was active in the Tourist Convention Committee of the Bellingham Chamber of Commerce. Later it
was called Whatcom County Chamber of Commerce. Our
president then was Mr. Nick Lidstone, a retired Admiral in
the Navy. He and Bob Stephens, the manager, were always
trying to find a way to re-start the Mt. Baker Marathon. This
had been a race in the 1920s when men raced with a car to
Glacier, a town 25 miles up the Mt. Baker highway, then
walked up to Mt. Baker Glacier, though they did not go to the
top, turned around, came down and drove their buggies back
to Bellingham. It was mass start, and the first back in
Bellingham would be the winner. It was supposed to have
been a very popular race, where the whole county would come
out to watch it. As the car traffic increased in later years it
was no longer possible to close off the Mt. Baker Highway for
this race and it was abandoned.

During the winter of 1973 I skied with my friend Joe
Gmuender, a Swiss, at Mt. Baker. Joe, who lived in Vancouver, B.C., just by chance mentioned that in Switzerland they
held a team relay race each year on a certain mountain where
they ski down a hill, then a bicycle racer takes over a baton
and finally two in a canoe or one in a kayak on a river races to
the finish line. It hit me like a lightening bolt. I knew then,
that this would be the Race which would fit the bill to replace
the Mt. Baker Marathon from the days in the 1920s. It was
not really a marathon, but a relay race. When I mentioned it

at the next Tourist Convention Committee meeting and told them of this race , they were enthused immediately, and after some discussions, Bob Stephens said to me, "Franz, do whatever is necessary to get this race off." Our president Nick Lidstone, Bob Stephens, Vivien and Fred Elsethagen, and others helped me plan to get publicity out and the ball rolling. I had never seen such enthusiasm as on that day. We all felt that this would be the replacement race for the Mt. Baker Marathon. The first thing I asked the office of the Chamber do was to send out invitations to all the high schools in Northwest Washington and the lower mainland of British Columbia for a poster design depicting a skier, bicycler, kayaker or canoer. It was kind of a gimmick. What we wanted was publicity and to let them know that this race was coming up. The local news media jumped on the wagon at once; response was unbelievable. A local group came up with a beautiful design for the poster; the winner got $50.00. The Chamber office at once ordered a hundred or more posters to distribute to ski and sport shops in the Northwest. I shall not take credit for the original idea of this Ski to Sea Race; it came from my Swiss friend Joe Gmuender, but I brought it to the attention of our Tourist Convention Committee and told them I would be willing to organize it.

With enthusiastic support from dozens of local businesses, especially the Komo Kulshan Ski Club who did all the timing, this race was born. It was not perfect, but did Henry Ford make a perfect car the very first time he had one made?

Each team had a sponsor who had to pay $25.00 per team; the money was used for prizes, and many more were donated by local businesses.

The first year in 1973, 73 teams had entered in ladies and men's divisions. The start of the race was on top of Pan Dome chair lift at the Mt. Baker Ski Area. From there, the downhill skier went down over Austin Pass and finished near the Mt. Baker Day Lodge. At that time the Forest Service was not prepared yet to close off the portion of Mt. Baker Highway for a runner for the seven-mile run down to the Nooksack river for a baton exchange. The ski race was timed separately, and the time added to the bicycle and canoe time. On the bottom of the mountain, seven miles away, the bicycle racers started off and raced to Nugents Corner where two in a canoe or a one in a kayak took the baton and ran to the Nooksack River and paddled down river to near the Guide Meridian, the finish line. The time of the skier was added to the bicycler and the canoers or kayaker. The winners had the shortest time. With the entry fee money a bicycle, a kayak and a pair of skis, ski boots, poles, bindings, packsacks and dozens of other prizes were bought to hand out to the winners and (losers). It reminded me of the prizes handed out in Innsbruck in 1936 when there were four Leica cameras for boys from 12 to 18 years of age. Now, it is common to have two thousand or more competitors entering this race from all over the globe. Bellingham's sister cities Nachodka in Siberia and Tatayama in Japan send a team every year. The race has also added many more types of sports to a team—mountain biking, running and sailing—and the finish is now in Old Bellingham near the cruise ship terminal.

In the early 1970s there was trouble in the Gabl marriage. Of course this happens only to other people! My wife Audrey, who was born and raised in Alberta, Canada, was homesick for her homeland, and I felt it might be best for her to return there, before more serious complications developed. I sold my sport shop and moved north because I had a financial interest in the Mt. McKenzie Ski Area in Revelstoke, British Columbia, and wanted to be near our two daughters. Son Charles stayed in Bellingham and never moved away. One of my saddest recollections was when they left for Calgary. Though Audrey insisted that Rosemary and Sarah visit me any time I asked. Audrey was very generous in this respect. It was a friendly parting, though the divorce came a dozen years later.

The manager at Mt. Mckenzie Ski Area asked me if I would be interested in running his place. I agreed and signed a contract to run it and hoped to succeed. Some of the board members were involved in another ski area in this town which had to close because of lack of skiers . Their hill was just one very steep run, nothing else. The reason of course was our new ski area. They sold the poma lift to Mt. McKenzie, our ski area, but wanted to be represented on the board of directors. They didn't forget, and when they didn't follow through with the contract I had with them, I packed my things and went to Alberta for a few months and, eventually, came back to Washington which was my plan to begin with. For two years I drifted around and took in the 1976 Olympics in Innsbruck, Austria.

Eventually I settled down in Seattle where I became a painting contractor. My training at home in my father's business and experience was a great asset. I had to turn down many a lucrative contract. The situation with journeymen was not too good. The good men and women were with firms who operated year round. I just closed the business for the winter season and went ski racing in Europe and on this continent to collect "silverware." Most weekends there were also masters ski races in the Northwest; any ex-racer who had not participated in them missed great fun and camaraderie.

From the years 1979 to 1984 I went to Europe each winter season to race in the Masters ski race circuit. My friend from Seattle Kris Berg, who hailed from Norway, but was a semiretired contractor and apartment mogul in Seattle, joined me, and we raced in Italy, France, Germany, Switzerland and Austria. We made our headquarter in my sister Kathi's apartment in Innsbruck, Tyrol. Bob and Virgie Hayden, my longtime friends from Bellingham, joined us for two seasons, though they didn't race. One day we went to St. Moritz and Virgie and Bob both went down on the 1948 Olympic downhill run. Bob went as far as saying it was a picnic!

The trophies they handed out at those races in Europe were like I had seldom seen before, some weighing 16 pounds.

Seattle, the Emerald city in the Evergreen State, had everything, and the weather is so much milder then many places I have lived in. It is also the boating capital of America. The mountains are wooded to near the top, except Mt. Rainier's 14,210-feet high top dwarfs all others, looking down on the city like a white haired-ghost. Lake Washington in the midst of surrounding cities is warm in summer and ideal for swimming and boating. The location of my house, just being a stone's throw away from Lake Washington, was ideal for boating, water skiing and swimming. Nearby Seward Park had facilities for tennis, picnicking, bicycling and walking. The space needle, 600 feet high, is a reminder of the 1964 Worlds Fair. From its top one can see the city, lakes, ocean and mountains with a 360-degree view. In the west looms the Olympic Mountain range in the almost inaccessible rain forest of Olym-

pic National Park. The other beautiful city, 140 miles to the
north, Vancouver, British Columbia, where I had lived many
years earlier, shares similar features.

RETIREMENT IN BELLINGHAM

In the spring of 1990 I felt the time had come and started
to relax. I sold my home in Seattle and moved back to
Bellingham. I bought an older duplex and started to fix it up;
it was a job I really enjoyed, being handy with tools.

During the winter my itch to race was still there, and the
races had a more local character, though the competition was
as tough as ever. It was surprising how many of the racers,
even in their eighties took racing very seriously.

In 1994, I met Ruby Slatten in Anacortes at a Western
Music Fest, and we immediately were attracted to each other.
It was not skiing though, because Ruby doesn't ski; she was a
golfer, and I enjoyed golf myself for many years, though not
like skiing. Ruby and I travel now frequently all over the
west, visiting my daughter Rosemary and Jim with their children in Alberta, Canada. Sarah and Andre' and their children moved to Langley in British Columbia to be near me.
Charles, my oldest son, stayed in Bellingham when my ex-
wife moved back to Alberta in 1974, her birthplace. He lives
with his family near Bellingham with wife Juli and her two
children Lindsey and MacKenzie which he also adopted.
Ruby's children we visit less frequently, as they are in Indiana and Anacortes, and we even go to Europe, seeing my relatives. Four of my sisters are still living whereas my two brothers Karl and Pepi both passed away many years ago in St.
Anton.

In March 1999, I felt some burning sensations on my body
which hurt quite badly; I had no idea what this was. I went
to my doctor who thought it might be shingles. The medication didn't do much good, so I was sent to a neurologist in
Seattle for further tests. It turned out to be myelitis. When I
tell you that I lost 28 pounds within a few weeks, then you
know the pain. It hurts more than had I ever experienced in
my life. Now after nine months I can feel it gets better all the
time. Hopefully after one year I will be fit again and do some
skiing and golfing. Without my three children's support, it

would have been real hell. All my children watched over me at one time or another; one cannot imagine how much that meant to their father. If I ski again is questionable, but should I be able, you bet I will be on the slopes before too long. Though racing I will leave to the younger generation.

Auf Wiederseh'n!

Ruby Slatten, my companion for many years.

Ruby, son Charles with family, Sarah and Rosemary, 1998

Ruby, Juli, Charles, McKenzy, Lindsey, and Franz.

Our cat Boo-Boo.

Niece Gertrude Gabl, 1969 World Cup Alpine Skiing champion, who died in an avalanche, January 1976.

Daughter Sarah and her husband Andre and family.

Castle Laudegg in Ladis.

St. Anton am Arlberg, Homecoming of cows from alpine meadows in the fall.

Edelweiss.